100

Days of Blessing

Devotions for Wives and Mothers

NANCY CAMPBELL

CAMPBELL HOUSE PUBLISHING

Unless specified, all Scriptures used in this book are from the King James Version. Other translations mentioned and abbreviated in the text are as follows:

AMP	Amplified Bible
AMPC	Amplified Bible, Classic Edition
Berkeley	The Berkeley Version in Modern English
BSB	Berean Study Bible
CSB	Christian Standard Bible
Darby	The Darby Translation by John Nelson Darby
ESV	English Standard Version
Fenton	Translation of the Holy Scriptures by Ferrar Fenton
GW	God's Word Translation
HCSB	Holman Christian Standard Bible
JBP	The New Testament in Modern English translated by J. B. Phillips
Knox	The Holy Bible translated by Monsignor Knox
Moffat	The Moffat Translation of the Bible
MLB	Modern Language Bible
MSG	The Message, a paraphrase of the Bible by Eugene H. Peterson
NASB	New American Standard Bible
NET	New English Translation
NKJV	New King James Version
NLT	New Living Translation
RSV	Revised Standard Version
TLB	The Living Bible
TPT	The Passion Translation, translated from Hebrew, Greek and Aramaic texts by Dr. Brian Simmons
WAY	The Letters of St. Paul translated by Arthur S. Way

*To my beloved husband who has always encouraged
me to fulfil the Titus 2 mandate to teach wives and
mothers His plan and purpose for their lives.*

*To my daughters, granddaughters, and great-granddaughters
who have been, and are, the blessing and glory of my life.*

*To all wives and mothers who are in the throes of
raising your families. You are not insignificant.
You are determining the destiny of the nation.*

*May you be encouraged and inspired as you read
these devotions that are written especially for you.*

*May you be strengthened and nourished to fulfil
the greatest career ever given to women—Motherhood!*

Contents

Alphabetical Contents

Introduction

Welcome to the fourth volume of 100 DEVOTIONS. These devotions do not succumb to the culture of our society but are true and faithful to the living Word of God. We are living in an hour of deception when even the elect can be deceived. The only sure remedy against deception is the ultimate truth of God's Word.

These devotions bring you back to God's Word. They plant you on a sure foundation. They fill your mind with a biblical worldview. When you get to the end you'll want to go back and read them again. One reading is not enough.

We often hear the word "brainwashed," usually in a negative sense. But it is a biblical word when we use it positively. God wants to "wash" us with His transforming Word (John 15:3; Romans 12:2; Ephesians 5:26; and Titus 3:5).

Washing our brains daily with God's eternal truths will save us from deception. As we make our pilgrimage toward the eternal city, we daily fill our minds with God's eternal truths.

In my Introduction to Volume 3, I wrote about the wonderful Greek word *perisseuo* which means "to superabound, to be excessive, exceed, excel, abundant, enough and to spare, over and above." We see this word again in Matthew 13:12: *"For whosoever hath, to him shall be given, and he shall have **more abundance** (perisseuo): but whosoever hath not from him shall be taken away even that he hath."* It is difficult to understand this biblical principle. We naturally think God would give to those who don't have rather than those who do. But God knows better.

We see this same principle in the way we hear God's Word. Jesus said in Mark 4:24, 25: *"Take heed **what ye hear**: with what measure ye mete, it shall be measured to you: and unto you that hear shall more be given. For he that hath to him shall be given, and he that hath not, from him shall be taken even that which he hath."*

Jesus gave this principle again in Luke 8:18, this time warning us how we hear: *"Take heed therefore **how you hear**; for whosoever hath, to him shall be given, and whosoever hath not, from him shall be taken even that which he seemeth to have."*

God knows our hearts. If we carelessly and lightly read His Word, He will not give us revelation and enlightenment. But if He sees our hearts and minds eager for His truth, open to receive His words, and coming into His presence with awe, trembling, and humility He will give us a feast from His table. The more we seek, search, and knock the more He gives. We will receive an abundance— superaboundingly—and more than we could dream.

May you feast as you read. Look up the Scripture references. Meditate on them. Check out the Further Study at the end of the book. If you want to read more, read the whole chapter of the verse for the day. When you get to the end of the devotion, say the prayer and affirmation ALOUD. They will both have far more impact upon your life when you say them aloud.

You will want to read this volume again. But make sure you also get Volumes 1, 2, and 3.

In His love,
NANCY CAMPBELL
www.aboverubies.org

1

WHERE ARE YOU?

"The LORD God called to the man and said to him, 'Where are you?'"
(Genesis 3:9 ESV).

God loves to ask questions. We notice that during Jesus' earthly stay He loved to ask questions too. Of course, God always knows the answer, but He wants to hear a personal answer from us.

The first question God asks in the Bible is: *"Where are you?"* After Adam and Eve took of the forbidden fruit, they realized they had sinned. When they heard the LORD God walking in the garden they freaked out and hid themselves among the trees. God knew where they were, but He wanted to hear from Adam and Eve.

God still asks this question. *"Where are you?"*

"Are you hiding from My presence?"

"Are you too busy to read My Word?"

"Do you think My thoughts? Are you obedient to My ways or are you more in sync with the thinking of this world?"

God knows the answers, but He wants us to answer Him. He keeps calling to us in the midst of this distorted and deceived society in which we live. He constantly calls us back to Him, His truth, and His ways.

It is interesting that God didn't ask this question the moment Adam and Eve sinned. He came at the end of the day. The toil of the day was over, and a comforting breeze blew gently about them. It was time to rest. The time for fellowship.

Genesis 3:8 says: *"And they heard the voice of the LORD God walking in the garden in the cool of the day: and Adam and his wife hid themselves from the presence of the LORD God amongst the trees of the garden."*

This is the time of the day that God still wants to visit us and fellowship with us. It's the time when we gather to eat together as a family. It's the time when we sit around the table to fellowship and discuss things together. It's the time when we invite God's presence to our table. And we wouldn't leave the table without opening His precious Word to allow Him to speak to us and to spend time praying and calling out to Him.

God longs to come to us. Do we long for His presence? Or do we hide? Just as Adam and Eve hid from the presence of the LORD, many families continue to hide from God's presence.

The enemy of God and of our souls tries to keep us from this daily appointment. Sports and extra lessons all vie for this time. This is the time of the day we should be home preparing the evening meal and gathering our family together. This is the time of the day God established to specifically communicate with His people.

Instead, we are out in the car, fighting traffic, and away from home. No time to prepare a meal. Let's grab some fast food. Eat while looking at the head of someone in front of you in the car! This is not how we are meant to eat meals. God wants us to sit around a table where we can see one another's faces and truly communicate. Mealtimes should be "face to face table fellowship."

Satan loves to stop us from reading God's Word together. He lures us into a lifestyle where won't be home to pray together as a family—the most powerful, nation-changing and world-changing thing we can do as a family. He knows that there is nothing we can do as powerful as praying together.

Don't let good things prevent you from doing the most powerful thing. Don't let Satan trick you into "hiding" from God's presence when He delights to be with your family in the *"cool of the day."*

Are you and your family where God can find you or are you hiding?

PRAYER:
"Dear Father, I thank You that You long to fellowship with us as a family. Give me strength and tenacity to make this daily appointment happen. We want to experience Your Presence at our table. Amen."

AFFIRMATION:
We are not a hiding family. We make time together to sit with God each day.

2

GO FACE THE CHALLENGE

*"Jesus therefore, knowing all things that should come upon him,
went forth, and said unto them, Whom seek ye?"*
(JOHN 18:4).

Jesus knew what was ahead. He had just come from the Garden of Gethsemane where He sweated drops of blood as He agonizingly faced the taking upon Himself the sins of the world. He prayed that His Father would take *"this cup"* away from Him. But knowing all He would face, He went forth. He went forth to face the agony. He didn't hold back.

This is a challenge to me. We will never have to face what Jesus faced. But what do we do about the problems we face each day? Do we cringe from them? Do we turn a blind eye? Do we go into depression and self-pity?

Perhaps you find it hard to get up out of bed and even face going out to the kitchen each morning. Do you have a hard time facing dishes and the big pile of laundry? Or that room that is in such a mess? Can I encourage you to get up and "go forth," even as Jesus did?

Tackle your task little by little. Don't think you have to do the whole overwhelming task all at once. Make a start and keep going until you finish. Perhaps you face a huge challenge in your life—a mountain that looks impossible in front of you. Mountains look impossible to us, but they are nothing to God. Go forth in His name and His power.

I think of a chorus that we used to sing as young people:

Got any rivers you think are uncrossable?
Got any mountains you can't tunnel through?
God specializes in things thought impossible;
And He can do what no other can do.

The above chorus was inspired by the Panama Canal builders who faced a nearly impossible task and where well over 25,000 people died during its building.

You may be facing a raging battle in your life. It seems too much for you. It is bigger than what you can handle. Don't look at the size. Read the instructions God gave to the Israelites when they faced battles and armies who were far bigger than them. In Deuteronomy 20:3 (Knox) God tells them not to be afraid because He will be with them: *"There must be no faint hearts among you, no flinching, no yielding, no trembling."*

Of course, you can't win this battle on your own, but God will fight for you. Trust Him. Go into the battle, not in your own strength, but trusting totally in God.

Jesus said in John 5:17 (NLT): *"My Father is always working, and so am I."* God, who lives in you by His Holy Spirit works in you to do His will.

Philippians 2:13 says: *"For it is God which worketh in you both to will and to do of his good pleasure."*

Will you allow Him to work in you? Will you allow Him to "go forth" in you? He will face your problems with you. He will go with you and help you.

Perhaps you are facing a cross. Can I encourage you to embrace your cross and go forth? Go forth by faith! Go forth knowing that Jesus lives in you. He has faced more than you will ever face, and He lives in you. He is in you to help you. You can go forth in His name.

Do you remember the challenge King Asa faced? An Ethiopian army of one million men! Asa had 580,000 soldiers, only half as many. He cried out to God: *"LORD, it is nothing with thee to help, whether with many, or with them that have no power: help us, O LORD our God; for we rest on thee, and in thy name we go against this multitude. O LORD, thou art our God; let no man prevail against thee* (2 Chronicles 14:11).

God answered his desperate cry and *"The LORD smote the Ethiopians before Asa and before Judah; and the Ethiopians fled"* (2 Chronicles 14:12).

I love the hymn Edith G. Cherry wrote about this story:

We rest on Thee, our Shield and our Defender!
We go not forth alone against the foe;
Strong in Thy strength, safe in Thy keeping tender,
We rest on Thee, and in Thy Name we go.

We go in faith, our own great weakness feeling,
And needing more each day Thy grace to know:
Yet from our hearts a song of triumph pealing,
We rest on Thee, and in Thy Name we go.

PRAYER:

"Thank You, Father, that You see what's ahead. Thank You that You help me to accomplish things I never dreamed of doing. Your path for me is bigger and brighter than I could ever imagine. Amen."

AFFIRMATION:

God is bigger than all the challenges I face.

3

HOW DO YOU LOVE YOUR HUSBAND?

"She will do him good and not evil all the days of her life"
(PROVERBS 31:12).

Some time ago I asked my Above Rubies Facebook readers to share the little things they do to show their husbands they love them. The following are some of the replies I received. Each one of us has a different personality and therefore we show our love in different ways. You may not do everything written in this list but please take time to read it through. You are sure to pick up some ideas that you are not currently doing and which you can incorporate into your marriage.

Because I love my husband I . . .

Love to serve him.

Love to cook his meals.

Love to have a wholesome meal prepared for him when he arrives home in the evening.

Love to make and serve him breakfast.

Love to make his lunch to take to work.

Love to think of ways to romance him.

Love to have a clean and fresh smelling house for him when he comes home.

Love to keep an orderly home for him.

Love to make sure he always has clean laundry.

Love to make him coffee.

Love to encourage him and affirm him.

Love to purchase the special goodies that he loves.

Love to buy him his favorite dark chocolate.

Love to do extra nice things for him.

Love to smile at him.

Love to ravish him and satisfy him sexually.

Love to follow him even though I may not agree with him.

Love to praise him instead of criticizing him.

Love to wake up and cuddle with him.

Love to greet him passionately when he comes home from work.

Love to run a bath for him.

Love to encourage and compliment him with my words.

Love to make him smile and laugh.

Love to tell him that he is the best.

Love to text him during the day to remind him how much I love and appreciate him.

Love to speak well of him to my friends and to praise him in front of others.

Love to be his best and closest friend.

Love to be his only confidante.

Love to pray for him and with him.

Love to respect him and his decisions.

Love to pay attention to him when he talks to me.

Love to look at him adoringly.

Love to help the children do special things for him.

Love to give him massages.

Love to softly tickle him.

Love to rub his back, shoulders, legs, and feet.

Love to be with him while he works.

Love to do what he asks me with a smile and cheerful attitude.

Love to listen to his dreams and ideas and support them.

Love to raise the children in the way that pleases him.

Love to take an interest in his passions.

Love to do everything I can to keep him healthy.

Love to kiss him when he comes near me during the day.

Love to blow him kisses.

Love to give him surprises.

Love to appreciate him for working hard so I can stay home with our children.

Love to hold hands with him at every opportunity.

Love to admire and adore him.

Love to be faithful to him until death or we meet the Lord face to face.

Never be content with a boring marriage. Get out of your rut. Think of new and exciting ways to love your husband. Surprise him with something you've never done before. And do it today.

PRAYER:

"Thank You, God for giving me a husband to provide for me and protect me. Help me to do good things for him each day of my life. Amen."

AFFIRMATION:

I am my husband's proudest cheerleader.

ONE ANOTHERING LIFESTYLE
Part 1

*"Let us think of ways to **motivate one another** to*
acts of love and good works"
(HEBREWS 10:24 NLT).

Family life is togetherness. It is participating in one another's lives. God created us to be a social people, to interact with one another. He knew we would need reminding about this and therefore gave us many Scriptures about how He wants us to interact with one another. We could call our family life our "one anothering" lifestyle.

True Christianity is also a "one anothering" lifestyle. It is an extension of our family lives. Paul wrote to the believers in Romans 1:12: *"That I may be comforted **together** with you by the **mutual faith** both of **you and me.**"* This is a powerful Scripture. Paul revealed three things to these new believers in this Scripture:

1) Our Christianity is a *"together"* lifestyle.

2) Our faith is not only a personal faith, but a *"mutual faith."*

3) Our faith is a *"you and me"* faith.

It is God's design for us to live together as families. God doesn't want people to live on their own. He sets the solitary in families (Psalm 68:6). This is why God commands that we meet together as believers and *"do not forsake the assembling of ourselves together"* (Hebrews 10:25).

You will love the Passion translation of Romans 1:11, 12: *"I yearn to come and be face-to-face with you and get to know you. For I long to impart to you some spiritual gift that will empower you to stand strong in your faith. Now, this means that when we come together and are side by side, something wonderful will be released. We can expect to be co-encouraged and co-comforted by each other's faith!"*

Wow, don't you love that? Our walk with the Lord is a *"face to face"* and *"side by side"* walk. It's a *"together"* walk. It's a *"co-encouraging and co-comforting walk."* God is not into social distancing. God wants social interacting with one another. Our faith grows stronger as we walk together. Remember, it's not just me—it's *"you and me!"* Selfishness and isolation do not belong in the kingdom of God.

The Greek word for the words "mutual faith" is *allelon* which means "re-duplicated, one another, each other, together." Can you believe it? I found 41 "one anothering" mandates that God wants us to do to one another—in our homes and in our church life. As you read them, take time to look up the Scriptures, meditate on them, and ask God to show you how to put them into practice in your marriage, your family life, and among the believers with whom you fellowship and worship.

If we sow the seeds of these commandments in one another's lives, we will reap the fruit of a wonderful revival in our families and communities.

Gather your children to do this study with you so your whole family will be blessed. Talk together about what each one means. You may like to look up each one of these "one another" Scriptures in different translations which will give you even more understanding. Here we go:

1. **ADMONISH** and counsel one another (Romans 15:14 and Colossians 3:16). This literally means to admonish with reproof, to warn. Read also Acts 20:31; 1 Corinthians 4:14; Colossians 1:28; and 1 Thessalonians 5:14). I am sorry to begin with one that sounds a little negative, but I am giving them to you in alphabetical order.

2. **BEAR** one another's burdens (Galatians 6:2 and Colossians 3:13). The Amplified Version states: *"Bearing graciously with one another."*

3. **BLESS** one another (Matthew 5:44 and 1 Peter 3:9).

4. **CARE AND CONCERN** for one another (1 Corinthians 12:25). The NET translation says: *"Have mutual concern for one another."*

5. **COMFORT** one another (Romans 1:12; 1 Thessalonians 4:18; 5:11; and 2 Corinthians 1:3, 4).

6. Have **COMPASSION** on one another (1 Peter 3:8).

7. **CONFESS YOUR FAULTS** one to another (James 5:16).

8. **CONSIDER** one another (Hebrews 10:24).

9. **DO GOOD** to one another (1 Thessalonians 5:15; Ephesians 6:10; and Hebrews 13:16). The Passion translation says: *"Always pursue doing what is beautiful to one another and to all the unbelievers."*

10. **ENCOURAGE** one another (Hebrews 3:13 and 10:25).

11. **EDIFY** one another (Romans 14:19; 15:1-3; 2 Corinthians 12:19; and 1 Thessalonians 5:11). This means to build up and strengthen one another. Love builds up; knowledge puffs up!

12. **ESTEEM AND DELIGHT** in one another (Psalm 16:2-3 and Philippians 2:3).

13. **FELLOWSHIP** with one another (Malachi 3:16; Acts 2:42; and 1 John 1:7). We take time to fellowship with one another at the meal table. We don't scoff our food, leave the table, and run. We linger and enjoy one another's company. We don't go off to church and rush home. We hopefully have a fellowship meal together with the saints. If your church doesn't do this, invite another family home to have lunch with you after church and enjoy fellowship together. This is a biblical thing to do (Acts 2:46, 47).

14. **FORBEAR** with one another in love (Ephesians 4:2 and Colossians 3:13).

15. **FORGIVE** one another (Matthew 6:14, 15; 18:21-35; Ephesians 4:32; and Colossians 3:13). The Amplified Version states: *"Willingly forgiving each other."*

We will continue discovering more "one another" Scriptures tomorrow.

PRAYER:

"Thank You for showing me, Father that You want my faith to be a mutual faith. You have shown me that I will grow stronger in my faith as I encourage others and they encourage me. Help me to always be seeking the good of others, rather than only thinking of myself. Amen."

AFFIRMATION:

I am creating a lifestyle of "face to face" and "side by side" interaction in my home and with fellow believers.

5

ONE ANOTHERING LIFESTYLE
Part 2

"Discover creative ways to encourage others and to motivate them toward acts of compassion, doing beautiful works as expressions of love. This is not the time to pull away and neglect meeting together, as some have formed the habit of doing. In fact, we should come together even more frequently, eager to encourage and urge each other onward as we anticipate that day dawning"
(HEBREWS 10:24, 25 TPT).

Today we continue looking at more things God wants us to do to one another in our families and in our church life. Did you realize there were so many?

16. **HELP** one another with your gifts and abilities (1 Peter 4:10).

17. **HONOR** and **PREFER** one another (Romans 12:10 and Philippians 2:3, 4).

18. Show **HUMILITY** to one another (Ephesians 4:2; Philippians 2:3; and 1 Peter 3:8).

19. Practice **HOSPITALITY** to one another (Acts 2:41-47; Romans 12:13; and 1 Peter 4:9). Hospitality is not optional. It is a biblical doctrine that begins in Genesis and weaves through the pages of the Bible until Revelation. It is an extension of your mothering and homemaking ministry. It is the lifestyle of the kingdom of God. Are you living this lifestyle?

20. Be **KIND** to one another (Romans 12:10; Ephesians 4:32; and Colossians 3:12).

21. **LAY DOWN YOUR LIVES** for one another (1 John 3:16).

22. Be **LIKEMINDED** to one another (Romans 15:5 and 12:16). Most other translations say: *"Live in mutual harmony with one another."*

23. **LOOK OUT FOR ONE ANOTHER'S INTERESTS**, not just your own (Philippians 2:4 and 1 Corinthians 10:24).

24. **LOVE** one another (John 13:34, 35; 15:12, 17; Romans 13:8; 1 Thessalonians 3:12; 4:9; 1 Peter 1:22; 3:8; 4:8; 1 John 3:11, 17, 18, 23; 4:7, 11, 12; and 2 John 1:5). We notice that loving one another has more Scriptures than any other virtue.

25. Have **PEACE** with one another (Mark 9:50).

26. **PRAY** for one another (1 Samuel 12:23; Romans 1:9; 2 Timothy 1:3; and James 5:16).

27. **REALIZE** we are members one of another (Ephesians 4:25).

28. **RECEIVE** one another as Christ as received us (Romans 15:7). Other translations encourage us to **ACCEPT** and **WELCOME** one another. The Greek word is *proslambana* and means "to take to oneself, take as a friend, give food, and show hospitality."

29. **REJOICE** with one another (Romans 12:15 and 1 Corinthians 12:26).

30. **SERVE** one another (Matthew 20:26-28; 23;11; and Galatians 5:13).

31. **SPEAK AND SING** to one another with psalms and hymns and spiritual songs (Ephesians 5:19).

32. **SPEAK** truth to one another (Ephesians 4:25).

33. **STIR UP** one another to love and good works (Hebrews 10:24). Loads of other translations say: *"STIMULATE one another to love and good deeds."* The Living Bible says: *"LET US OUTDO each other in being helpful and kind to each other."* The NET says: *"Let us take thought of how to SPUR ONE ANOTHER ON to love and good works."*

34. **SUFFER** with one another (1 Corinthians 12:26).

35. **SUBMIT** to one another (Ephesians 5:21 and 1 Peter 5:5).

36. **TEACH** and instruct one another (Colossians 3:16).

37. Be **TENDERHEARTED** to one another (Ephesians 4:32).

38. **THINK MORE HIGHLY** of one another than you do of yourselves (Philippians 2:3 AMP).

39. **WASH** one another's feet. Jesus admonished us to do this to one another which is symbolic of serving one another, no matter how servile the task (John 13:14-17).

40. Be on the **WATCH** to look after one another (Hebrews 12:15 AMPC).

41. **WEEP AND MOURN** with one another (Romans 12:15).

Romans 12:5 (NLT) sums it all up: "*We are many parts of one body, and we all belong to each other.*" Your home can be a place of heaven on earth as you fulfil these "one anothering" admonitions together. There is more than one for every day of the month. You won't run out. You may like to work on one as a family for a whole month or perhaps one each day.

THINGS GOD DOES NOT WANT US TO DO TO ONE ANOTHER

God gives far more positives in His Word than He does negatives, but we also need to remind ourselves of the things God does not want us to do to one another.

1. Do not judge one another (Romans 14:13).

2. Do not have lawsuits among one another (1 Corinthians 6:7).

3. Do not bite and devour one another (Galatians 5:15).

4. Do not provoke or envy one another (Galatians 5:26).

5. Do not lie to one another (Colossians 3:9).

6. Do not forsake assembling yourselves together with one another (Hebrews 10:25).

7. Do not speak evil of one another (James 4:11).

8. Do not hold a grudge against one another (James 5:9).

PRAYER:

"Dear Father, Thank You for showing me how You want me to serve my family and others around me. Please help me to think of others, rather than always thinking of myself. Please help me to look out for the interests of others, not just my own. Help me to live beyond myself by having a serving attitude. Amen."

AFFIRMATION:

"Others, Lord, yes others, let this my motto be,
Help me to live for others, that I may live like Thee.
~ Charles D. Meigs

6

AN EDEN HOME

"Build ye houses, and dwell in them; and plant gardens,
and eat the fruit of them"
(JEREMIAH 29:5).

God built the first home. The predominant thing about this home is that it was a garden—the garden of Eden (Genesis 2:15). The word Eden means delight. The first home was a prototype of all homes to come. Consequently, God wants our homes today to also be places of delight. We should seek to make our homes lovely, whether small or big. Of course, we know there is more to a home than the beautiful architecture and the décor. A beautiful looking home can have a cold and hateful atmosphere whereas a little hut can be filled with the atmosphere of heaven.

But there is something we shouldn't forget. The first home was a garden. God wants our homes to be more than brick and timber. He wants them to be gardens too.

And guess who was the first Gardener? Yes, it was God Himself. Genesis 2:8 says: *"And the LORD God planted a garden eastward in Eden."* Do you get it? God put His hands into the soil and planted! He was the first gardener. He showed us the way.

The garden was part of God's plan for the home. It adds beauty to the home, but it also supports the home. The Knox translation of Jeremiah 29:5 states it clearly: *"I would have you . . . plant yourselves gardens of your own to support you."* We often forget about gardens today because every kind of food we need from anywhere in the world is available at the local supermarket. We don't really need a garden. Or do we?

I am a great believer in keeping to the plan that God established in the beginning. Therefore, an important part of our homemaking is to feed our families from the home garden. It provides for the family. It saves money. The nutritional benefits far surpass any vegetables or fruit you can purchase at the supermarket. Most of them are sprayed with chemicals, and even if you could afford to buy organic vegetables, how long have they been sitting on the shelf? There is nothing more wonderful than going to the home garden, harvesting vegetables straight from the plants, and preparing them for the meal immediately. This is the ultimate plan.

"Just a minute," you exclaim. "I can't have a garden. I live in an apartment. This doesn't relate to me." Or maybe you live in a high-rise. How can you have a garden? If you don't have room to grow a garden outside, you can grow herbs and vegetables in pots on your verandah or deck. You can grow herbs in pots on your windowsill. And if, for some impossible reason, you can't do this, grow some sprouts! Grow something. Bring greenery into your home. Make it a garden. Make it a delight.

In our home in New Zealand, we had a huge inside tree/plant which filled one corner of our lounge and beside it a beautiful painting of a tree from ceiling to floor. A dear friend painted it for me, and it included the Scripture: *"And he shall be like a tree planted by the rivers of water"* (Psalm 1:3). It was the saddest thing to leave behind when we left the shores of New Zealand.

Even when you do have room for a garden, there are still challenges to face. When we moved to our land in Tennessee over 21 years ago, we had plenty of room for a garden, but we still couldn't grow anything. Our soil consisted of clay and stones. We had to purchase soil which we continue replenishing year by year with compost and manure.

There are many Scriptures relating God with gardens. Where did God fellowship with Adam and Eve at the end of each day? In the garden! Read Genesis 3:8-10.

Song of Solomon 8:13 tells us that our Heavenly Bridegroom *"dwellest in the gardens."* Jesus was crucified, laid in the tomb, and rose from the dead in a garden (John 19:41 and 20:15, 16).

Isaiah 51:3 says: *"For the LORD shall comfort Zion. . . and he will make her wilderness like Eden, and her desert like the garden of the LORD; joy and gladness shall be found therein, thanksgiving, and the voice of melody."*

Genesis 13:10 also talks about *"the garden of the LORD."* Don't you think we should also have Nancy's garden, Susie's garden, Debbie's garden, and so on?

What's your garden like?

PRAYER:

"Thank you, Lord, for showing me that a garden is part of the home. Please show me the best way to grow a garden in my situation. Amen."

AFFIRMATION:

Gardening is God-like, and I want to be like God.

7

WHERE THERE'S A WILL, THERE'S A WAY

"This book of the law shall not depart out of thy mouth; but thou shalt meditate therein day and night, that thou mayest observe to do according to all that is written therein: for then thou shalt make thy way prosperous, and then thou shalt have good success"
(JOSHUA 1:8).

You may be saying, "I want to spend time in the Bible, but I have all these little children to care for. How can I find the time?"

I also faced this dilemma as a young mother. Before children came along, I would rise at 5.00 am and spend three hours reading God's Word and praying before I started each day. I wrote pages of revelation as God showed me wondrous things as I meditated on His Word. I still have these hard-covered notebooks. But when I entered the new adventure of motherhood, I could no longer find that time. What could I do now?

GRAB

At first, I lamented that I couldn't spend hours alone with God but grumbling over what I couldn't do didn't help. I realized that God was not limited to my quiet hours with Him, yet He wanted to be very much part of my life as a mother. He wanted me to abide in Him and live in His presence as I cooked meals, changed diapers, and cleaned toilets, etc.

I discovered a little secret. I found that I could still get desperately needed nourishment from God's Word by grabbing little bits here and there throughout the day. I could read when I nursed the baby (if I wasn't reading stories to the other children). I could snatch a verse from the psalms when visiting the bathroom. I could keep Bibles in these certain places in my home.

I remember one time feeling such a need to grab some nourishment for my soul. I took a few toys and four little ones with me into my bedroom and knelt by my bed with my Bible. I was hardly aware of the children climbing all over me when I got a loud knock on my bedroom door with the words, "Can you keep those children quiet?"

Our boarder, who was in the room next to me, was home from work as he was sick. He couldn't sleep because of the noise of the children in the bedroom and yet I wasn't even aware of it! Your "Quiet Time" may not always be quiet, but we mothers can learn to hear from God even in the midst of children and noise all around us.

THE WINDOWSILL

In my young mothering days, I would put a Bible on the windowsill above my kitchen sink where I spent hours preparing meals and doing dishes. I opened the Bible to the Psalms or the Proverbs, and from time to time, I could look up for a moment, read a verse, and meditate upon it.

I remember one moment in my mothering days in New Zealand. As I washed the dishes at the kitchen sink, I had sunk into a self-pity trip. The tears rolled down my cheeks! Suddenly, I looked up. My Bible was open to Psalm 103, and I read: *"Bless the LORD, O my soul: and all that is within me, bless his holy name. Bless the LORD, O my soul, and forget not all his benefits: Who forgiveth all thine iniquities; who healeth all thy diseases; Who redeemeth thy life from destruction; who crowneth thee with lovingkindness and tender mercies."*

I was convicted and immediately confessed my sin. "I'm sorry, Lord. I repent of these deceptive, self-pitying thoughts. I resist them in the name of Jesus. I thank You for all my blessings. Thank You for my salvation. Thank You for my home. Thank You for my husband. Thank You for these wonderful children you have given me. I am a blessed woman."

As I praised and thanked the Lord my negativity disappeared. It wasn't my circumstances after all! It was my deceptive thoughts! What delivered me? The powerful word of God!

WRITE ONE SCRIPTURE

I no longer had time to write pages of revelation, but I could find time to write one verse! This became a lifesaver for me. I purchased a journal with two or three days to a page with room enough to write one Scripture. This was all I could do in that season. Dear busy mother, I think you can find time to write ONE VERSE!

My season has changed again and now I find time to write more. Each New Year I purchase a hard-covered journal that has a full page to write. I don't use this journal to write my schedules, but to write God's revelation to me each day. If you were to ask me at the end of the day what God told me in the morning, I may have forgotten, but I can always check my journal. That's why I love to write. I don't want to forget one word God speaks to me. Every word is life to me.

BIBLE BASKET

This is another wonderful idea for you in your baby/toddler season (and for the rest of your life). I continue this today. Find a suitable basket you can carry with you. Put in it your Bible and hard-covered journal, a Daily Devotional of your choice (perhaps this one you are reading or Volumes 1, 2, or 3) and maybe an old hymn book. Some of the old hymns have wonderful words to meditate upon. Don't forget to put in two or three pens so there is always one when you are ready to write. And extra paper and notebooks for a child or children to draw who may be with you.

You can pick up your basket and take it with you anywhere in the house—your kitchen table, where you nurse your baby, your bedroom, outside under a tree while you watch the children play, or wherever you want to go. It's all in the basket. You don't have to run around finding everything when you find another cozy nook somewhere.

My Bible basket continues to do the rounds of my bedroom, my kitchen table in the early morning, and my Above Rubies office downstairs every day. It's beside me right now.

PRAYER:

"Father, I thank You for Your Word which is life-sustaining. You know I don't have hours of time to read, but I ask You to speak to me in the moments I find. I long to hear from You and I am listening and ready. Amen."

AFFIRMATION:

I am ready and listening for God's voice.

8

LEAVING AND CLEAVING
Part 1

*"Therefore shall a man leave his father and his mother,
and shall cleave unto his wife: and they shall be one flesh"*
(GENESIS 2:24).

To be married, we must do three things: leave, cleave, and become one flesh.

We are going to discover what it truly means "to cleave." However, before we can cleave, we must first leave. The word "leave" is *azab* and means "to loosen, relinquish, forsake." This doesn't mean that we forget about our parents. We continue to enjoy a loving and close relationship with them. However, we must understand that when we get married, we begin a new family.

The husband is now responsible to provide for his wife. He doesn't rely on his parents to provide for her. He must leave the dependence upon his parents for provision to "man up," work hard, and provide for his new wife and coming family. The wife no longer relies upon her parents for provision, but upon her husband. He is now her provider and protector. She now looks to her husband for her needs instead of her parents.

She no longer looks to her parents for protection and leadership. She looks to her husband, and he must be ready to rise to this privilege and responsibility.

Both leave behind their single lives which have often been motivated by selfishness. The young husband cannot do what he likes and when he likes any longer. He is responsible for his wife—and preparing to provide for children to come. And if the couple are not thinking about coming children, they are not yet ready for marriage.

The couple leaves behind their single socialness. Of course, they will enjoy friendships with other couples and families, but never again will they go on a date, or even for a cup of coffee with a friend of the opposite sex. Marriage is "forsaking all others." There are too many couples who think they can spend time on their own with the opposite sex. It never works. It destroys the marriage. When you get married you are no longer two people, but one (Matthew 19:5).

The couple no longer hang out with their single friends in the way they did before. They leave behind this lifestyle. It is a new lifestyle. Once again, it doesn't mean they will discard their old friends. They will invite them to meals at their home or to come to functions with them, but they won't spend time "hanging out" with them on their own when they could be with their spouse.

When a new baby is born, someone cuts the umbilical cord so the baby can grow into its new life in this world. When a daughter or son marry, they also cut the umbilical cord to their parents so they can experience the fulness of their new life as a married couple.

We leave when we begin the marriage, but I believe we continue leaving all throughout our marriage. We make the decision to leave when other relationships could take precedence over our marriage relationship. If friendships with others are overclouding our marriage relationship, we step back and leave!

It can often be a temptation when difficult financial times arise in a marriage to go back to wealthy parents. Many parents will help their married children financially, but when they do, the married couple should accept with gratefulness but not rely upon it. Parents can encourage and bless with wisdom but should not exercise final authority.

When you face a dilemma in your marriage, you will often know the answer by adhering to the "leave and cleave" truth. For example, "Do I need to leave this situation or relationship? If it will weaken your "cleaving relationship" in any way, the answer is leave.

"Will becoming involved in this organization or group weaken my "cleaving relationship" with my husband?" If so, don't do it.

"If I do this thing, will it help me to cleave more to my husband?" If not, don't do it. Get the picture?

It is interesting to note that when God established this principle of *therefore shall a man leave his father and mother,* there was yet no father and mother on the earth! God was laying down His foundation of truth for marriage for all future generations.

This message is so important that Jesus emphasized it again in Matthew 19:4-6, and Paul revealed the truth again in Ephesians 5:22-33. Paul spoke of marriage as the great mystery, revealing the relationship of Christ and His beloved bride, the church. Verses 31 and 32 say: *"For this cause shall a man leave his father and mother, and shall be joined unto his wife, and they two shall be one flesh. This is a great mystery: but I speak concerning Christ and the church."*

When we come to Christ, we leave behind our old life, our old relationships, and our old ways. We are now joined to Christ and one with Him. We have entered a new kingdom, the kingdom of Christ, and we embark on living a totally new lifestyle. Our marriage relationship pictures this great truth. It is imperative that we do not disfigure this beautiful picture.

PRAYER:

'Thank You, dear Father, that marriage is Your design. You chose this earthly way of revealing Your heavenly and ultimate plan of the marriage of Jesus Christ to His bride, the church. Please help me to live in such a way that I show a true example of this truth through our marriage. Amen."

AFFIRMATION:

I joyfully leave any situation or any organization that weakens cleaving to my husband.

9

CLEAVING
Part 2

"Draw me, we will run after thee . . ."
(SONG OF SONGS 1:4).

Now that we have learned how important it is to leave, we must discover what it truly means to cleave. This Hebrew word *dabaq* is translated by 10 different English words in the King James Bible. As we look at each one, we come to a greater understanding of how to cleave.

1. CLEAVE

The word cleave is used in the King James Bible in Genesis 2:24. It means "to cling to, to adhere to, to be stuck to, to hold fast, and to be joined." Most modern translations use the word "united" which I don't think is as strong as cleave.

I love this quote of John Piper: "There has never been a generation whose view of marriage is high enough." I believe this is true. I don't think any of us understand the fullness and glory of God's value of marriage. God speaks of being married to Israel and uses "cleave" to reveal this relationship between Him and His people Israel, and in the New Testament of Christ and His bride, the church.

Let's look at some Old Testament Scriptures. As you read them, relate the words to your marriage.

Deuteronomy 10:20: *"Thou shalt fear the LORD thy God; him shalt thou serve, and to him shalt thou cleave."* Also read Deuteronomy 11:21, 22 and 30:19, 20.

Deuteronomy 13:4: *"Ye shall walk after the LORD your God, and fear him, and keep his commandments, and obey his voice, and ye shall serve him, and cleave unto him."* Go back and read this Scripture again. Can you count six things God wants us to do toward Him?

Notice six things again in Joshua 22:5: *"But take diligent heed to do the commandment and the law . . . to love the LORD your God, and to walk in all his ways and to keep his commandments, and to cleave unto him, and to serve him with all your heart and with all your soul."* Did you count six?

Jeremiah 13:11 tells us: *"For as the girdle cleaveth to the loins of a man, so have I caused to cleave unto me the whole house of Israel and the whole house of Judah, saith the LORD; that they might be unto me for a people, and for a name, and for a praise, and for a glory."* This is the relationship God wanted with His people Israel. This is the relationship God wants us to have in our marriage. When we cleave to one another in marriage, we reveal the picture of our relationship with God and Christ. And when we live this lifestyle, our marriages will be a praise and glory to God in this world.

2. OVERTAKE

Judges 18:22 tells how the Israelites pursued the Benjaminites and "*overtook* (dabaq)" them in the battle. How did they overtake them? They had to chase after them. I can't imagine them idling along as though they were out for a Sunday school picnic. They chased after them with every ounce of their strength. Now ladies, this is the same word that is used to describe your marriage relationship. Are you chasing after our husband with love, kindness, and encouragement?

3. PURSUE

We read this word in the battle of Benjamin and the rest of Israel. Judges 20:45 tells us that they *"pursued (dabaq) hard after them."* You may have pursued your husband before marriage, but are you continuing to pursue him? That's the secret of a wonderful marriage.

4. FOLLOW HARD

This is the third word for *dabaq* that the Bible uses in the context of battle.

1 Samuel 14:22 tells how the men of Israel *"followed hard"* after the Philistines in battle and defeated them.

1 Samuel 31:2; 2 Samuel 1:6; and 1 Chronicles 10:2 tell the sad story of how the Philistines *"followed hard upon Saul and upon his sons."* This time the Israelites were defeated, and Saul and his three sons were killed.

David, who was one of the greatest warriors of all time used the same analogy of chasing the enemy for his passion for chasing after God. In Psalm 63:8 he says: *"My soul followeth hard after thee."*

Are you getting the picture of what it really mans to cleave? It's not a casual thing. When warriors *"follow hard"* after the enemy, they exert every ounce of their physical strength and mental concentration. Their adrenaline pumps. The sweat pours off them. They are not thinking of another thing except how to defeat the enemy.

We learn two things from these words. Firstly, we must be vigilant in pursuing the devil and his cohorts who want to bring down and defeat our marriages. The devil hates marriage. He wants to break up your marriage. Therefore, you must be alert. Pounce on any suggestion the enemy brings to your mind to weaken your marriage. Go hard after the enemy and kick him out.

1 Peter 5:8 says: *"Be sober, be vigilant; because your adversary the devil, as a roaring lion, walketh about, seeking whom he may devour: Whom resist steadfast in the faith . . ."*

Secondly, on the positive side, we must "follow hard" after our spouse. Do you notice that it doesn't say to follow, but to follow hard? Does your love feel a little cold in your marriage? Chase after your husband with love and devotion. Think of new and creative ways to show your love to him. Exert every bit of your physical and mental strength. Chase him like a warrior in battle.

PRAYER:

"Oh God, I am sorry for taking my marriage lightly. Please help me to understand how You see marriage. Please help me and show me how to chase after my husband with tangible ways of loving him. Amen."

AFFIRMATION:

I am not settling for an average marriage. I'm pursuing my husband with all my mind and strength.

10

CLEAVING
Part 3

"His mouth is most sweet: yea, he is altogether lovely. This is my beloved, and this is my friend, O daughters of Jerusalem"
(SONG OF SONGS 5:16).

We continue looking at the words to describe cleave.

5. FOLLOW CLOSE

God warned the people through the prophet Jeremiah that He would send them to Babylon. This was God's judgment upon them because of their sin. However, they thought they could avoid judgment by going down to Egypt. But Jeremiah spoke the word of the Lord in Jeremiah 42:16: *"The sword, which ye feared, shall overtake you there in the land of Egypt, and the famine, whereof ye were afraid, shall follow close (dabaq) after you there in Egypt."*

This time the Bible uses the words *"follow close."* This is also a lovely meaning of "cleave." We must follow close to our husbands. We don't allow rifts to come between us. Life is not perfect and neither husband or wife always say or do everything right. Often an aloofness comes between you because you feel hurt by the way your spouse has spoken to you or treated you. But we must not allow this aloofness to become a "cold front." Even if we don't feel like it, we all must do whatever we need to do to bring back the closeness. This is what it means to cleave, and this is what marriage is all about.

We don't automatically stay close. We *work* at staying close together. Have you allowed a distance to come into your relationship? What can you do today to bridge that gap again? It won't be easy, but this is what you must do. For your own sake. For the sake of your marriage. For the sake of your children. And for the sake of generations to come!

6. STICK TO/CLING TO

Psalm 119:31: *"I have stuck (dabaq) unto thy testimonies: O LORD put me not to shame."* The psalmist sticks to and cleaves to God's Word. This word is used in the context of sticking to our marriage, sticking to God's Word, and sticking close to God. That's why marriage is a picture of our relationship with God. Our marriage relationship reveals to others what our relationship with God is like.

What does it mean to stick to God's testimonies and stick to our marriages? Other translations say: "hold tight, hold fast, and cling tightly."

7. TAKE

The word *dabaq is* translated "take" in Genesis 19:19: *"I cannot escape to the mountain, lest some evil take me, and I die."* As we read this, we realize that "taking" is not a little tap on the shoulder but the complete capturing of someone.

We now look at another nuance of this word. When we marry, the husband captures his wife, and she becomes his. She belongs to no one else but him! The wife captures her husband, and he belongs to no one else but her! That's it. Period. *"I am my beloved's, and my beloved is mine"* (Song of Songs 6:3).

We confess this word in our vows on our wedding day. Do you remember?

"I TAKE thee to be my wedded husband, to have and to hold from this day forward, for better for worse, for richer for poorer, and in sickness and in health, to love and to cherish, and to obey, till death do us part according to God's holy ordinance, and thereto I pledge thee my troth."

By the way, you may not have said the word "troth" on your wedding day. These are the original wedding vows. But it's a good word and means "faithfulness and loyalty when pledging a solemn agreement."

"Cleave" or "take" is a verb. It's not passive. Not only on our wedding day, but each new day we "take" our husbands again for better for worse! I think it is more exciting to think of capturing our husbands. Why not capture your husband today and let him know tangibly how much you love him?

PRAYER:

"Dear Father, please teach me how to follow close to my husband and to reveal to our children and those around us a picture of the relationship of Christ and His church. Amen."

AFFIRMATION:

I take my husband without reservations today, tomorrow, and each new day.

11

CLEAVING
Part 4

"I am my beloved's, and my beloved is mine."
(Song of Songs 6:3).

Today we look at the last three words used for "cleave."

8. ABIDE/STAY CLOSE HERE

We find these words in the book of Ruth. Let's read Ruth 2:8, 23 (HCSB): *"Then Boaz said to Ruth, 'Listen, my daughter. Don't go and gather grain in another field, and don't leave this one, but stay here close (dabaq) . . . Ruth stayed close (dabaq) . . ."*

The Bible is not an ordinary book. Every line is alive with the power of God. Every story of a Bible character is not only a story about their lives but written for our example.

1 Corinthians 10:11 says: *"Now all these things happened unto them for examples: and they are written for our admonition, upon whom the ends of the world are come."*

Although the above words were spoken directly to Ruth, I believe God also speaks His word to every wife and mother through this Scripture. He says to us: "Don't go and glean in another field. I have given you your field in which to glean. It is my perfect and best will for you. Don't leave it. Stay close."

If God has given you children, then this is the field He has given to you. He doesn't give you children to give to someone else to look after. He gives them to you to love, nurture, train, and prepare for the future and for eternity.

Ruth could have looked over at other fields and thought, "Oh, there is so much more to glean over there, but now I am stuck here." Instead, she submitted to Boaz' words and ultimately received incredible blessings. What a blessing to marry Boaz. She became the great-grandmother of King David and in the Messianic line of the birth of Jesus.

These words, *"stay here close,"* also speak into our marriages. Once again, it is the same Hebrew word used in Genesis 2:24. God wants you to stay close to your husband. He doesn't want you to look at any other man. Or be jealous of someone else's marriage. When tempted, resist these destructive thoughts in the power of the name of Jesus. Stay close to your husband. Don't compare your marriage with another marriage. This is your marriage, and it will be different and special to you and your husband.

You can have the greatest marriage as you *make* it the greatest marriage. You will do this as you stay close. Don't look to other fields.

9. KEEP

Numbers 36:7, 9, 12 speak about keeping to your own inheritance. God wants you to keep to your own marriage. He wants you to find your sustenance, satisfaction, delight, and inheritance in your own marriage.

Read Proverbs 5:15-20 which is an allegory revealing the difference between private property versus common property. Verses 15 and 17 (AMP) say: *"Drink water from your own cistern (of a pure marriage relationship) and fresh running water from your own well . . . (Confine yourself to your own wife.) Let your children be yours alone, and not the children of strangers with you . . ."*

Our wedding vows also use the word "keep."

"Wilt thou have this man to be thy wedded husband to live together after God's ordinance in the Holy Estate of matrimony? Wilt thou love him, comfort him, honor and KEEP him, in sickness and in health, and forsaking all other keep thee only unto him as long as you both shall live?"

We covenant to keep ourselves only for our husbands.

10. CLOSELY SEALED

We find this word in the description about the leviathan in Job 41:15-17 (HCSB): *"His pride is in his rows of scales, closely sealed together (dabaq). One scale is so close to another that no air can pass between them."* They are joined so closely that they cannot be separated.

What do you think of that? God wants us as husband and wife to be joined so closely that no air can pass between us! Impossible to separate. What a great description of cleaving!

When Jesus was on earth, He confirmed Genesis 2:24. When answering the Pharisees about marriage, He said in Matthew 19:4, 5 (HCSB): *"'Haven't you read,' He replied, 'that He who created them in the beginning made them male and female . . . For this reason a man will leave his father and mother and be joined to his wife, and the two will become one flesh? So they are no longer two, but one flesh.'"*

Jesus not only confirmed God's original words but elevated them to a greater level: *"So they are no longer two, but one flesh. Therefore, what God has joined together, man must not separate"* (Matthew 19:6).

This means we are glued together, never to come apart. We are so stuck together that it's well-nigh impossible for anything or anyone to pull us apart.

My grandson said to me recently, "Nana, they call a husband and wife a couple. But doesn't God say they are one?

"Yes, you are absolutely correct," I replied.

Maybe, rather than saying, "Look at that lovely couple walking along," we should say, "What a lovely "oneness" walking together." Commenting on Matthew 19:5, John D. Garr, Ph. D. states: "Your 'twoness' has ceased to exist." I love that, don't you?

PRAYER:

"Dear Father, please help me to remember that my husband and I are not two but one. You want us to be one—physically, spiritually, mentally, and emotionally. Please help me to create this oneness together. Amen."

AFFIRMATION:

I'm keeping my own vineyard and my own marriage.

12

SOWING SEEDS OF PEACE
Part 1

"I am planting seeds of peace and prosperity among you."
(ZECHARIAH 8:12 NLT).

God spoke these words to encourage the people when rebuilding the temple of Jerusalem. You are also involved in a building program, the most important one in the nation. As you establish your family, you establish and strengthen the nation.

As you build your marriage and home, God wants to speak peace and prosperity to you too.

Sowing peace is God's character and His way. Because God created us in His image, it should also be our way. When we sow seeds of peace, we reap a harvest of peace.

How can we sow seeds of peace in our homes and families? The following are some seeds that I am sure will bring a harvest of peace to you personally and to your household. As you read these Scriptures you will notice there are conditions for peace. It doesn't automatically happen. We reap what we sow.

1. SEEK FOR PEACE

I believe this is the first thing we need to do. Every morning when we have devotions as a family, my husband prays for peace to fill our home. If we seek it, we are well on the way toward making it happen.

Psalm 34:14: *"Seek peace, and pursue it."* To pursue means "to run after." It's the same word that is used repeatedly in the Bible when soldiers were chasing their enemies. They pursued them with all their strength and energy! They didn't give up until they captured them.

Romans 14:19: *"Let us therefore follow after (pursue) the things which make for peace, and things wherewith one may edify another."*

Hebrews 12:14 (ESV): *"Strive for peace with everyone, and for the holiness without which no one will see the Lord."*

1 Peter 3:11 (NLT): *'Seek peace, and work to maintain it."*

2. SPEAK PEACE

We should not only seek peace but speak peace. Words have power; they release what we say.

As we were raising our older children, my husband constantly confessed: "I am a man of peace" or "I am for peace." We needed that confession with our very exuberant and outspoken children. Unfortunately, our children seem to have "loudness" in their genes. My husband comes from a family of nine children. They all serve God with all their hearts but have very loud voices, are very opinionated, and are not afraid to speak their ideas. Never a dull moment when we are together.

I come from a smaller family but just as loud. A friend of ours, who lived with us for a while as we raised our family often stated: "What hope do your children have with a "Crowin' Campbell" for a father and a "Blowin' Bowen" for a mother!" Amazingly, amid all our loudness, we mostly had an atmosphere of peace.

Speak the peace of God over your children. Walk into your kitchen with your "gospel of peace" shoes on your feet and release peace over each one of your children. Pray it over them. Confess it over them. Speak it into their lives. Be a peace-bearer rather than a tension-bearer.

I love the Jewish greeting of shalom, meaning peace. What a wonderful way to greet people. We read one of David's greetings in 1 Samuel 25:6: *"Peace be both to thee, and peace be to thine house, and peace be unto all that thou hast."*

Amasai's greeting to David in 1 Chronicles 12:18: *"Peace be unto thee, and peace be to thine helpers."*

Psalm 85:8: *"(God) will speak peace unto his people, and to his saints."*

John 20:19-21 tells us how Jesus greeted people when He came into a home: *"When the doors were shut where the disciples were assembled for fear of the Jews, came Jesus and stood in the midst, and saith unto them, Peace be unto you. And when he had so said, he showed unto them his hands and his side. Then were the disciples glad, when they saw the Lord. Then said Jesus to them **again**, Peace be unto you."* Also read Luke 24:36-40.

And Luke 10:5 tells how Jesus encouraged others to do the same: *"And into whatsoever house ye enter, first say, Peace be to this house."* Wouldn't it be a wonderful thing if we spoke words of peace to every house we enter?

PRAYER:

"Dear Father, I long for peace. I don't want tension in my home. Please teach me how to be a peacemaker. Amen."

AFFIRMATION:

I am a peace-sower in my home.

13

SOWING SEEDS OF PEACE
Part 2

*"Peace I leave with you, my peace I give unto you: not as the world giveth,
give I unto you. Let not your heart be troubled, neither let it be afraid"*
(JOHN 14:27).

Have you begun sowing and speaking seeds of peace in your home? You sowed a few seeds? That's great. You wished you could have sown more? Don't despair. Keep at it. Make it a habit and it will become a way of life. Here are some more seeds for you to sow:

3. FORGET YOUR WORRIES

Worry is the worst thing to spoil peace. When you worry, your mind is in turmoil, and you are miserable. And even worse, you put this misery on your husband and your children. God commands us to do the opposite:

Philippians 4:6, 7 (NASB): "***Be anxious for nothing*** . . . *And the peace of God, which surpasses all comprehension, will guard your hearts and minds in Christ Jesus.*" In other words, don't worry about anything! Easier said than done! But if we want peace in our hearts and homes, we must practice the habit.

Don't feed your worries and problems. Cast them away from you instead. Don't allow the following lines to be your testimony:

I made a nest for my worries and care;
They grew bigger because I fed them there.

Each time you face another problem, instead of worrying, turn it over to the Lord. Look to Him rather than your circumstances. It takes a while to get into this habit, but it will change your life. You can then walk in peace even during the storm.

4. PRAY FOR PEACE

Did you notice that I left some words out of Philippians 4:6, 7 (NASB)? Let me write it again for you: *"Be anxious for nothing: but in **everything by prayer and supplication** . . . let your requests be made known to God. And the peace of God, which surpasses all comprehension, will guard your hearts and minds in Christ Jesus."*

Here is another condition for peace—pray about everything! Not just some things, but everything! Every little thing and every big thing.

Corrie Ten Boom stated: "The wonderful thing about praying is that you leave a world of not being able to do something and enter God's realm where everything is possible." Prayer is the supernatural realm. Why stay in your earthly realm where you are full of despair and have no answers when you can enter God's supernatural realm of prayer? You will move into peace into this realm.

God commanded us to pray for the peace of His city, Jerusalem (Psalm 122:6). He also reminds us to pray for the city in which we live (Jeremiah 29:7). Therefore, it is just as important to pray for the peace of our homes. If every family prayed for the peace of God to be in their homes, we would experience more peace in our homes, in our cities, and ultimately our nation.

Can you say Amen with me?

5. KEEP A THANKFUL HEART

Can you believe it? I still left out some words from Philippians 4:6, 7. Important words too. They are *"with thankfulness."* We are not only to pray about everything, but to be thankful about everything. Check it in your Bible and underline it. There is no greater way to live in peace than to keep a heart filled with gratitude and thankfulness. You will eliminate so much stress and tension. God says you will begin to enjoy peace that *"passeth all understanding."* Do you think you could make it a habit of your life?

6. LOVE AND OBEY GOD'S WORD

We sow peace into our home when we love God's Word. Read the blessings we receive when we are obedient to God and His Word.

Psalm 81:13-16: *"Oh that my people had hearkened unto me, and Israel had walked in my ways!* (Notice the exclamation mark!) *I should soon have subdued their enemies, and turned my hand against their adversaries . . . He should have fed them also with the finest of the wheat: and with honey out of the rock should I have satisfied thee."*

Psalm 119:165: *"Great peace have they which love thy law: and nothing shall offend them."*

Isaiah 48:18: *"O that thou hadst hearkened to my commandments!* (Notice another exclamation mark!) *then had thy peace been as a river, and thy righteousness as the waves of the sea."*

It is not always easy to obey God's Word. His ways are usually the opposite of the way we feel, but obedience always bring peace.

Keep sowing seeds of peace. The more you sow, the more you will reap.

PRAYER:

"Dear Father, Thank You for showing me the way to peace. I want to forget my worries and bring everything to You in prayer. And keep a thankful heart. I thank You that I can trust You wholly. Amen."

AFFIRMATION:

A thankful and prayerful heart equal peace.

14

SOWING SEEDS OF PEACE
Part 3

*"These things I have spoken unto you, that in me ye might
have peace. In the world ye shall have tribulation:
but be of good cheer; I have overcome the world"*
(JOHN 16:33).

Henry Drummond writes: "The Christian life is not casual but causal."
To live in peace, we must sow seeds of peace. Jesus said: "Blessed are
the peacemakers." Peace doesn't just happen; we must make it happen.

Let's look at a few more peace-seeds to sow in our homes.

7. BLESS WITH PEACE

Psalm 29:11 tells us that God wants to bless His people with peace.
Therefore, we should also want to bless our household with peace. After
David and the people had enjoyed great celebrations when they brought
the ark back to Jerusalem, David thought of home. 2 Samuel 6:20 says that
"David returned to bless his household."

8. STAY YOUR MIND ON GOD

One of my favorite Scriptures is Isaiah 26:3, 4: *"Thou wilt keep him in
perfect peace, whose mind is stayed on thee: because he trusteth in thee. Trust
ye in the LORD forever: for in the LORD JEHOVAH is everlasting strength."*

What's your mindset? Do you keep it on your problems? Or do you fix it
upon the Lord? When we sow the habit of bringing our thought life to the
Lord, we experience peace. Not only peace, but perfect peace. It is a plural
word in the Hebrew meaning "peace, peace!

9. HOLD YOUR TONGUE

Perhaps this is one of the biggest ways to keep peace. It's easy to spout off words that cause discord. It's easy to react with words that cause pain or even incite rebellion. It's easy to answer back when accused. God's Word reminds us . . .

Proverbs 10:19: *"In the multitude of words there wanteth not sin: but he that refraineth his lips is wise."* The NLT doesn't mince words when it says: *"Too much talk leads to sin. Be sensible and keep your mouth shut."* In other words, the less we speak, the less we sin!

Proverbs 17:27, 28: *"He that hath knowledge spareth his words . . . Even a fool, when he holdeth his peace, is counted wise: and he that shutteth his lips is esteemed a man of understanding."*

Proverbs 29:11: *"A fool uttereth all his mind: but a wise man keepeth it in till afterwards."*

Proverbs 15:1: *"A soft answer turneth away wrath: but grievous words stir up anger."*

If you cannot give a soft answer, it is best not to open your mouth! One of the greatest disciplines of a godly woman is to learn how to hold her tongue! Let's pray that God will enable us to shut our mouths and hold back all words that are negative, ungodly, shallow, silly, hurtful, slanderous, unbelieving, and which do not inspire faith.

I am challenged by Jesus' reaction when he was accused:

Isaiah 53:7: *"He was oppressed, and he was afflicted, yet he opened not his mouth."*

Matthew 26:62, 63: *"The high priest arose, and said unto him, Answerest thou nothing? What is it which these witness against thee? But Jesus held his peace."* Other translations say: *"Jesus remained silent."*

Matthew 27:12, 13: *"When he was accused of the chief priests and elders, he answered nothing. Then said Pilate unto him, Hearest thou not how many things they witness against thee? And he answered him to never a word."*

1 Peter 2:23: *"Who, when he was reviled, reviled not again."*

10. LOVE RIGHTEOUSNESS

Psalm 85:10: *"Righteousness and peace have kissed each other."*

You can't have peace without righteousness. They are inseparable. But righteousness is more than turning away from evil. It is doing righteous deeds. Righteousness is not stagnant. It is alive. You reveal it in your facial features as you smile at your family and speak positive things. It comes out your fingertips as you work and toil for the blessing of your family or hug and embrace your children. It shows itself as you do good deeds for your family and others.

We see this in Isaiah 32:17: *"The **work** of righteousness shall be peace; and the effect of righteousness quietness and assurance forever."* Do you notice that righteousness is a work? And do you notice the cause and effect? The effect is peace!

Verse 18 states: *"And my people shall dwell in a peaceable habitation, and in sure dwellings, and in quiet resting places."*

If you want peace in your home, you must sow seeds of righteousness. That means saying No to certain TV programs, DVDs, and social media. It means taking a stand against the spirit of the world entering your home. Peace does not come by compromise or even by feeling good. Sometimes people equate peace with calm. Anyone can feel peaceful when everything is going perfect. True peace rests on a foundation of righteousness (Hosea 10:12).

PRAYER:
"Oh God, it is so easy to retaliate. Please help me to hold my tongue, and when I open my mouth, please help me to sow words of peace. Amen."

AFFIRMATION:
Peacemaking is my job today!

15

SOWING SEEDS OF PEACE
Part 4

"Depart from evil, and do good; seek peace, and pursue it"
(Psalm 34:14 and 1 Peter 3:11).

11. DISCIPLINE FOR PEACE

This doesn't sound very peaceful, does it? We often think that if we rock the boat, we won't have peace! But the opposite is true. Discipline precedes peace! Read that again. Yes, discipline precedes peace! If your children are playing up, disobeying, being defiant, and causing havoc in the home, you won't have any peace. To get peace, you must deal with the disobedience or bad behavior.

One of my favorite Scriptures for parenting is Proverbs 29:17: *"Correct thy son, and he shall give thee rest; yea, he shall give delight unto thy soul."*

Do you want rest and peace in your home? Don't gloss over disobedience. Deal with the issues. Sow loving but firm discipline for disobedient behavior and you will reap a reward of rest. Many parents have no rest. Their children are a constant hassle to them because they do not train them. They may yell at them, but yelling doesn't change their behavior.

Hebrews 12:11 reiterates: *"Now no chastening for the present seemeth to be joyous, but grievous; nevertheless, afterward it yieldeth the peaceable fruit of righteousness unto them which are exercised thereby."*

Romans 16:20 is an interesting Scripture: *"And the God of peace shall bruise Satan under your feet shortly."* You would think that when it speaks of God defeating the devil that He would be called the God of War or the Lord of hosts, which means "the Lord of Heaven's armies." It will not be a peaceful task to conquer Satan. It will be war and blood and tears. And yet the One who comes to conquer Satan is called the God of peace. I am sure this is because there can never be true peace while evil reigns and therefore it is the God of peace who wages war to bring peace.

You too may have a little war (or big war) before you experience peace. Don't be afraid. Covering over things will not bring peace. It is like a festering sore that will not heal until it is fully cleansed. If you don't deal with the problem and gloss over it instead, it always comes back to bite you.

12. RECONCILE FOR PEACE

You cannot have peace if you have estranged relationships. To enjoy peace, you must seek healing and restoration. Sow seeds of reconciliation. Don't let the sun go down while you are still angry. You won't have peace until you forgive and reconcile.

Ephesians 4:26 (ESV): *"Be angry and do not sin; do not let the sun go down on your anger, and give no opportunity to the devil."*

13. KEEP UNITY

Sow unity in your marriage relationship. If you don't have unity together, you won't have peace in your heart or home. Neither will your children know peace. When there is estrangement between you and your husband, the children bear the brunt of it.

Acknowledge the truth that God has made you one. Not two, but one! Sow seeds to make this oneness a reality. Say sorry. Forgive. Swallow your pride. Humble yourself. Shut your mouth. Speak soft words. Say "I love you" constantly. Submit for your own blessing. As you sow these seeds, you'll reap peace.

14. DON'T COMPROMISE

We often think that if we compromise, it will make things peaceful. Let me tell you, it never works. Compromise always boomerangs back upon you.

Do you remember how Eleazar the priest did not hesitate to act against the adulterous couple? He took a javelin in his hand and thrust it right through the couple. And God stopped the plague. God blessed Eleazar and said: *"Behold, I give unto him my covenant of peace: And he shall have it, and his seed after him, even the covenant of an everlasting priesthood; because he was zealous for his God"* (Numbers 25:12, 13).

15. ORDER YOUR HOME

It is difficult to have peace when you live in a mess. 1 Timothy 5:14

tells us that the young women are to *"guide the house."* The Greek word for this phrase is *oikodespoteo* coming from two words: oikos – home, and despotace – master. God has given you the responsibility to manage your home—to keep it in order and running smoothly.

Don't forget the principle of cause and effect. If you want peace, do things that will bring order and peace. If you have clutter everywhere and dishes and laundry piled up, you won't be able to think straight. Order brings serenity. Sow seeds for a harvest of peace by de-cluttering your home.

If you have loads of junk, it can be daunting to start on this venture. Take one room at a time. Be ruthless. Get rid of everything you don't need. Purge. The more you eradicate, the more serenity will come to your soul.

Sow seeds of peace daily and your harvest time will come.

PRAYER:

"Dear Father in Heaven, thank You for reminding me that You want me to make peace. Help me to be a peacemaker! As I sow seeds of peace, I know You will bring the wonderful harvest. Amen."

AFFIRMATION:

I aim for peace, but never by compromise.

NEW STRENGTH FOR EACH DAY

"For the eyes of the LORD run to and fro throughout the whole earth, to show himself strong in the behalf of them whose heart is perfect toward him."
(2 CHRONICLES 16:9).

STRENGTH FOR EACH NEW DAY

Deuteronomy 33:1, 24, 25: *"This is the blessing wherewith Moses the man of God blessed the children of Israel . . . Let Asher be blessed with children . . . and as thy days, so shall thy strength be."*

Let's read this Scripture in its true context! Immediately after the "blessing promise" that Asher would be blessed with children, comes the promise: *"As thy days, so shall thy strength be."* As God blessed Asher's family with children, so He provided daily strength and wisdom for the task!

This promise is tailor made for parenting. You may be thinking, "I can't cope with caring for my children," or "How on earth could I ever cope with another child?" But God has promised that when He blesses you with a child that He will give you the strength and enabling to care for this child. He gives new strength for each new day. He doesn't give the strength and ability before the baby arrives, but when this blessing comes from Heaven, He sends His daily strength. Isn't that wonderful?

Whatever responsibilities loom ahead of you, and you wonder how you will cope, don't despair. God will not give you the strength before you need it. When you face the task, you will find God's strength. You only need to get through today! Tomorrow God will come again, refreshing, and renewing you.

Matthew 6:34 (TLB): *"Don't be anxious about tomorrow. God will take care of your tomorrow too. Live one day at a time."*

STRENGTH FOR THE BATTLE

Maybe you are going through a battle in your life. Claim God's Word to you. He has promised to arm you with strength for the battle. He doesn't give you the strength before you face the battle, but when you face it, He will be right there with you!

Psalm 18:39: *"Thou hast girded me with strength unto the battle."*

Isaiah 28:5, 6: *"In that day shall the LORD of hosts be for a crown of glory, and for a diadem of beauty, unto the residue of his people . . . and for strength to them that turn the battle to the gate."*

STRENGTH IN TIME OF TROUBLE

Psalm 37:39: *"The salvation of the righteous is of the LORD: he is their strength in the time of trouble."*

Nahum 1:7: *"The LORD is good, a stronghold in the day of trouble; and he knoweth them that trust in him."*

Dear wife and mother, as you lean on God each new day, He will be . . .

Your strong arm (Psalm 89:10, 21; Isaiah 33:2; and Luke 1:51).

Your strong habitation (Psalm 71:3).

Your strong hand (Psalm 89:13; 136:12; Isaiah 40:10; and Jeremiah 32:21).

Your strong refuge (Psalm 71:7).

Your strong rock (Psalm 31:2).

Your strong tower (Psalm 61:3).

And here is a wonderful promise for you, one for every day of the week. You will find it in Isaiah 41:10.

"Fear not on Sunday,
I am with you on Monday,
Be not dismayed on Tuesday,
I am your God on Wednesday,
I will strengthen you on Thursday,
Yes, I will help you on Friday.
I will uphold you with my righteous right hand on Saturday."

God's strength is yours for today.

PRAYER:

"Dear God and Father, I thank You that I don't have to worry about tomorrow. I trust You for today. I thank You for Your strength for all my needs today. And tomorrow You will give me fresh strength. I thank You that whatever difficulty or pain I must endure, I can endure it in Your strength. Thank You in Jesus' name, Amen."

AFFIRMATION:

My strength is in God and God is my strength.

17

FREELY GIVE
Part 1

"As every man hath received the gift, even so minister the same one to another, as good stewards of the manifold grace of God"
(1 PETER 4:10).

God pours out His gifts upon us and He wants us to pour them out upon others. The word "gift" is the Greek word *charisma* which means a gift of grace. Each one of us has received grace from God, but God's grace is manifold. It is revealed in numberless ways as we need it. As God pours out His grace upon us in a certain way, He does not want us to keep it to ourselves, but to pour it out on others.

We must not do this in a haphazard way, but with a serving heart. The Scripture says that we are to minister the grace to one another. The word "minister" is the Greek word *diakonea* meaning "to serve with an emphasis on work; in a practical sense it means to wait on a table, to serve at dinner, to care for someone's needs." That relates to us as homemakers, doesn't it?

We see a lovely example of this when Jesus healed Peter's mother-in-law who was very sick with a fever. The moment he touched her the fever left her. She received a healing grace of God and immediately poured it back on others. After she was healed, she didn't sit back on the sofa with her feet up, glowing in the joy of her healing. Instead, *"she arose, and ministered unto them"* (Matthew 8:15). She immediately got up and prepared a meal for everyone in the home.

When you receive a spiritual blessing, show your gratefulness by serving others in a practical way. You can pour it back on your family by creating a special meal for them and serving them. When God graciously provides you with a home, either purchased or rented, minister back the grace you have received by showing hospitality and opening your home to others.

In Acts 19:22 Paul talks about Timothy and Erastus who *"ministered unto him,"* the word *diakoneo* again. Timothy and Erastus received the grace of salvation through the ministry of Paul. They returned this grace by serving Paul in a sacrificial and practical way.

Matthew 25:43 encourages us to pour out God's grace by serving those who are hungry, thirsty, naked, sick, in prison, or who are strangers.

Angels love to *diakoneo* (to serve). If they do, surely, we should too (Matthew 4:11 and Hebrews 1:14).

I loved reading this story about General William Booth who founded the Salvation Army along with his wife Catherine. During his last days, he was not able to attend a conference because of ill health. They asked if he would send a written message instead to inspire the people. The message arrived. Instead of a long exhortation, it contained one word: "Others."

Another thing we notice in our Scripture today is that we don't employ our gifts for money, but to serve one another. It is true that God gives talents to us which we can use to help finance the household. Many women have gifts to make all kinds of amazing things which they sell through a web page and therefore help finance the household. This is good, but I don't think we should always use our gifts for monetary gain. We should also give freely of our talents. The emphasis of the Scripture is that we do it to bless others, free of charge. It's good to do things for others freely.

It's important to teach our children this principle too. We teach them that God has given them gifts to help provide for their families one day (especially our sons), but we also teach them to use their gifts to help others. As we see their aptitudes developing, we should encourage them to use them to help those in need.

Do you have the gift to write beautiful script? You may like to make cards and write powerful quotes in them to give or send to those who need encouraging and building up. Do you love to paint? You can not only beautify your own home, but other homes with your wonderful gift. Do you love to cook? Make cookies or your specialty foods to bless tired young mothers and those in need. Perhaps you have the gift of organization. You can use this to help many people in different ways. And so it goes on.

The New English Translation says: *"Just as each one has received a gift, use it to **serve one another** as good stewards of the varied grace of God."*

The New Living Translations says: *"**Use them well** (your gifts) to serve one another."*

Next time God blesses you, which is sure to happen today, because

God pours His grace upon us continually, respond by pouring it out upon someone else.

PRAYER:

"Father, I am a continual recipient of Your grace. Please help me to pour Your grace out upon others, especially those in my own home. Amen."

AFFIRMATION:

I am not keeping all my blessings and abilities to myself but pouring them out on those around me.

18

FREELY GIVE
Part 2

"Freely ye have received, freely give"
(MATTHEW 10:8).

We are learning that as God pours His grace upon us, He wants us to respond by pouring it out on others.

Let's read Ephesians 2:8, 9 as we think more about this: *"For by grace are ye saved though faith; and that not of yourselves; it is the gift of God: not of works, lest any man should boast."* God's grace of salvation is free. It is a gift. No matter how many good works we do, we can never earn it. God gave His Only Son freely. Jesus gave His life freely. He endured pain, persecution, suffering and death to pay for our sins.

> Was it the nails, O Savior,
> That bound Thee to the tree?
> Nay, 'twas Thine everlasting love,
> Thy love for me, for me.

But what happens after we receive this gift of salvation? Although we do not need works to earn our salvation, it propels us into a life of good works. Ephesians 2:10, the Scripture following the truth of free salvation, tells us: *"For we are his workmanship, created in Christ Jesus **unto good works**, which God hath before ordained that we should walk in them."*

There is nothing we can do before the cross, but on the other side of the cross we discover we are now re-created to do good works. These works do not earn our salvation, but they show our thankfulness for our salvation. This is the life God has planned for us.

Were the whole realm of nature mine?
That were an offering far too small,
Love so amazing, so divine,
Demands my soul, my life, my all.

We receive the grace of God freely. Now we freely give it to others. We did not receive salvation because we deserved it. The opposite. Therefore, we pour out grace and blessing on those around us even when they don't deserve it. We prove that we have received the free grace of God by freely giving it to others.

We have opportunities to serve, give, and love freely in our homes as we raise our children! This is our sphere to fulfill good works. Way's translation of Titus 2:5 says that the older women are to teach the younger women *"to recognize that their sphere is home."*

Serve freely in your home today. Pour out God's grace freely. Give lavishly.

He might have doled His blossoms out quite grudgingly,
He might have used His sunset gold so sparingly,
He might have put but one wee star in all the sky,
But since He gave so lavishly, why should not I?
Why should not I?

Luke 6:38 (NLT): *"Give, and you will receive. Your gift will return to you in full—pressed down, shaken together to make room for more, running over, and poured into your lap. The amount you give will determine the amount you get back."*

And what spells joy?

Jesus first,

Others second,

Yourself last!

PRAYER:

"Oh God, please save me from being so mean and stingy. Enlarge my heart to give freely, to pour out Your grace moment by moment. Help me to be a lavish giver. Amen."

AFFIRMATION:

I am looking for opportunities to bless others with the gifts God has given to me. This is my JOY.

19

FOLLOW THE PATTERN

"The LORD our God made a breach upon us,
for that we sought him not after the due order"
(1 CHRONICLES 15:13).

The tabernacle in the wilderness, and later Solomon's temple, were built according to God's heavenly pattern. They were a shadow or type of the heavenly dwelling place of God (Hebrews 8:2-5 and 9: 23, 24). God gave many ordinances for the running of His earthly tabernacle and temple.

Moses followed God's pattern of the heavenly sanctuary to establish God's house on earth. We no longer have need for a tabernacle or temple because Christ now dwells in the hearts of those who receive Him and acknowledge the shedding of His precious blood for their sins.

Because God is a dwelling God, He wants to not only dwell in our hearts but in our homes too. Our greatest privilege is to make our homes a dwelling place for God. Therefore, as we have this vision, we should also follow the pattern God showed for His earthly house. We notice that it didn't run haphazardly. God established daily ordinances, laws, statutes, and set times.

This is the question we must ask ourselves: if God established ordinances and laws to efficiently order His house, surely, we need plans and ordinances to efficiently run our homes?

I don't like to run a rigid household. I want to fill my home with joy and spontaneity. However, I have proved, as I am sure you have too, that I cannot run an efficient household without certain guidelines that everyone in the home must heed.

Ordinances bring order to the home, but they also give freedom to accomplish many projects and visions. What is the result of a home out of order, in a mess, everyone doing their own thing at their own time, and duties left undone? Turmoil. Confusion. Overwhelmingness. No one can accomplish anything of great significance because everyone's mind is in a muddle.

In 1 Chronicles 28:11-13, it tells us how David gave to Solomon the pattern for building the temple. How did David decide on the pattern? He received it *"by the Spirit"* (verse 12). I love that, don't you? God showed him, right down to the exact duties for the priests and Levites, their times, and courses, and even for all the vessels they would use. Every practical detail. Isn't that amazing?

God will also show you how He wants you to order your home. Take time to let Him speak to you by His Holy Spirit and put into action what He reveals to you. It's not enough to get a vision, you must implement your vision. You must make it happen in your home. My constant affirmation is: Nothing just happens; you have to make it happen!

It won't be easy. You may receive opposition. Children invariably want to do their own thing—the little ones and older ones. It's the way of the flesh. However, keep establishing the laws until they are the habit of their lives. Ultimately, they will bring freedom and joy to their lives.

Start life at the beginning of the day. All children should be up, dressed, and ready for breakfast by a certain time. You will establish the time for your home. Those who are old enough should also make their beds before coming to breakfast. Institute this habit. I don't allow beds to stay unmade in my home. We have Morning Devotions after breakfast, but the only way I can make this happen is to have everyone up in time for breakfast.

I am amazed that in some homes, teens are allowed to sleep in and get up when they like. This does not train them for diligence or for one day running their own home. The easiest way for homes to become a mess is to sleep in. Everything stays out of order for the rest of the day.

After breakfast appoint chores for each member of the family to get the kitchen cleaned and the laundry humming in the machine. All children need to be involved from the youngest to the oldest. When you start your tasks in the morning, aim for a finishing time. No dawdling about! Teach your children to work hard and fast. You are training them for the future! They should learn how to work hard, fast, and joyfully!

Establish a time when you begin preparing the evening meal and the time you eat together as a family. Keep to it. If you leave it to the last minute to prepare, you will not be able to make it the enjoyable, restful gathering time it is meant to be. Once again, we like to have our evening devotions at the end of supper time. This won't happen unless I have the meal ready on time, the table set, and prepare the way for this appointment with God.

It is important to have times for all mealtimes. I also have a law in my home that we only eat meals at the table. If children want snacks during the day, they must eat them in the kitchen, not in the lounge or bedrooms. This causes more cleaning as crumbs and spills end up all over the home.

God also gave orders for Ezekiel's temple. Ezekiel 44:5: *"Son of man, **mark well,** and behold with thine eyes, and hear with thine ears all that I say unto thee concerning all the ordinances of the house of the LORD, and all the laws thereof; and **mark well** the entering in of the house, with every going forth of the sanctuary."*

What ordinances do you have in your home? Each home will be different, and you will pattern it according to your husband's schedule and the children's seasons of life.

Did you notice that you are to "mark well" the coming in and going forth of your home? You must guard the gates of your home. God will show, by His Spirit, the pattern of how He wants you to establish this in your family too.

PRAYER:

"I thank you, dear Father, that You are a God of order. The whole universe runs according to Your divine order. You set decrees for the sea and all of creation. Help me to also run my home in an orderly way that will bring glory to Your name. Please reveal to me by Your Holy Spirit, the plans and ordinances You have for my home. Amen."

AFFIRMATION:

I am walking away from disorder and into God's order.

FURTHER STUDY:

"According to the pattern" (Exodus 25:9, 40 and Numbers 8:4).

According to God's "order" (Leviticus 24:8; 1 Chronicles 6:32; 15:13; 23:31; 24:19; 25:2; 2 Chronicles 8:14; 13:11; 29:35; Psalm 110:4; Luke 1:8; Hebrews 5:6, 10; and 7:11, 17, 21).

God wants order in the gathering together of God's people (1 Corinthians 14:40).

Christ orders His kingdom (Isaiah 9:6, 7).

20

DO YOU SPOON-FEED YOUR CHILDREN?

"Ye are become such as have need of milk, and not of strong meat. For every one that useth milk is unskillful in the word of righteousness: for he is a babe. But strong meat belongeth to them that are of full age, even those who by reason of use have their sense exercised to discern both good and evil"
(HEBREWS 5:12-14).

When a baby begins to eat solid food around nine months, or perhaps six months with a hungry baby, it is a joy to feed them. Sometimes they won't eat their food and we play all kinds of games to make them eat it. The spoonful of food becomes an airplane, or the poor little kitten out in the cold waiting to come into the warm home, and so on.

However, the time comes when they grab the spoon away from us and want to feed themselves. They want their independence. It's normal. We anticipate the time when they will eat on their own. If we were still spoon-feeding our children at five or ten years old, we would be in despair.

Yet isn't it amazing that we often continue to spoon-feed our older children their spiritual food. Some are still spoon-feeding in their teens. Many adults are still spoon-feeding!

Just as a little baby nurses at the breast and then begins to receive food from the spoon, so a newborn babe in Christ must also be nurtured with food. They cannot feed themselves. But growth is part of God's plan—for physical babies and spiritual babies.

As parents, we love to see our children grow physically. We are excited to see them take their first steps, say their first word, develop into adolescents and then adults, filled with all the wonderful talents God has given them. We should have this same excitement about growth in their spiritual lives.

If they are going to grow, we must teach them to feed themselves. They will stay babies if we keep spoon-feeding them.

Many children in Christian homes are taken to Sunday School or Children's Church every Sunday, or perhaps a Bible club during the week, and the parents feel they are catering for them spiritually. These are good things, but they are spoon-feeding. We have a responsibility to teach our children how to feed themselves, how to read God's Word themselves, and how to listen for God to speak to them personally as they read.

I am glad I was taught this principle growing up in my home. We were taught that the normal daily feeding pattern was to start the day with a "Quiet Time" where you take time to read God's Word and pray. We went to church, Sunday School, and Bible clubs, but that didn't suffice. We learned to read the Bible personally.

I learned to read the Word in faith. I read with expectancy, anticipating God to speak to my heart, and because I did not want to forget what God said to me, I wrote what God said to me in a journal. I wrote the Scriptures that spoke to my heart, what God spoke to me personally through them, and then I wrote a responding prayer to the Lord. I continue this habit to this day. As I write the Scriptures, I receive more revelation than when I first read them. As I write what God is saying, more understanding and revelation floods my soul. My spirit is filled up and nourished.

You can teach your older children how to do this by doing it with them each day. You may like to do it as you commence homeschooling each morning. Choose a book of the Bible and ask each one to read the chapter of the day (or a half chapter) silently to themselves. Encourage them to eagerly look for the Scripture that speaks to them. To listen with their inner ears to the voice of the Holy Spirit.

Then ask them to write the Scripture that God illuminated to them in their hard-covered notebook (which you provide for them). Encourage them to write the understanding of the Scripture and what God is saying personally to them and then write a prayer.

The next step is even better. Ask each one to read aloud (including you as the mother) what God has spoken to them. We not only write but speak out what God shows us.

Don't let your children be spiritual dwarfs with stunted growth. Teach them how to independently hear from God each new day. If you can encourage them to establish this habit, they will keep growing all through their lives.

PRAYER:

"Dear Father, help me to have a healthy appetite for Your precious Word. I cannot survive without the daily nourishment You have for me. Help me to teach my children how to personally feed from Your Word so that they will grow strong in the Lord too. Amen."

AFFIRMATION:

I am not raising spoon-feeders. I am raising children who are mature enough to feed from God's Word themselves.

21

SECRETS TO SUCCESS
Part 1

"'As for Me, this is My covenant with them,' says the LORD: 'My Spirit who is on you, and My words that I have put in your mouth, will not depart from your mouth, or from the mouth of your children, or from the mouth of your children's children, from now on and forever,' says the LORD."
(ISAIAH 59:21 HCSB).

Does God want us to prosper? Yes. And He shows us the principles. I found three different Hebrew words for the word success and prosper.

a) *Tsalach* meaning "to press forward, to break out."

b) *Sakal* meaning "to have good success, to be wise, intelligent, have intellectual comprehension, to act in a prosperous manner, skill, understanding, and insight."

c) *Shalah* meaning "to be successful."

I know it's your desire to prosper in life. Even more, you long for your children to prosper. Let's look at the principles God gives us to live a successful life.

1. MEDITATE IN GOD'S WORD DAY AND NIGHT

Joshua 1:8: *"This book of the law shall not depart out of thy mouth; but thou shalt **meditate** therein day and night, that thou mayest observe to do according to all that is written therein: for then thou shalt make thy way **prosperous** (tsalach), and then thou shalt have **good success** (sakal)."* This Scripture uses both words for prosperity.

Our immediate thought about prospering is to send our children to college to get a degree so they are prepared to prosper in life. But God gives us a different plan. He tells us to meditate in His Word day and night.

God's Word should be our life. Our daily guide. Our counsellors for every question and need we have. Our wisdom and knowledge rather than the humanistic wisdom of this world.

Hosea 8:12 says: *"I have written to him the **great** things of my law, but they were counted as a strange thing."* God has given to us His great and amazing, life-giving Word, filled with the treasures of wisdom and knowledge. And yet God's Word is a "strange thing" to many Christians today. It's unrelated to their lives. They are not familiar with it. Many young people know more about the latest movies and actors than they do of God's Word.

The other evening, we had some boys from a Christian family around our table. As we enjoyed Family Devotions together at the end of our evening meal, my husband began to read John 3:16 and asked the boys to finish the Scripture. To our chagrin, they did not even know it! And they came from a "Christian" home. And one was a teenager. How can God's Word be strange to someone growing up in a Christian home?

How much time do you and your children spend in God's Word?

2. KEEP GOD'S WORDS IN YOUR MOUTH

Joshua 1:8: *"This book of the law **shall not depart out of thy mouth** . . . for then thou shalt make thy way prosperous, and then thou shalt have good success."*

When will you have good success? When God's Word is **in your mouth.** Not only in your heart but in your mouth! In your mouth, ready to speak out at any time and in any situation.

What about your children? Do you really want them to be successful in life? Begin **now** to get God's Word into their mouths. Read it together. Talk about it together. Memorize it together.

When you and your children have God's Word in your hearts and in your mouths, you are on the way to success. God always prospers His Word. Therefore, when you speak His Word from your mouth, that Word will prosper in the situation or person into which you speak.

Isaiah 55:11 states: *"So shall my word be that goeth forth out of my mouth: it shall not return unto me void, but it shall **accomplish** that which I please, and it shall **prosper** in the thing whereto I sent it."*

Did you read the Scripture at the beginning? Can I ask you to read Isaiah 59:21 again? These words are a mandate from God for parents. Take hold of them for you and your family. Put them into practice.

PRAYER:

"Dear Father, I confess that Your precious Word has not been pre-eminent in our home life. Please give to me, my husband, and our children a renewed love for Your Word. Help us to be faithful to get it into our hearts and into our mouths. We want Your Word to be the most preeminent treasure in our home. Amen."

AFFIRMATION:

God's Word is going to be the foremost and most celebrated, distinguished, eminent, grandest, greatest, highest, important, matchless, outstanding, predominant, unrivaled, unequaled, and incomparable feature in our home!

22

SECRETS TO SUCCESS
Part 2

"If you seek Him, He will be found by you,
but if you forsake Him, He will reject you forever"
(1 CHRONICLES 28:9 HCSB).

6. NEVER GIVE UP SEEKING GOD

We learn this principle for success from two kings of Judah, Asa and Uzziah. Both began seeking God, but sadly their lives ended tragically.

Asa began his reign over Judah with great gusto. He did that which was good and right in the sight of the Lord. He stood strong against evil. He smashed down the altars of the strange gods, chopped down the Asherah poles, and removed the pagan shrines and incense altars. And he commanded the people to seek God. And because they sought God with all their hearts, He gave them rest.

In 2 Chronicles 14:7 Asa told the people: *"Because we have sought the LORD our God, we have sought him, and he hath given us rest on every side. So they built and prospered."*

He also trained a great army of 580,000 who were all brave warriors. But in this time of peace and blessing a huge army of one million men and 300 chariots came against them from Ethiopia. They were outnumbered. What would they do? Asa was in the habit of seeking the Lord, so he cried out to God: *"LORD, it is nothing with thee to help, whether with many or with them that have no power: help us, O LORD our God; for we rest on thee, and in thy name we go against this multitude. O LORD, thou art our God: let not man prevail against thee"* (2 Chronicles 14:11).

God heard his cry, and He smote the Ethiopians and they fled before Judah. All because he sought the Lord.

God wanted Asa to keep seeking Him so it would become a habit in his life. After this victory, He sent a prophet to him with the word of the Lord:

"Hear ye me, Asa, and all Judah and Benjamin; The LORD is with you, while ye be with him; and if ye seek him, he will be found of you: but if ye forsake him, he will forsake you" (2 Chronicles 15:2).

At that time Asa and all the people *"entered into a covenant to seek the LORD God of their fathers with all their heart and with all their soul; That whosoever would not seek the LORD God of Israel should be put to death, whether small or great, whether man or woman. And they sware unto the LORD with a loud voice, and with shouting, and with trumpets, and with cornets. And all Judah rejoiced at the oath: for they had sworn with all their heart and sought him with their whole desire: and he was found of them: and the LORD gave them rest round about"* (2 Chronicles 15:12-15).

What a wonderful revival! But after Asa had been reigning for 36 years, he became complacent and stopped seeking the Lord. The king of Basha came against him and instead of crying out to the Lord as he did with the Ethiopian army, he contacted the king of Syria (a foreign king) to help him!

Another prophet of the Lord came to Asa and said: *"Because thou hast relied on the king of Syria, and not relied on the LORD thy God, therefore is the host of the king of Syria escaped out of thine hand. Were not the Ethiopians and the Lubims a huge host, with very many chariots and horsemen? Yet because thou didst rely on the LORD, he delivered them into thine hand . . . Herein thou hast done foolishly: therefore from henceforth thou shalt have wars"* (2 Chronicles 16;7-9).

Then Asa became *"diseased in his feet, until his disease was exceeding great: yet in his disease he sought not to the LORD, but to the physicians"* (2 Chronicles 16:12).

What a sad ending to a man who began pursuing God with his whole heart. This story is a great warning to us all that we must **continue** seeking God. We must never give up until the day we die.

Psalm 105:4: *"Seek the LORD, and his strength: seek his face evermore."*

The New English Translation says: *"Seek the LORD and the strength he gives! Seek his presence continually."*

You can read the full story of Asa in 2 Chronicles, chapters 14 – 16.

PRAYER:

"Dear Father, I want to seek Your face daily. And I want to keep seeking Your presence in my life until the day I see You face to face. Please keep tugging at me if ever I move away from Your presence. Amen."

AFFIRMATION:

We are a family who seeks God's presence daily.

23

SECRETS TO SUCCESS
Part 3

"As long as he sought the LORD, God made him to prosper"
(2 Chronicles 26:5).

Today we continue talking about No. 6 Principle, NEVER GIVE UP SEEKING GOD.

King Uzziah was only 16 years old when he began his reign. He began well. He *"did that which was right in the sight of the LORD . . . And he sought God in the days of Zechariah . . . and as long as he sought the LORD, God made Him to prosper"* (2 Chronicles 26:4, 5).

The secret to prosperity is to seek the Lord. Because Uzziah sought the Lord, *"God helped him"* (v 7). Verse 15 tells us that *"his name spread far abroad; for he was marvelously helped, till he was strong."*

And now we have another "but"! 2 Chronicles 26:16 tell us: *"But when he was strong, his heart was lifted up to his destruction."* Remember how King Asa became complacent and forgot to seek God, determining his ruin? God marvelously helped Uzziah to become strong, but when he became powerful, he also became proud, and it led to his destruction.

What happened? Although he was king, he was forbidden to do the work of the priests. But he thought he was beyond the law and went into the Holy Place in the temple to burn incense upon the golden altar of incense.

The priests of the Lord were aghast! Azariah the high priest went running in after him, plus 80 other priests of the Lord, all brave and valiant men. Can you imagine it? Eighty-one priests confronting King Uzziah!

"Get out of the sanctuary," they yelled. "Only the priests who have descended from Aaron have been consecrated to do this sacred task."

In his pride, Uzziah became furious, but as he held the censer in his hand, suddenly leprosy appeared in his forehead. They immediately thrust him out and he was a leper for the rest of his life. He had to live in a separate house and his son Jotham governed in his stead. You can read his whole story in 2 Chronicles, chapter 26.

We dare not ever give up seeking God.

Do you want your children to be successful? Teach them to get into the habit of seeking God each day and to never stop seeking God and relying wholly on Him for the rest of their lives.

7. WORK FOR THE LORD WITH ALL YOUR HEART

We see this principle in the life of Hezekiah. 2 Chronicles 31:21 says: *"And in every work that he began in the service of the house of God, and in the law, and in the commandments, to seek his God, **he did it with all his heart, and prospered.**"*

What service of the Lord are you involved in? If God has blessed you with children, your service to Him is to mother and train your children. Therefore, embrace this high calling and do it with all your heart—even the homely duties of each day that may seem insignificant.

God wants us to not only work with our hands but work with our soul. The Williams translation of Colossians 3:23 says: *"Whatever you may do, work **wholesouledly** for the Lord and not for men, for you know that from the Lord you will receive the inheritance as your remuneration; you are working for your Master Christ."* I've never read the word *"wholesouledly"* before, but I like it, don't you?

The Fenton translation says: *"Working from your soul."*

AMP: *"Work from the soul."*

NET: *"Whatever you're doing, work at it with enthusiasm."*

HCSB: *"Whatever you do, do it enthusiastically."*

TPT: *"Put Your heart and soul into every activity you do."*

Teach this principle to your children. Teach them how to do their chores, not only with their hands but their souls. Train them to work hard with a happy attitude. Don't give up on this training for it is the secret to their future success. If they do not learn to work with all their hearts when they are young, they will not be in the habit when they are older and will deprive themselves of success.

PRAYER:

"Dear Father, You show me clearly from Your Word that I dare not forget to seek You. Please save me from ever getting out of this habit. I do not want to become complacent or proud, but wholly rely upon You. Amen."

AFFIRMATION:

We are a wholesouled family, seeking the Lord wholesouledly, and working for the Lord wholesouledly.

SECRETS FOR SUCCESS
Part 4

"Keep thy heart with all diligence; for out of it are the issues of life"
(PROVERBS 4:23).

8. LIVE IN THE PRESENCE OF THE LORD

We either live our lives independently, trust in ourselves, or rely upon God moment by moment. This is the picture of abiding in Christ, living in His presence, walking with Him.

We read the example of four different men who lived in God's presence.

ABRAHAM

When Abraham told Eliezer, his servant, to go and find a bride for his son, Isaac, he said: *"The LORD, before whom I walk, will send his angel with thee, and prosper thy way, and thou shalt take a wife for my son of my kindred and my father's house"* (Genesis 24:0).

What a beautiful testimony! Wouldn't you love to have that testimony spoken over your life? Because Abraham walked with God each day, He knew His God. He knew he could trust Him to give Eliezer success to find a bride for his son.

Other translations say:

AMPC: *"The Lord, in Whose presence I walk (habitually), will send His Angel with you and prosper your way."*

NLT: *"The LORD, in whose presence I have lived . . ."*

JOSEPH

Although Joseph went through much suffering, being cast out from his family as a teenager, thrown out of Potiphar's house because of lies, and then put in prison and forgotten, yet in every situation God made him successful because he acknowledged Him in everything he did.

Read the whole chapter of Genesis 39 to see how God was with Joseph: *"And **the LORD was with Joseph**, and he was a prosperous man, and he was in the house of his master the Egyptian. And his master saw that **the LORD was with him**, and that the LORD made all that he did to prosper in his hand. . . The keeper of the prison looked not to anything that was under his hand: because **the LORD was with him**, and that which he did, the LORD made it to prosper."*

HEZEKIAH

Hezekiah's testimony was that he cleaved to the Lord walked in God's presence.

2 Kings 18:3-5: *"He trusted in the LORD God of Israel . . . For he cleaved to the LORD, and departed not from following him, but kept his commandments . . . And **the LORD was with him**; and he prospered withersoever he went forth."*

ASA

King Asa also had this testimony in the days when he sought after God. 2 Chronicles 15:9: *"They fell to him out of Israel in abundance, when they saw that **the LORD his God was with him**."*

Do our children see that we live in the presence of the Lord? Do people around about us see that the Lord is with us?

9. KEEP A SOFT HEART

How important it is to keep a soft heart before the Lord. This is one of the great secrets to success.

Job 9:4: *"Who hath hardened himself against him, and hath prospered?"* This is a rhetorical question. The answer is obvious. We will never prosper if we don't let go of hardness and bitterness.

Proverbs 29:1 (NKJV): *"He who is often rebuked, and hardens his neck, will suddenly be destroyed and that without remedy."*

Proverbs 29:1 (TPT): *"Stubborn people who repeatedly refuse to accept correction, will suddenly be broken and never recover."*

Proverbs 29:1 (NET): *"The one who stiffens his neck after numerous rebukes will suddenly be destroyed without remedy."*

We remember Jesus' words to us in Matthew 19:8 that *"hardness of heart"* leads to divorce. We must take the warning of this Scripture to heart.

Life is not perfect. Marriage is not perfect. There will be times when your husband says and does things that hurt you. You can either get hard and bitter which, if you let hardness fester, can lead to divorce and destruction. Or you can ask the Holy Spirit to work in your heart, melt the hardness, and give you a soft heart.

A soft heart is beautiful thing. It leads to life, peace, and blessing.

PRAYER:

"Dear Father, I want to keep a soft heart before You in every situation. Please expose any hardness in my heart that grieves Your Holy Spirit. Amen."

AFFIRMATION:

To keep a soft heart is my daily desire,
I won't stay cold for my heart's on fire.

25

SECRETS FOR SUCCESS
Part 5

"Keep thy heart with all diligence; for out of it are the issues of life"
(PROVERBS 4:23).

We look at the last point for success today.

10. DO NOT COMPROMISE

Sometimes Christians may be tempted to compromise for the sake of success. They lower their standards to the standards of the world. They stay silent when they should speak up for truth. All because they may not receive the favor of the world around them. But if we want God's prosperity upon our lives, we must never compromise.

Young Hananiah (Jehovah is gracious), Mishael (Who is he that is God?), and Azariah (God has helped) were dragged from their beloved homeland of Judah to the foreign land of Babylon. They were now captives. These young men, along with Daniel (and maybe others), were chosen for training and indoctrination into Babylonian life. Their original Hebrew names were changed to the names of Babylonian gods—Shadrach, Meshach, and Abednego. Most commentaries say that they would have only been 11 – 13 years of age when they came to Babylon, 15 years at the most.

For three years the court officials indoctrinated them against their Hebrew faith and immersed them in Babylonian culture and deception.

But when King Nebuchadnezzar set the image of gold and commanded everyone to worship it, these young men would not bow. Not even in the face of a torturous death. They would not bow to another god. They would not compromise their faith.

Listen to their confession before the king: *"O Nebuchadnezzar, we do not need to defend ourselves before you. If we are thrown into the blazing furnace, the God whom we serve is able to save us. He will rescue us from your power, Your Majesty. But even if he doesn't, we want to make it clear to you, Your Majesty, that we will never serve your gods or worship the gold statue you have set up"* (Daniel 3:16-18 NLT).

The king did not relent. They threw them into the furnace which they heated seven times hotter! But God miraculously delivered them. Daniel 3:30 says: *"Then the king promoted (prospered) Shadrach, Meshach, and Abednego in the province of Babylon."*

God prospered them because they would not compromise. Sometimes our success may not come in this lifetime. If not, it will come in the eternal realm, which is the real world.

May God help us to have this same spirit. We live in a culture of humanism, feminism, socialism, and many other isms. The Bible is opposite to these man-made isms. Let's stand true, even in the face of persecution.

And what about our children who are growing up in this deceived culture? Are you filling their minds, hearts, and mouths with God's truth? Our task as parents is a powerful one. We must make them strong in truth in order to face the deception and maybe persecution one day. We must prepare them to stand strong, even in the face of death.

The story of this courageous mother in the time of the Maccabees is such a challenge. The evil king commanded her son to be killed because he would not forsake the name of God or His ways. Not just killed, but cruelly tortured. They cut out his tongue, scalped him, cut off his hands and feet, and while maimed and helpless, fried him alive! In the same manner, they tortured and killed her second and third sons. The third son cried out: *"I have received these limbs from heaven, and I give them up for the sake of God's laws."* Another cried out: *"We are prepared to die rather than sin against our ancestral laws"* (2 Maccabees 7:2, 11).

Because they would not bend and turn from God's laws this dear mother watched as Antiochus tortured her fourth, fifth, and sixth sons the same way. The mother had only one son left, her beloved youngest. Antiochus tried to influence the mother to save his life. He promised he would make him rich and prosperous and even a political advisor.

She obliged by turning to her youngest son saying: *"Son, pity me who carried you in the womb nine months, nursed you for three years, nurtured you, and brought you into this stage of life with care. I beg you, child . . . Don't fear this killer but prove worthy of your brothers. Accept death so that in God's mercy I should recover you with your brothers."* She watched her last son die before she herself died (2 Maccabees 7:27-41).

This mother was a nurturing and caring mother. But she had a vision for her children beyond this earth. She raised her sons to fear God rather than man. She raised them to stand for truth, no matter what the consequences. She raised them to see beyond this earth to the endless life of the heavenly.

May God help us to be courageous mothers. May He save us from raising wimpy, mediocre children who are seduced by the humanist and feminist lies of an ungodly society. May He anoint us with the mighty power of God to raise children who will have the courage to stand for God and for truth, no matter what persecution they face.

And what about Daniel? We know he did not compromise but continued to pray three times a day, even though it meant death. They threw him into the lion's den, but God delivered him and Daniel 6:28 states: "*So this Daniel prospered in the reign of Darius, and in the reign of Cyrus the Persian.*"

A BONUS SECRET

We have now learned 10 secrets of success using the words *tsalach* and *sakal* which mean "to prosper and succeed." Here is one more Scripture that uses *shalah* which also means "successful."

Psalm 122:6: "*Pray for the peace of Jerusalem: they shall prosper that love thee.*" Do you and your family pray for Jerusalem and Israel in your home each day? It's a bonus secret for you to be blessed.

PRAYER:

"*Oh God, I live in a deceived world. Please save me from giving into the deceptions which are so prevalent around me. I want to be true to You. I want to be true to Your words. I do not want to compromise. Please help me to be a courageous mother, always standing for truth, and teaching my children to stand strong for truth. In Jesus' name. Amen.*"

AFFIRMATION:

Never bending, never bowing to the world around.
Sticking fast to God's Word, I'll never be dumbed down!

26

BLESSING YOUR
HOME WITH FOOD
Part 1

"I will feed my flock, and I will cause them to lie down, saith the Lord God"
(EZEKIEL 34:15).

God is the true Shepherd of his flock. As we parent in His likeness, He shows us how to shepherd the little flock that He has graciously given to us. There are many things we do as a shepherdess in watching over our flock, but there are two main things. The Knox translation of Ezekiel 34:15 says: **"Food and rest**, *says the Lord God, both these will I give to my flock."* Above everything else, the true shepherd provides food and rest for his flock. They are the most important.

To feed our families is an especially important part of motherhood. Many mothers despise the hours spent preparing and cooking meals. It seems endless. You can never get away from it. It is day after day. I want to remind you that this task is not unimportant, even though it may seem thankless at times. It is the chief role of the shepherd.

We read the testimony of a shepherdess/mother in 1 Timothy 5:10. The first attribute it mentions is that she *"brought up children."* The Greek word for "brought up" is *teknotropheo*, which means "to nurture, to feed, to nourish, to pamper with food." Providing food is a very big part of bringing up children.

The true shepherdess/mother will not give any kind of food to her family. She provides them with good food, *"rich feed for them to graze"* (Ezekiel 34:14 Knox). She leads her children to eat wholesome foods to nourish their bodies. She turns them away from all junk food—the devitalized and refined foods that lack nutrients. She throws out all white bread, white flour, white rice, white sugar, and so on. She would not dream of leading her children to pastures of sugary cereals, soda, and pop. The true shepherdess leads her family into wholesome pastures.

God says in Psalm 81:16 (NLT): *"I would feed you with the best of foods."*

Good food is enjoyable and should also be eaten with joy. In the Scriptures we see how God links eating with joy and gladness.

Esther 9:19: *"A day of feasting and gladness . . ."*

Psalm 103:1, 5: *"Bless the Lord, O my soul . . . who satisfieth thy mouth with good things; so that thy youth is renewed like the eagle's."*

Ecclesiastes 9:7: *"Eat thy bread with joy, and drink thy wine with a merry heart."*

Acts 2:46-47: *"And they, continuing daily with one accord in the temple, and breaking bread from house to house, did eat their meat with gladness and singleness of heart."*

Acts 14:17: *"He did good, and gave us rain from heaven, and fruitful seasons, filling our hearts with food and gladness."*

But there is more to feeding our family than food for their bodies. The responsible shepherdess/mother also provides wholesome food for her children's souls and spirits. She provides rich food in conversation, teaching, excellent books, and music. She does not lead them to the destroying diet of worldly TV and video games but provides them with wholesome DVDs that will nourish their souls. She does not keep any junk food among their books, music, or DVDs. Everything in her home inspires, enriches, and nourishes.

When raising our children, I continually prayed Paul's prayer for the Thessalonians: *"I pray God your whole spirit and soul and body be preserved blameless unto the coming of our Lord Jesus Christ"* (1 Thessalonians 5:23). It is not enough to care for your children's physical needs. We must enrich their souls and spirits too.

Psalm 107:9 tells us that God *"satisfieth the longing soul, and filleth the hungry soul with goodness."* Good food for the body and good food for the soul and spirit.

PRAYER:

"Oh, dear Father, please help me to be an enricher of my children's souls and spirits as well as their physical bodies. Show me how to fill my home with good food. Amen."

AFFIRMATION:

Junk food out; good food in!

FURTHER STUDY:

To discover 25 different things God associates with food, go to: https://tinyurl.com/FoodTwins

27

BLESSING YOUR HOME WITH REST
Part 2

*"Thus saith the LORD, Stand ye in the ways and see,
and ask for the old paths, where is the good way, and walk therein,
and ye shall find rest for your souls"*
(JEREMIAH 6:16).

The second thing God wants a shepherdess to provide for her flock is to lead them into **rest**.

Does this mean the children can loaf around and do what they like? No, this is not talking about laziness. It is a rest of peacefulness. It is rest from tension and strife. The shepherdess leads her family into a restful atmosphere.

Ezekiel 34:13, 14 (Knox): *"They shall have pasture on the hill-sides of Israel, by its water-courses, in the resting-places of their home. Yes, I will lead them out into fair pastures, the high mountains of Israel shall be their feeding-ground, the mountains of Israel, with soft grass for them to rest on."*

It is delightful to lie down in soft grass, isn't it? Who can lie down in prickly grass? No one. The shepherdess/mother seeks to eradicate all prickliness from the atmosphere of her home. She works as a peacemaker against all contention. She leads her family to soft grass. It's beckoning. It's comfortable.

Of course, life is never perfect. There will always be conflicts to overcome in the home. There are often arguments and upsets. The enemy is always lurking around to disrupt the peace and make the grass prickly.

But the shepherdess is also a watchwoman. She guards her family from the attacks of the enemy. She uses the weapon of intercession to push back the enemy of discord. She prays in the anointing of God's Holy Spirit to put out the fires of discord and bring harmony and peace.

Proverbs 18:6 often challenges me: *"A fool's lips enter into contention."* We can dissipate many conflicts if we hold our tongues!

The shepherdess who safely "folds" her flock makes sure everything is clean and orderly in her home. It is difficult to rest in a home that is out of order. We need to remind ourselves that God calls the home a *resting place.*

Numbers 10:33 tells us that God went before the children of Israel to search out a "resting place" for them.

Proverbs 24:15 gives a strong warning to anyone who destroys the peace and rest of a godly home: *"Lay not wait, O wicked man, against the dwelling of the righteous, spoil not his **resting place**."*

Isaiah 32:18: *"My people shall dwell in a peaceful habitation, and in sure dwellings, and in quiet **resting places**."*

Jeremiah 50:6: *"My people . . . have gone from mountain to hill, they have forgotten their **resting place**."*

Hosea 11:11 (Knox): *"And in their own home, says the Lord, **I will give them rest**."* Do you feel overwhelmed? Life is turmoil? Maybe you ae trying to do too many things outside your home. God promises that He will give you rest in your home, not running to activities outside your home.

COME HOME!
To your nesting place!
To your resting place!
To your investing place!

May you live in rest in your home of rest.

PRAYER:
"I pray, dear Lord God, that You will help me to make the grass soft for my children to lie in. Help me to lead them away from prickly grass. Help me to create an atmosphere of rest in my home. Amen."

AFFIRMATION:
In meadows green my children nest,
Where the grass is soft to lie and rest!

28

EXERCISE COURAGE

"But the people that do know their God shall be strong, and do exploits"
(DANIEL 11:32).

I love twins. I am blessed to have twins. I always used to say when my twins were little, "There's only one thing better than having a baby and that's having two babies!"

I also love twins in the Bible. Did you know there are many twins in the Bible? Yes, there are physical twins, but there are biblical twins such as Faith and Love, Grace and Truth, Peace and Righteousness, and so on. These things dovetail together. They need one another.

Here is another pair that you wouldn't pick up reading your English Bible, but we find them in the Hebrew.

ASAH AND CHAZAQ

The names of these twins are Asah and Chazaq. God couples them together. We need them working together in our lives. *Asah* is an action word meaning "to do, to make, to take action." The Bible is an action book. We don't just read it. We DO it. We asah it. This word occurs 2,630 times in the Old Testament.

Chazaq is a powerful word meaning "to be strong, courageous, valiant, to conquer, to hold fast."

When God tells us to do something, it's usually something we don't find easy to do in the natural. We need *chazaq* to do it. Conversely, we don't need courage just for the sake of having it. We need courage to *asah* it, to execute it! We need both these attributes working together.

EXCERCISE YOUR COURAGE MUSCLE

Courage is far more than an attribute. It's a muscle that gets stronger with use. If we don't exercise courage, we atrophy and stay weak and wimpy. It takes courage and effort to do something that is not easy. Even if we only have a little courage, if we exercise it, our muscle courage will grow stronger and we'll find it easier to do difficult things, to stand up for truth, and to resist evil and tyranny.

We face tyranny in this world at this current time. We know there will be a time in the future when we will face the Mark of the Beast. If we do not exercise courage to stand up against tyranny now, how will we stand strong and resist when that day comes? We must prepare now. We must say No to the tyranny our governments illegally put upon us. We dare not give in to the submitting of our bodies to foreign substances. Each time we exercise courage, it grows stronger, and we will be prepared for more difficult days ahead. If we have succumbed in every trial run, we'll more easily succumb to the Mark of the Beast.

I think of the great heroes of the faith in Hebrews 11. Verse 34 tells of those who *"out of weakness were made strong, waxed valiant in fight, turned to flight the armies of aliens."* They didn't start out strong. They were weak in faith and courage. But they became stronger. They *"became strong out of weakness, became mighty in war . . ."* (Darby translation).

Let's look at some examples:

Joshua encouraged the Israelites in Joshua 23:6: *"Be ye therefore **very courageous** (chazaq) to keep and **to do** (asah) all that is written in the book of the law of Moses."*

David encourages Solomon to build the temple in 1 Chronicles 28:20: *"Be **strong** (chazaq) and of good courage, and **do** (asah) it: fear not, nor be dismayed: for the LORD God, even my God, will be with thee; he will not fail thee, nor forsake thee, until thou hast finished all the work for the service of the house of the LORD."*

Ezra exhorts the offenders to put away their foreign wives: *"Be of **good courage** (chazaq) and **do** (asah) it."*

Daniel tells us in Daniel 11:32 that in the midst of those who are corrupted by lies and flatteries, *"the people that do know their God shall be **strong** (chazaq) and **do** (asah) exploits."*

CHAYIL AND ASAH

There's also another set of twins that are very similar, Asah and Chayil. God puts these two together also.

YOU ARE IN A BATTLE

Chayil is a battle word just like *chazaq*. It means "might, strength, valiant." It is mostly used in the context of an army or soldiers. Interestingly, it is the word that is translated "virtuous" in Proverbs 31:10: *"Who can find a virtuous woman for her price is far above rubies."* She is a woman of strength.

Do you feel timid to share your faith? Do you feel frightened to be bold for truth? Do you fear belonging to the minority? God is with you. He will give you courage and power to do it. Let's begin exercising our courage muscle and leading our children into this lifestyle. We have a responsibility to prepare them for what is ahead.

PRAYER:

"Dear Father, please strengthen me to be courageous in the face of evil and deception. Please save me from caving into the devil's plan. Please help me to rise up with chazaq and chayil like the men and women in Your Word. Amen."

AFFIRMATION:

I am exercising my courage muscle a little more each day. I want to be strong and ready for whatever lies ahead. And I am preparing my children for the future.

29

WINDING PATHS

"The voice of him that crieth in the wilderness, Prepare ye the way of the LORD, make straight in the desert a highway for our God. Every valley shall be exalted, and every mountain and hill shall be made low: and the crooked shall be made straight, and the rough places plain: And the glory of the LORD shall be revealed."
(ISAIAH 40:3-5).

We read in Luke 3:3-6 that John the Baptist came as *"the voice of one crying in the wilderness"* to prepare the way of the Lord. Each one of the Gospel writers confirms this—Matthew 3:1-4; Mark 1:1-2; and John 1:23. The last verses of the Old Testament in Malachi 4:5, 6 also prophesy it and Luke 1:16-17 and 76 fulfill the prophecy.

Luke 1:17 explains in more detail exactly what it means to prepare the way for the Lord: *"And he shall go before him in the spirit and power of Elijah, to turn the hearts of the fathers to the children, and the disobedient to the wisdom of the just; to make ready a people prepared for the LORD."*

To prepare the way for the coming of the Lord Jesus Christ, John the Baptist had to make the way straight. He was anointed to *"turn the hearts of the fathers* (which includes the mothers too) *to their children."* But the prophetic word of Malachi 4:5-6 says that it will happen again *"before the coming of the great and terrible day of the LORD."*

We are getting closer to this time. It is time to prepare. It is time to straighten the paths.

When the hearts of fathers and mothers do not turn to their children, they are on a crooked path. There are many deviant paths in this humanistic world. There are luring detours off the straight road. They may look enticing. They may even seem the right way, but they are often subtle "windings" to steer us away from God's perfect plan.

Are you on a winding path? Sometimes you don't even realize it until you get lost. You wake up to find that the devil's tempting ways are not what they seem. Your family life is out of order, and you wonder why. Perhaps, without realizing it, you have landed up on a winding path of independence from your husband. You are too busy to serve him and your family.

Perhaps you veered on to a crooked path of busyness—running here and there, attending this meeting and that, getting involved with this organization and that. You are in a whirlwind of activity. It may seem fulfilling but where is this winding path taking you? What will be the final result?

It's a long way off the path God planned for you as a mother—to be nestled in the heart of your home. And what are your children learning? That life consists of going to this and that, being involved in this sport and that organization, and rarely having time to sit around the dinner table together?

Are they learning the ways of the home? It is in the home they learn the patterns to pass on to the next generation. It is in the home that they learn to create, think great thoughts, and bask in the joy of home and family life.

Our children will follow the path we take. We dare not take them down winding paths of deception. The decisions we make and the paths we choose will determine the course of not only our children, but generations to come.

Keep alert for these crooked roads and remember that we only prove the salvation and deliverance of the Lord on the straight path. It is only on the straight path that God reveals His glory.

Isaiah 35:8 tell us: *"And an highway shall be there, and a way, and it shall be called The way of holiness; the unclean shall not pass over it . . ."*

God wants to show His power in your life. He can bridge the lonely valleys with His love and compassion. He wants to level every mountain that looks impossible in the natural. He wants to cut a straight path of truth through all the windings that crisscross over and back through God's straight road. Will you let Him lead you?

I love the Way's translation of 2 Timothy 2:15: *"Be earnest . . . a laborer who needs not to blush for his work, but who drives the ploughshare of truth in a straight furrow."*

PRAYER:

"Father, I ask You to help me to keep on Your straight path, never turning to the right or the left. Please expose every winding path that beckons me away from Your truth." Amen."

AFFIRMATION:

I will plough a straight furrow in my life and the life of our family.

30

IT'S ALL ABOUT HOLINESS

"But as he which hath called you is holy,
so be ye holy in all manner of conversation"
(1 PETER 1:15).

HOLY MARRIAGE

When a couple stand before the minister to take their marriage vows, he begins with the words: "Dearly Beloved, we are gathered together here in the sight of God, and in the face of this company, to join together this man and this woman in **holy matrimony** . . . and therefore, is not by any, to be entered into unadvisedly or lightly – but reverently, discreetly, advisedly, and solemnly. Into this **holy estate** these two persons present now come to be joined."

Marriage is a holy estate. Because God ordained it, it is sacred and to be set apart for Him. It is not something we take lightly because we are taking part in a God-ordained holy institution.

Hebrews 13:4 (NET): *"Marriage must be honored among all and the marriage bed kept undefiled, for God will judge sexually immoral people and adulterers."*

HOLY MOTHERHOOD

God also ordained motherhood and therefore it is a sacred calling. The humanistic programming of today, masterminded by Satan, relegates motherhood to the "common" or even the "inferior." This is a lie. It is time we saw motherhood as God sees it, a holy and elevated estate.

1 Timothy 2:15 (BSB) reminds us that women will be *"saved through childbearing—if they continue in faith, love, and **holiness**, with self-control."* The Scriptures connect motherhood with holiness. This word is translated "sanctification" in other places and literally means to be purified. Motherhood is certainly a role that exposes our flesh and our need to be purified, doesn't it?

There is an interesting verse in the Apocrypha. The Apocrypha was not included in the canon of Scripture, but it is good reading. Ecclesiasticus 1:16 (Knox) says: *"Wouldest thou be wise, the first step is fear of the Lord . . . it goes with **holy motherhood.**"*

Mother, God sees your work as holy. You are called into holy employment! You are set apart by God for a sacred task, the mightiest career in the nation. Motherhood is what keeps civilization going. Motherhood determines the rise or fall of the nation. Motherhood is eternal. God has divinely called you to not only train your children to spread the kingdom of God on this earth but to prepare them for the eternal realm.

You may think that much of what you do in the home is mundane and worthless. Wrong thinking! Everything you do in your home—scrubbing toilets, changing diapers, teaching your children, or preparing meals are all part of the holy estate of motherhood. Every task is holy, no matter how lowly.

HOLY HOME

Did you know that God wants your home to be holy too? Wow, that's a huge undertaking, isn't it? Especially when our homes are filled with sinners. We are sinners and our children are sinners. Even though we are sinners saved by grace, we are still prone to sin. But as we invite God to come and dwell in our live and our homes, He woos us to holiness.

Hebrews 9:1 tells us: *"Then verily the first covenant had also ordinances of divine service, and a worldly sanctuary."* That's King James language, not always easy to understand if you are not used to it.

Let's read it in the J. B. Phillips' translation: *". . . and it had a sanctuary, a holy place in this world for the eternal God."* Don't you love those words? Let's read them again: ***"a holy place in this world for the eternal God."***

Back in those days, God dwelt in the midst of His people, Israel. God dwelt in His Shekinah glory in the Holy of Holies in the tabernacle, and later the temple. Today, God does not live in a temple in Jerusalem, but He still wants a dwelling place on earth. He now comes to dwell in our hearts, and He also wants to dwell in our homes (1 Corinthians 6:19, 20 and 2 Corinthians 6:16).

The eternal God desires your home to be a holy place for Him on this earth. Can you seek to make your home a holy place for Him?

But there's more. God not only wants our homes to be holy, but all the area around our homes. Talking about Ezekiel's temple in Ezekiel 43:12 it says: *"This is the law of the house; Upon the top of the mountain the whole limit thereof round about shall be **most holy**. Behold, this is the law of the house."* You may only have a little backyard, or you may own many acres. Whatever God has given to you, He wants it all to be holy.

We not only guard what goes on in our homes but what goes on around our homes. Who hangs out with our children? What is happening on the inside? What is happening on the outside?

God wants every material thing in our homes to be anointed with His presence. Even our pots and pans (Zechariah 14:20, 21).

Fill your home with everything that promotes holiness and cast out every evil thing.

Holiness begins with you, dear wife and mother. You are the heart of the home, and it is your responsibility to make it holy. Make holiness your vision.

Hebrews 12:14: *"Follow peace with all men, and holiness, without which no man shall see the Lord."*

PRAYER:

"I thank you, Dear Father God, that I have been called into a divine and holy calling. Help me to remember each day that mothering and homemaking are sacred callings in Your eyes. Amen."

AFFIRMATION:

I am called to holy employment! On this bit of earth, in the neighborhood where I live, I am making a holy place for the eternal God. This is my mission!

31

DAILY GRIND OR DAILY REST?

"Come unto me, all ye that labor and are heavy laden,
and I will give you rest. Take my yoke upon you, and learn of me;
for I am meek and lowly in heart: and ye shall find rest unto your souls.
For my yoke is easy, and my burden is light"
(MATTHEW 11:28-30).

When God told the Israelites about the Promised Land, He was taking them to, He said: *"For the land that you are entering to take possession of it is not like the land of Egypt, from which you have come, where you sowed your seed and irrigated it, like a garden of vegetables. But the land that you are going over to possess is a land of hills and valleys, which drinks water by the rain from heaven, a land that the LORD your God cares for. The eyes of the LORD your God are always upon it, from the beginning of the year to the end of the year"* (Deuteronomy 11:10-12 ESV).

They could not rely on the rain from heaven in the land of Egypt. They had to do all their irrigation by hand, or I should say, by foot. They dug man-made channels for the water which they forced along by wheels operated by their feet. It was hard and laborious work. It was a daily grind. They didn't have to do this in the Promised Land. They relied totally upon God to send the rain to water the crops.

Egypt is a type of the world. It is a type of walking in the flesh and doing things by our own energy. This contrasts with our new life in the kingdom of God where we walk in the Spirit and trust God instead of our own resources.

How are you living each day? Are you still living back in Egypt or are you basking in the rest of the Lord? Often mothers feel their life is a daily grind, with no joy or hope. They live like the Israelites when they were slaves in Egypt. But we are no longer slaves. We are free people, saved by the blood of Jesus Christ. He died to deliver us from relying upon the flesh.

"But don't you realize the financial difficulties we are going through? I have to work this extra job to help my husband pay all our bills." Has God asked you to take on your husband's responsibility? Or are you taking it on yourself?

"But don't you realize how many things I have to do? I'm pregnant! I'm homeschooling my children. Plus, I'm involved in this Ladies' group at church and I'm also helping with the Sunday school." Did God tell you to get involved in these activities or was it pressure from people?

Many times, our lives become a daily grind because we take on things that God hasn't told us to do. We can't live our lives by what everyone else wants us to do. Instead, allow the Holy Spirit to lead you. Romans 8:1 says: *"There is therefore now no condemnation to them which are in Christ Jesus, who walk not after the flesh, but after the Spirit."*

God promises in Isaiah 40:11 that He *"gently leads those that are with young."* If you are pregnant or have little children, God doesn't expect you to keep up with everything you were doing before. Apart from your mighty and divine calling of nurturing and raising your children for Him, He doesn't expect you to be involved in extra church and other activities (unless your children are growing older).

"But don't you realize that I take Susie to ballet lessons, Grace to violin lessons, Johnny to soccer, and Brian to baseball, as well as keep up with the home and everything else? I'm constantly in the car." Did God command you to take your children to all these things? Or are you trying to keep up with the Joneses who think that their children should be involved in everything that is going?

We are conditioned to think that our children will not make it in life unless we take them to extra lessons and sports. That is not true. God can make a way for your children without putting extra pressure on your life and your gadding about in the car everywhere.

"But don't you realize? I supervise my children finishing their lessons that I have given them for the day and on top of all that, I have to get this done and that done." Who said you must complete all your children's lessons? Is this what God planned for the day or your own exacting plans? Are you teaching your children what God wants them taught, or what you think others expect of you?

Life is hard work, but it does not have to be a grind. It can be drudgery when we do it in the energy of the flesh. God wants us to live by the power of His Spirit. The Israelites worked in the Promised Land, but they enjoyed their work, because they were cast upon God's resources, not their own energy. They no longer irrigated the way they did in Egypt. They relied on God to send their rain.

Which land ae you living in?

PRAYER:

"*Father, I thank You that You have brought me into a new kingdom, a kingdom where I cannot rely on my own strength, a kingdom where I must trust you wholly. Please show me where I am doing things in my own energy because I want to be led by Your Holy Spirit. Thank You that You are watching over my life and Your eye is upon me from the beginning of the year to the end of the year. I can trust you to lead me. Amen.*"

AFFIRMATION:

No more condemnation! I'm tired of walking in the flesh; I'm now walking in the power of the Holy Spirit.

32

ARE YOU IN A WILDERNESS?
Part 1

*"The LORD thy God . . . Who led thee through that great and terrible
wilderness, wherein were fiery serpents, and scorpions, and drought,
where there was no water . . . that he might humble thee,
and that he might prove thee, to do thee good at thy latter end"*
(DEUTERONOMY 8:14-16).

Are you going through a desert time in your life? Does it seem a *"great
and terrible"* experience? Perhaps you feel as though God has forsaken you. Your life seems dry and meaningless.

Please don't despair. Your wilderness experience is not a time to grovel and complain. It is your opportunity to see the power and provision of God. You can experience more miracles from God in your wilderness than at any other time. The children of Israel did not accidentally land up in the wilderness. God led them there. They were in His perfect will.

Granted, it was not a smooth road! They faced serpents and scorpions. They endured hunger and thirst. They could not survive without the help of God. Nor can you. But look up! As you take your eyes off your "terrible" wilderness and trust in God, you will be in for some SURPRISES.

Let me show you what happens in the wilderness.

1. GOD LED HIS PEOPLE INTO THE WILDERNESS

Ezekiel 20:10: *"Wherefore I caused them to go forth out of the land of Egypt, and brought them into the wilderness."*

God led His people into the wilderness, through the wilderness, and out of the wilderness. He will lead you **through** your wilderness too. And remember, your wilderness is only for a season. His plan is to prove you in your wilderness so He can bring you out into a good place. The above Scripture says: *"that he might prove thee, to do thee good at thy latter end."* Look beyond your difficulties to where God is taking you.

2. GOD GUIDED HIS PEOPLE IN THE WILDERNESS

Psalm 78:52 tells us that God *"guided them in the wilderness like a flock."* All through the wilderness God guided His people like a shepherd. Trust God. He is guiding you in your wilderness too.

3. GOD INSTRUCTED HIS PEOPLE IN THE WILDERNESS

Deuteronomy 32:10 tells us that *"He instructed him"* in the wilderness. The Hebrew word for "instruct" is *bin* which means "understanding, insight, and discernment." You will have insight into God's ways in your wilderness experience far more than when you are on the easy path.

God had much to teach His people in the wilderness. They were not ready to live in the Promised Land when they first came out of Egypt. They were still a broken people. They had a slave mentality. God had to ingrain into them His laws, statutes, and commandments and make them into a set-apart, holy people with a conquering spirit.

Moses lived 40 years in Pharaoh's household receiving the education of Egypt. God had to take him out into the wilderness into Jethro's household for 40 years to unlearn his humanistic education and receive God's education. This happened again when Moses brought out the Israelites from Egypt. They needed 40 years to unlearn their Egyptian ways and change their Egyptian mindset to God's mindset.

Sometimes God takes us into the wilderness to unlearn much of our worldly education and to open our hearts and minds to His ways (Isaiah 55:8, 9). God cannot use us for His purposes until we are filled with His truth and understand His ways.

4. GOD SPOKE TO HIS PEOPLE IN THE WILDERNESS

Nehemiah 9:13 (NASB) states: *"You came down on Mount Sinai, and **spoke with them from heaven**; You gave them just ordinances and true laws, good statutes and commandments."*

Isn't this amazing? They were out in the wilderness, but God spoke to them from Heaven! What more could you want? Sometimes God takes you into a desert place in your life so that you can hear Him speak to you.

The desert is quiet and free from distractions. You can hear His voice more clearly than when taken up with the busy rat-race of this life.

Where did God speak to Moses and give him direction to deliver His people from the Egyptians? Out in the backside of the desert (Exodus 3:1-14). Sometimes you may think you are in a wilderness hidden away in your home. Well, look forward to God speaking to you!

Let's look at some ways God speaks in the wilderness.

Shakingly: *"The voice of the LORD shakes the wilderness; the LORD shakes the wilderness of Kadesh"* (Psalm 29:8 NASB). God gets your attention in the wilderness. Sometimes He may have to shake you up!

Face to Face: *"I will bring you into the wilderness of the people, and there will I plead with you face to face. Like as I pleaded with your fathers in the wilderness of the land of Egypt, so will I plead with you, saith the Lord God"* (Ezekiel 20: 35, 36). Sometimes God takes you into the wilderness to plead with you face to face. But what could be more wonderful than meeting face to face with God? We know that we cannot literally see His face, but "face to face" speaks of His intimate presence. It's worth being in the wilderness to experience God's intimate presence in our lives.

Tenderly and Kindly: *"I will allure her, and bring her into the wilderness, and speak tenderly to her"* (Hosea 2:14 ESV).

Prophetically: Balak, the king of Moab, was afraid of the children of Israel. Therefore, He asked Balaam, a prophet, to come and prophecy curses over God's people. However, every time Balaam opened his mouth, God spoke His words of blessing through his mouth. Four times he spoke powerful and prophetic blessings over Israel and even spoke of the coming of Jesus saying, *"there will come a Star of Jacob."* Read all the great prophetic words in Numbers 23:8-10; 18-24; 24:1-9; and 15-19.

Expect God to speak to you prophetically in your wilderness too.

More surprises tomorrow.

PRAYER:

"Oh Lord God, I thought I was finished, but now I see this is just the beginning of Your dealings with me. I thank You that even in my hopeless situation You will speak to me and reveal more of Yourself to me. I am listening, dear Father. Amen."

AFFIRMATION:

Even in my desert times I am listening for God to speak to me.

FURTHER STUDY:

God led His people throughout their whole journey in the wilderness: Exodus 13:8; 29:42; Deuteronomy 8:2, 15; 29:5; 32:10; Nehemiah 9:12, 19; Psalm 78:53; 136:16; and Amos 2:10.

33

ARE YOU IN A WILDERNESS?

Part 2

"Forty years you sustained them in the wilderness, and they lacked nothing. Their clothes did not wear out and their feet did not swell" (NEHEMIAH 9:21 ESV).

When our daughter, Evangeline, gave birth to her eighth baby, she wanted to call her Sahara. At first her husband did not like the idea of calling her after the name of a desert. However, as they thought of all the mighty things God does in the desert, they realized that it was an amazing name to call their child and they decided on the name of Sahara Oasis.

We continue to discover more wonderful surprises you will encounter in your wilderness experience. Claim these great promises. Lean on them. Confess them. Believe them.

5. GOD DID NOT FORSAKE HIS PEOPLE IN THE WILDERNESS

Do you feel that God has forgotten you?

Be encouraged by these words: *"They refused to listen, and did not remember Your wondrous deeds which You had performed among them; so they became stubborn and appointed a leader to return to their slavery in Egypt. But you are a God of forgiveness, gracious and compassionate, slow to anger and abounding in lovingkindness; And* **You did not forsake them.** *Even when they made for themselves a calf of molten metal and said, 'This is your God Who brought you up from Egypt,' And committed great blasphemies, You, in your great compassion,* **did not forsake them in the wilderness"** (Nehemiah 9:17-19 NASB).

Dear daughter of God, as you face trials and difficulties in your life, remember that God's Word is always true. You can claim this promise. He will not forsake you in your wilderness.

6. GOD MANIFESTED HIS PRESENCE IN THE WILDERNESS

The children of Israel had no shops, no marketplaces, no modern conveniences, and no lush fields to grow vegetables and yet God dwelt in their midst. In the tabernacle, which was in the center of the camp, God dwelt between the cherubim in the Holy of Holies in all His Shekinah glory. The divine pillar of cloud covered them in the daytime and the children of Israel could look out at night and see the divine pillar of fire rising from above the Holy of Holies.

Imagine seeing the glory of God in your midst? And this is in the wilderness!

When they completed the tabernacle, God came and filled it with His glory. This happened at other times too. They were privileged to see the glory of God in the wilderness (Exodus 40:34-38 and Numbers 14:10).

God said in Exodus 25:8: *"Let them make me a sanctuary; that I may dwell among them."*

God said in Exodus 29:43-45: *"I will meet with the children of Israel, and the tabernacle shall be sanctified by my glory . . . And I will dwell among the children of Israel and will be their God."*

Are you in a *"howling wilderness"* that Deuteronomy 32:10 talks about? Look to your God. He will manifest His presence to you too. And there is nothing more precious than the presence of God, no matter what trial you are going through.

7. GOD KNEW HIS PEOPLE IN THE WILDERNESS

Deuteronomy 2:7: *"He knoweth thy walking through this great wilderness: these forty years the LORD thy God hath been with thee."*

Hosea 13:5: *"I did know thee in the wilderness, in the land of great drought."* God intimately knows what you are going through. He never leaves you. What more could you want?

8. GOD KEPT HIS PEOPLE AS "THE APPLE OF HIS EYE" IN THE WILDERNESS

The description of *"the apple of his eye"* in Deuteronomy 32:10 reveals God's tender care for His people. The pupil is the most sensitive part of the eye. Even in the worst times, God tenderly watched over His people.

The HCSB says: *"He found him in a desolate land, in a barren, howling wilderness; He surrounded (encircled) him, cared for him, and protected him as the pupil of his eye."*

When you go through your wilderness experiences God encircles you and watches over you with tender care. You may not feel His presence, but you can count on it!

9. GOD SUSTAINED HIS PEOPLE IN THE WILDERNESS

Nehemiah 9:21 testifies: *"Yea, forty years didst thou sustain them in the wilderness."* God will sustain you too. Forty years is a long time, isn't it? I am sure your wilderness won't be that long.

10. GOD CARRIED HIS PEOPLE IN THE WILDERNESS

Deuteronomy 1:31: *"And in the wilderness, where thou hast seen how that the LORD thy God bare thee, as a man doth bear his son, in all the way that ye went."* God carried His people all the way through the wilderness. Not once did He let them down until He brought them to the Promised Land.

I love the Knox translation: *"Your own eyes have witnessed how the LORD your God carried you through the desert as a man carries his little son."* Isn't that so beautiful? You are God's little daughter, and He is carrying you through your wilderness.

11. GOD GAVE HIS PEOPLE GRACE AND REST IN THE WILDERNESS

Jeremiah 31:2: *"Thus saith the LORD, The people which were left of the sword found grace in the wilderness; even Israel, when I went to cause him to rest."* How did God show His favor and kindness? By giving them rest. There is also a rest in God for you in your wilderness.

More surprises again tomorrow.

PRAYER:

"Dear Father, I thank You that You are the God of the wilderness. This is where You love to manifest Your power and Your presence. I thank You that I can experience Your power and presence, even in my "terrible" wilderness. Amen."

AFFIRMATION:

I'm living in the rest of God while in my wilderness.

ARE YOU IN A WILDERNESS?
Part 3

"And the LORD went before them by day in a pillar of cloud, to lead them the way; and by night in a pillar of fire, to give them light; to go by day and night: He took not away the pillar of the cloud by day, nor the pillar of fire by night, from before the people"
(EXODUS 13:21, 22).

We have been discovering all the wonderful things God did for the children of Israel in the wilderness. "But that was just for them," you say. "Can God do these things personally for me?"

Let's look at more testimonies.

12. GOD FED HIS PEOPLE IN THE WILDERNESS

God led His people to a barren wilderness. It wasn't long before they were crying, complaining, and demanding food! But God did not let them down. We know the wonderful miracle of how God sent the manna to them. He didn't send it to them for one day, but for 40 years! There wasn't a day that God wasn't faithful to provide food for them until they reached the Promised Land.

Exodus 16: 35 says: *"And the children of Israel did eat manna forty years, until they came to a land inhabited; they did eat manna until they came unto the borders of the land of Canaan."* Also read Joshua 5:10-12.

But they had to trust God for each new day. He wanted to teach them that *"Man shall not live by bread alone, but by every word that proceedeth out of the mouth of God"* (Deuteronomy 8:3 and Matthew 4:4).

What a faithful God we have. He hasn't stopped being a faithful God. And even when you are going through a drought and you've got hardly anything to eat, you won't starve. You may not feast, but you will eat!

During our lives, God allows us to have times of lean eating (just enough for our needs) and other times of feasting. Even Paul knew how to abound and to be in need (Philippians 4:12, 13).

Do you remember that it was also in a desert place that Jesus fed 5,000 plus people (Mark 6:31-44)?

13. GOD GAVE HIS PEOPLE WATER IN THE WILDERNESS

Nehemiah 9:20: *"Thou . . . gavest them water for their thirst."*

Isaiah 35:6: *"In the wilderness shall waters break out, and streams in the desert."*

Isaiah 41:18: *"I will make the wilderness a pool of water, and the dry land springs of water."*

Isaiah 43:20: *"I give waters in the wilderness, and rivers in the desert, to give drink to my people, my chosen."*

Isaiah 48:21: *"And they thirsted not when he led them through the deserts: he caused the waters to flow out of the rock for them: he cleaved the rock also, and the waters gushed out."* Are you dry and thirsty? Even in the desert God will satisfy you with water.

On two separate occasions God brought water out of the rock for them (Exodus 17:6 and Numbers 20:10, 11).

You may feel parched, dry, and desolate. Look up. Jesus is your living water, even in desert times.

14. GOD PROVIDED ALL THE NEEDS OF HIS PEOPLE IN THE WILDERNESS

Can you imagine it? For 40 years their shoes and clothing did not wear out. He provided a pillar of cloud to protect them from the sun by day and a pillar of fire to give them warmth and light at night. They didn't enjoy the mod-cons we take for granted today They had no shops. They couldn't run down to the supermarket for an item they think they needed. They had no entertainment centers. They had no "extra" things, but God says in Nehemiah 9:21 that *"they lacked nothing."* Also read Deuteronomy 2:7; 8:4; and 29:5.

You may not have all the things you covet or even think you need, but if you have food, clothing, and a roof over your head, you lack nothing! Remind yourself of what Jesus says to you in Matthew 6:25-34.

15. GOD REVEALED HIS MIRACULOUS POWER IN THE WILDERNESS

The children of Israel lived miraculously every day. Every day they walked out and gathered angels' food to keep them healthy and strong. Apart from all the miracles we have been reading in the above points, they saw more manifestations of the power of God.

At the beginning of their journey they arrived at Marah, parched with thirst, but could not drink the waters because they were bitter. God showed Moses a tree which he cast into the water, and immediately they became sweet (Exodus 15:23-25).

They saw God open the ground and swallow up the tents and all the families of Korah, Dathan, and Abiram, because they revolted against Moses. Read this breathtaking story in Numbers 16.

In Numbers chapter 17 we read of when the people revolted against Moses. God instructed the prince of each tribe to take a rod. Moses laid their rods and his rod in the presence of the Lord. The next day Moses' rod had budded, blossomed, and yielded almonds! The others were all dry.

You can expect miracles in your wilderness experience.

16. GOD GAVE LIGHT TO HIS PEOPLE IN THE WILDERNESS

Nehemiah 9:19: *"The pillar of the cloud departed not from them by day, to lead them in the way; neither the pillar of fire by night, to show them light, and the way wherein they should go."* God didn't leave them stranded. He didn't leave them in the dark.

As we go through our wilderness season, God never leaves us in the dark either. He has given us His Son who is the light of the world and His Word which is a lamp to our feet and a light to our path (Psalm 119:105).

Are you in the dark and you can't see any way out of your tunnel? Take hold of God's Word. Clasp it to you, read it, stand on the word God gives to you, and don't let it go. It will be your light in the darkness.

"Who is among you . . . that walketh in darkness, and hath no light? Let him trust in the name of the LORD, and stay upon His God" (Isaiah 50:10).

PRAYER:

"I thank You, Lord God, that You are bringing me through the wilderness. Please help me to have the right attitude. Help me to see that this is all part of Your plan and that You are preparing me for Your highest purposes. Amen."

AFFIRMATION:

I am walking through my wilderness, rejoicing that God is with me.

FURTHER STUDY:

GOD PROVIDED FOOD IN THE WILDERNESS:

Exodus 16:11-36; Numbers 11;1-9; Deuteronomy 8:3; 16; Nehemiah 9:20; Psalm 78:19; and John 6:31, 32.

GOD PROVIDED WATER IN THE WILDERNESS:

Deuteronomy 8:15; Psalm 78:15, 16; 105:41; 107:35; Isaiah 35:6, 7; 41:18-20; and 43:19, 20.

GOD PROVIDED MANNA IN THE WILDERNESS:

Exodus 16:4-35; Numbers 11:6-9; Deuteronomy 8:3, 16; Joshua 5;10-12; Nehemiah 9:15, 20; Psalm 78:22-25; 105:40; John 6:31-58; 1 Corinthians 10:31; and Hebrews 9:4.

ARE YOU IN A WILDERNESS?
Part 4

"Behold, I will do a new thing; now it shall spring forth;
shall ye not know it? I will even make a way in
the wilderness, and rivers in the desert"
(Isaiah 43:19).

17. GOD MAKES A WAY FOR HIS PEOPLE IN THE WILDERNESS

Can you see no way out of your difficulties? It's easy to get lost in the wilderness. There are no road signs but keep trusting God. He will make a way for you.

Isaiah 43:19 is a promise for you: *"I will even make a way in the wilderness, and rivers in the desert."* Do you believe God's words? It is impossible for Him to lie. Thank Him that He will make a way for you and remember that His way is always better than your way.

18. GOD PROVED HIS PEOPLE IN THE WILDERNESS

Deuteronomy 8:2: *"And thou shalt remember all the way which the LORD thy God led thee these forty years in the wilderness, to humble thee, and to prove thee, to know what was in thine heart, whether thou wouldest keep his commandments, or no."*

Our wilderness experience is a test to see what is really in our hearts. This is a good thing because God is always leading us on to higher things. His purpose is to conform us to the image of His Son (Romans 8:29). He doesn't want us to stay in our rut of sin, doubt, unbelief, and ignorance of His ways. He brings us into the wilderness to show us His ways.

19. GOD SHOWED MERCY TO HIS PEOPLE IN THE WILDERNESS

Nehemiah 9:19 tells us that He revealed His *"manifold mercies"* to them in the wilderness. What are manifold mercies? They are abundant, exceeding, abounding, and plenteous mercies.

20. GOD KEPT HIS PEOPLE SAFE IN THE WILDERNESS

Ezekiel 34:25 tells us that *"they shall dwell safely in the wilderness."* We are always safer with God in the wilderness than a comfortable situation without God. The safest place on earth is in the will of God.

21. GOD PREPARES US FOR HIS PURPOSES IN THE WILDERNESS

It was in the far side of the wilderness that Moses had his first an encounter with God. He stood on holy ground in the desert. God kept him in that wilderness for 40 long years, but he came out ready to deliver a nation from the tyranny of Egypt (Exodus 3:1-15 and Acts 7:30-38).

David was forced into the desert to hide from the wrath of King Saul, but while in that desert he raised an army of men and came forth in God's time to be king and to reign over all Israel (2 Samuel 5:3).

John the Baptist prepared the way for the coming of the Lord in the wilderness. (Mark 1:1-7 and Luke 1:15-17).

After Paul's conversion, he went into seclusion—into the desert of Arabia, where he met with God and heard *"unspeakable words"* (2 Corinthians 12:1-7 and Galatians 1:17). From his wilderness experience he came forth to fulfil his destiny and to be the mighty apostle to the Gentiles.

Sometimes you feel like you are in a wilderness as you feel forgotten in your home. Be encouraged, God is preparing you and anointing you for greater nurturing in the future and also to prepare your children to come forth to fulfil the destiny God has for them.

22. GOD PREPARES US FOR BATTLE IN THE WILDERNESS

Exodus 13:18: *"But God led the people about, through the way of the wilderness of the Red sea: and the children of Israel went up harnessed out of the land of Egypt."* The NLT says they went forth *"like an army ready for battle."*

The word "harnessed" is *chamush* and means "able-bodied soldiers, armed men, equipped." It is translated *"armed men"* in the other three passages in the Bible where this word is used. But where did the Israelites get their weapons? They were slaves and under the hard bondage of the Pharaoh. Some commentators believe they went forth in an organized way, at least looking like an army. I am sure that as God was sending the plagues upon Egypt that Moses and the elders were planning their exit, right down to the very last detail. The NKJV says they went out in *"orderly ranks."*

Exodus 12:37 tells us that 600,000 men on foot, besides women and children came out of Egypt. Most commentators believe that would have been about 2. 5 million people. To tell you the truth, I believe it could have been more the way the Bible says they were populating in Egypt (Exodus 1:7-12). Perhaps three to four million? It must have been an incredible sight.

I am sure they stripped the bodies of the slain Egyptians for weapons after they drowned in the Red Sea. They faced a battle with Amalekites soon after which they won with the help of God. However, they were not yet ready to conquer the land of Canaan. They were fresh out of slavery. They were still fearful and bowed down in spirit. They had to learn how to trust God and become strong in faith.

Read how their fear and unbelief kept them from entering the Promised Land for another 40 years—and then only two of them got in! (Numbers 13 and 14). The next generation needed training for the big battles ahead.

We are also in a fight against the powers of darkness. In the wilderness God teaches us to be strong and courageous and how to fight the enemy His way, not our own way.

PRAYER:
"Thank you, dear Father, for showing me that I need the wilderness to prepare me for what You have ahead for me. I need the wilderness to learn how to fight against the enemy. Amen."

AFFIRMATION:
I will not reject but embrace my wilderness experience.

FURTHER STUDY:
DAVID'S PREPARATION IN THE WILDERNESS:
1 Samuel 22:2; 23:14-15, 24:1; 26:3; and 1 Chronicles 12:1-15.

36

ARE YOU IN A WILDERNESS?
Part 5

*"Who is this that cometh up from the wilderness,
leaning upon her beloved?"*
(SONG OF SONGS 8:5).

Today we complete the 27 surprises about how God is with us in our wilderness times.

23. GOD TEACHES US TO OVERCOME IN THE WILDERNESS

Jesus won the victory over Satan in the wilderness and came forth to minister in the power of the Holy Ghost. (Matthew 4:1-11) Notice that the Holy Spirit led Jesus into the wilderness. He was not out of God's will but in the very center of His will while in that desert.

24. GOD RELEASES JOY AND SINGING IN THE WILDERNESS

You don't have to lose your joy in your wilderness experience.

Isaiah 51:3: *"He will make her wilderness like Eden, and her desert like the garden of the LORD; joy and gladness shall be found therein, thanksgiving, and the voice of melody."*

Instead of giving into the gloom of your situation, step out in faith and sing. Praise the Lord. Thank Him that He is with you in your wilderness. Rejoice in His faithfulness.

25. WE LOSE OUR DESIRE FOR WORLDLY THINGS IN THE WILDERNESS

After being in the wilderness for 40 years, Moses went back into the pride and wealth of Egypt, but it no longer held any hold upon him.

Hebrews 11:24-26 states: *"By faith Moses, when he was come to years, refused to be called the son of Pharaoh's daughter; Choosing rather to suf-*

fer affliction with the people of God, than to enjoy the pleasures of sin for a season; Esteeming the reproach of Christ greater riches than the treasures in Egypt: for he had respect unto the recompense of the reward."

26. WE LEARN TO WALK BY FAITH IN THE WILDERNESS

Psalm 78:17-19: *"And they sinned yet more against him by provoking the most High in the wilderness. And they tempted God in their heart by asking meat for their lust. Yea, they spake against God; they said, 'Can God furnish a table in the wilderness?"*

They did not believe God could provide for them. But God did not let them out of the desert until they learned the walk of faith. Trust God and thank Him that He is faithful in every detail of your life. And He is well able to furnish your table.

27. WE LEARN TO DEPEND ON GOD IN THE WILDERNESS

What a beautiful picture we see of the bride of Christ in our Scripture for today, Song of Solomon 8:5: *"Who is this that cometh up from the wilderness, leaning upon her beloved?"*

During the wilderness experience, God's people learned to rely totally on His strength. There was no other way. Moses tried to help his people in his own strength when he killed the Egyptian, but it failed. God had to work on him for 40 years in the desert before he was ready to deliver his people from the power of Egypt.

Are you going through a difficult wilderness experience right now? Don't despair. Remember, you are going **through**! There is an end! But according to your attitude to your problems you will either die (spiritually) in your wilderness or come out victorious. You will come forth hurt and bitter or with the sweet anointing of the presence of God upon you.

Because the children of Israel were full of unbelief, grumbled, and complained about their hardships and challenges they had to face, they all died in the wilderness. This is a great challenge to us, isn't it? Joshua and Caleb were the only two of the generation that came out of Egypt to enter the Promised Land.

Joshua came forth to lead God's people into battle and to take the Promised Land (Joshua 1:6-7).

Caleb came forth ready to take mountains and tackle giants (Joshua 14:6-15).

Later, David came forth from his wilderness experience ready to reign over Judah and later all of Israel (2 Samuel 5:3)

Paul came forth from his time in the desert of Saudi Arabia to be a mighty apostle.

How will you come through?

The wilderness is a place of miracles. In fact, after reading all these points, it makes you want to be in a wilderness!

PRAYER:

"Dear faithful Father God, help me not to look at the hardships I face, but to trust You, knowing that You will bring me through. The problems I face are bigger than me, but You are bigger than the problems. I can rejoice and sing in the wilderness, knowing that it is all Your plan, and You are working out the greater plan for my life. Thank You. In the name of Jesus. Amen."

AFFIRMATION:

I am coming through my wilderness leaning on my Beloved.

37

PAY UP!

"But if any provide not for his own, and especially for those of his own house, he hath denied the faith, and is worse than an infidel"
(1 TIMOTHY 5:8).

We are living in an entitlement society where many people want everything for nothing, especially young people who are currently educated in our colleges. They are consistently brainwashed in extreme socialism where they think they should get everything free without working for it. They want free education, free housing, free health care, etc. They don't even use their brains to think where the money would come from.

I believe we should live with an attitude of expectation that God is going to do good things. That's the meaning of hope and hope is a godly attitude. But when things cost money, we should always be prepared to pay our share. This is a biblical principle.

When the children of Israel passed through the land of Seir, God told them to make sure they paid for anything they ate or drank.

Deuteronomy 2:6: *"Ye shall buy meat of them for money, that ye may eat; and ye shall also buy water of them for money, that ye may drink."*

The same happened when they passed through the land of the Moabites. When they came to the land of Sihon, Moses told King Heshbon: *"Thou shalt sell me meat for money, that I may eat, and give me water for money that I may drink"* (Deuteronomy 2:28). They were ready to take responsibility for what they used.

God gives us a biblical principle for everything in life. We should always seek to pay for what we need, for what we eat and drink, and for what we use. If we break something that belongs to someone else, we should replace it. If we lose something that belongs to someone else, we should replace it.

If a family invites us for dinner, we should bring something toward the meal. If the hostess says not to bring anything, we could purchase flowers, or make a little gift, or write a card etc.

Don't keep your table only to yourselves. Invite others to share your meal table.

Let's not take everything for granted.
Away with entitlement mentality!

Paul, the great apostle, worked hard at a low-grade job to provide for his own needs and the needs of others! Let's read about his attitude.

Acts 20:34, 35 (NLT): *"You know that these hands of mine have worked to supply my own needs and **even the needs of those who were with me.** And I have been a constant example of how you can help those in need by working hard. You should remember the words of the Lord Jesus: 'It is more blessed to give than to receive.'"*

1 Thessalonians 2:9 (NLT): *"Don't you remember, dear brothers and sisters, how hard we worked among you? **Night and day we toiled** to earn a living so that we would not be a burden to any of you as we preached God's Good News to you."*

2 Thessalonians 3:8-10 (NLT): *"We never accepted food from anyone **without paying for it. We worked hard day and night** so we would not be a burden to any of you . . . Even while we were with you, we gave you this command: 'Those unwilling to work will not get to eat.'"* Read also Acts 18:3; 1 Corinthians 4;12; 2 Corinthians 11:9; and 12:13-15.

The Bible certainly makes it clear how God wants us to live, doesn't it?

Let's look at the example of David when he wanted to purchase the threshing floor of Araunah to build an altar to the Lord. Araunah offered it freely to David. He told David: "Take the threshing floor. And look, here are oxen for you to use. And here are the threshing instruments. Use them all freely."

What did David answer? *"I will surely buy it of thee **at a price:** neither will I offer burnt offerings unto the LORD my God of **that which doth cost me nothing.** So David bought the threshing floor and the oxen for fifty shekels of silver"* (2 Samuel 24:21-24). May God help us to always have this same kind of attitude that David had.

PRAYER:

"Dear Father, please help me to be responsible before You and to do what is right toward my fellowman. Save me from being selfish and thinking of only my needs. Amen."

AFFIRMATION:

I will take responsibility for my own needs and also the needs of others.

38

THE ORDINATION OF MOTHERHOOD
Part 1

"Ye have not chosen me, but I have chosen you,
and ordained you, that ye should go and bring forth fruit,
and that your fruit should remain"
(JOHN 15:16).

I wonder if you understand the power of your calling as a mother. Did you know that were ordained, designed, and designated for this great career?

Let's seek further understanding:

1. GOD *CREATED* YOU FOR THIS CAREER

It's not hard to understand when we observe our female bodies that they were created for the ultimate purpose of motherhood. And yet isn't it amazing that many women spurn the way they were created? God created us physically with a womb where we have the privilege to conceive and grow a baby. We have breasts to nurture and feed the baby.

However, we are not only physically created for the job, but innately. We are inherently born with a nurturing heart. It is part of every female, even those who refuse children. If they don't have children, they'll have pets, because it is instinctive to nurture. It is part of being a woman.

God created us perfectly (Deuteronomy 32:4; Psalm 18:30; and Job 37:16). Because He chose to create us female, the most obvious thing in the world is to embrace our womanhood and femininity with our whole being.

I often think how sad it is for someone to go through life and not ful-fil the plan God has for them. If God created us female, it is as a female we will fulfil the destiny He planned for us before the foundation of the world. Therefore, let's acknowledge and live out our womanhood and motherhood. This is how we glorify the God who created us.

We either dampen the image of God or reveal the image of God through the way we live.

Isaiah 45:9-12 (NET) says: *"One who argues with his creator is in grave danger . . . The clay should not say to the potter, 'What in the world are you doing? Your work lacks skill!' Danger awaits one who says to his father, 'What in the world are you fathering?' and to his mother, 'What in the world are you bringing forth?' This is what the LORD says, the Holy One of Israel, the one who formed him, concerning things to come: 'How dare you question me about my children! How dare you tell me what to do with the work of my own hands! I made the earth, I created the people who live on it.'"*

Also read these powerful Scriptures: Psalm 100:3; 111:1-8; 119:73; 139:14; Isaiah 10:15; 29:16; 64:8; and Revelation 4:11.

2. GOD *CHOSE* YOU SPECIFICALLY FOR THIS CAREER

The career of motherhood is specifically and uniquely female. God did not give the career of motherhood to men. He has a different role for them. He wants them to fulfil their fatherhood anointing—to father their children, not mother them. I hope you understand that there is a difference between fathering and mothering. That's why children need a father and a mother. They receive different blessings, affirmations, and parenting from each parent. It's not the same! I minister to my children far differently from my husband. Our children need us both.

You are the only one who can truly mother your children. It is unique to YOU. Don't for a minute give in to this genderless society. Genesis 3:20 says: *"And Adam called his wife's name Eve (life-giver); because she was the **mother** of all living."* At this stage Adam had never seen a mother, so what was he talking about? He spoke under the inspiration of God. God called Eve the mother, not Adam the male.

When Jesus answered the Pharisees in Matthew 19:4, He stated: *"Have ye not read, that he which made them at the beginning made the male and female."* The word Jesus used for "female" was the description of a "suckling mother." A man is not a suckling mother. It is the female!

PRAYER:

"Dear Father, I thank You so much that You purposely and uniquely chose me to reveal Your nurturing heart to the world and to be the mother of my children. Please help me to glorify Your wonderful name as I embrace my female mothering. Amen."

AFFIRMATION:

I am ordained for the ministry of mothering as much, or even more, than any person ordained to be the minister of a church!

THE ORDINATION
OF MOTHERHOOD
Part 2

*"Take heed to the ministry which thou hast
received in the Lord, that thou fulfill it"*
(COLOSSIANS 4:17).

3. GOD *COMMISSIONED* YOU FOR THIS CAREER

Motherhood is not an idle pastime. You are part of a mighty army in the home. In Psalm 68:11, 12 the psalmist talks about two armies:

a) The men who go out to fight the battles to protect their homes, families, and their land.

b) The army of women who dwell at home, the mothers who hold the home fort and build strong families. Mothers who proclaim the Word of truth. Mothers who prepare soldiers for the army. Mothers who divide the spoil and share the blessings.

Song of Songs 6:10 (NLT) is a picture of a mighty woman fulfilling her commission: *"Who is this arising like the dawn, as fair as the moon, as bright as the sun, as majestic as an army with billowing banners?"*

4. GOD WANTS YOU TO BE *COMMITTED* TO YOUR CAREER

You are not tossed about by each new trend in society. You are not moved by negative statements from family and friends. You are not moved when facing hardships or financial stress. You've counted the cost. Your heart is fixed, trusting in the Lord. You are unshakable. You are immoveable. You know you are in the perfect will of God. You know your purpose. You stand true to your convictions.

Your heart is like David's heart: *"My heart is fixed* (established), *O God, my heart is fixed: I will sing and give praise"* (Psalm 57:7 and Psalm 108:1).

When Nehemiah went back to Jerusalem to repair and build the gates of Jerusalem, he faced continual persecution and ridicule. His enemies did everything in their power to thwart him from his great purpose. When they asked him to come down, he refused to stop his great work. Instead, Nehemiah 6:3 tells us that he sent messengers to them, saying:

> "I am doing a great work,
> so that I cannot come down:
> why should the work cease,
> whilst I leave it, and come down to you?"

Make this your confession too. I would encourage you to write or type these words out in big letters and pin them up in an appropriate place in your home.

Colossians 4:17 (Moffat): *"Attend to the duty entrusted to you . . . and discharge it to the full."*

Colossians 3:12, 12 (JBP): *"Whatever you do, **put your whole heart and soul into it**, as unto work done for God, and not merely for men – knowing that your real reward, a heavenly one, will come from God, since **you are actually employed by Christ**. "*

5. GOD WANTS YOU TO *COMPLETE* YOUR CAREER

In this great work of mothering, we are committed to the end. Ecclesiastes 7:8 says: *"Better is the end of a thing than the beginning thereof."* As children grow up, many mothers think they have come to the end of motherhood. They fling off their motherhood mantle and set out into the world for a new life. This is not God's plan. He doesn't want us to stop half-way through or just before we get to the finishing tape. He created us physically and innately to be mothers, and we are mothers to the end.

Jesus Himself gave us the example. He stated in John 4:34: *"My meat is to do the will of him that sent me, and to **finish** his work."*

Jesus prayed in John 17:4: *"I have glorified thee on the earth: I have **finished** the work which thou gavest me to do."* We bring glory to God by finishing the task He gives us to do.

In biblical days, the watchman watched over the cities to be aware of any enemy activity. They divided the watches into four times:

First watch:	6.00 pm – 9.00 pm.
Second watch:	9.00 pm – 12.00 pm (midnight).
Third watch:	12.00 pm – 3.00 am.
Fourth watch:	3.00 am – 6.00 am.

No watchman was permitted to sleep on his watch. It was a very responsible assignment. Many people today use these times as prayer watches as they pray and watch over the nation in this "night season." However, I would like to relate these watches to our mothering seasons of life.

Tomorrow we'll begin with the FIRST WATCH.

PRAYER:

"*Thank you, dear Father, for giving me this great career of motherhood. Thank You for the precious children You have entrusted to my care. Help me to be a faithful mother to the end. Amen.*"

AFFIRMATION:

I have the greatest career on earth and I'm in for the long haul!

THE FIRST WATCH

"He shall feed his flock like a shepherd: he shall gather the lambs with his arm, and carry them in his bosom, and shall gently lead those that are with young"
(ISAIAH 40:11).

THE FIRST WATCH (1 – 5 YEARS)

The first watch is the beginning of mothering. The glorious moment, although sometimes bewildering and even frightening to many new mothers, is when your first baby arrives. Everything is new. You are learning a whole new lifestyle. You are gradually learning how to lay down your self-life and pour out your life for someone else. This is a new experience, isn't it? And it happens "little by little." Unless you are really prepared for motherhood, it takes time to change from a life of selfishness to a life of selflessness.

Although I loved my first baby with such an intensity of love that I had never experienced before, I hadn't yet learned how to live a selfless life. I learned more with each baby that came along.

This watch is also the time of more babies coming. It may be the most physically exhausting time of motherhood when we have little ones to care for (maybe one, two, or even three) and no extra help! I remember what that was like. I had three in 17 months because twins arrived unexpectedly with my second pregnancy! Can you believe it? I didn't know I was having twins until my first twin was born! No ultrasounds in those days.

GOD GENTLY LEADS YOU

These times can be physically exhausting, but God will never forsake you. Dear precious mother, as you keep the right attitude and embrace your role, you will find joy and delight, even in this busy time. God cares for you as a young mother. He is with you moment by moment.

Read again the Scripture for today. Isaiah 40:11: *"He shall feed his flock like a shepherd: he shall gather the lambs with his arm, and carry them in his bosom, and shall gently lead those that are with young."*

God gently leads you. He doesn't expect you to be at the front of flock, keeping up with everything you were doing before you gave birth to your baby (or babies). Forget about all those other things. You have a new career now. You are nursing a little lamb that takes all your care, night and day. You don't have time to do all those extra things. And God doesn't expect you to do them. So, relax. Put your feet up and nurse your baby again. Bask in the joy of this season.

I remember when I was learning how to be a mother. I wanted to change the world, but suddenly I was stuck in the home with three little babies, then four under four, and later more! What had happened to me? Was my life finished? God had to show me that I was in His perfect will. As I embraced it, I began to enjoy it and all my frustrations gradually left.

I would write my "To Do" list for each day. But I don't think I ever crossed off one of the things on the list. It took my whole day to care for my babies! I had to learn that I accomplished everything I was meant to do for the day, even if I thought I had done nothing! Caring for my little ones was a powerful career in God's eyes.

I am sure, like me, you will wonder how to even accomplish the most basic duties of the home and how to get meals ready with a little fussy baby. You will find a baby carrier such a blessing. It's amazing what you can accomplish wearing your baby. It's a good idea to put a meal in the crockpot early in the day so food is ready for the evening, as it is usually in the evening when baby is most fussy.

YOU CREATE THE FOUNDATION FOR THEIR LIVES

In this first watch of one to five years, you will teach your little ones so much. You are establishing a foundation for their whole lives. You will teach them how to hear and obey. They can't learn to obey you until you first teach them how to listen carefully. You teach them this habit of listening and obeying in these early years. If you get them into this habit of listening attentively when they are young, you won't have to keep on teaching them this for the rest of their lives.

In these early years, you will teach them about Jesus and His ways. Young children can be saved and born again at three to five years of age when they live in a home where the parents daily read God's Word daily to the family (2 Timothy 3:15).

You'll be teaching them how to pray. As soon as they can speak, they can pray. God gives them the gift of speech not only to communicate with people but ultimately to communicate with Him. Praying should be as normal as breathing in their lives.

During this early age you enhance their ability to distinguish between good and evil. Each new baby is born with a God consciousness. Jesus lights every person that comes into the world (John 1:9), but you will fan this light each day as you teach them God's ways and how to know what is evil and what is good.

Dr. Henry C. Thiessen writes about the conscience: "It is the presence in man of this sense of right and wrong . . . conscience in man reveals both the existence of God, and to some extent the nature of God. That is, it reveals to us not only that He is but that He sharply distinguishes between right and wrong." You, as the mother, help to sharpen their conscience.

As you gather for mealtimes, they'll firstly sit on your knee, and then in a highchair, but gradually you'll teach them to sit at the table and not jump up and down every few minutes. This is an important habit to teach them that prepares them to be able to sit in church. Some children are still jumping up and down when they are older as they have never been taught when they were young.

Embrace your FIRST WATCH.

PRAYER:

"I thank You, dear Shepherding Father, that You have blessed me with my precious children. Thank You for showing me that this is my new, full-time career. I embrace motherhood with all my heart, knowing that I am serving and pleasing You as I care for Your little lambs. Amen."

AFFIRMATION:

I'm not neglecting my watch. My little ones are my life and joy.

41

THE SECOND WATCH

*"But grow in grace, and in the knowledge
of our Lord and Savior Jesus Christ"*
(2 PETER 3:18).

THE SECOND WATCH (5 – 12 YEARS)

Your little ones are growing. It's time to officially begin schooling. I say "officially," because you have been teaching your children from the time they were born. It is inherently within you to teach. You talk to them and tell them about life. You teach them the parts of their body. You teach them the names and sounds of all the animals in the world and the names of everything around them. You are a full-time teacher.

YOU ARE THEIR BEST TEACHER

Now it's time to teach them to read, teach them math, and undergird them in a basic education and understanding of life. You begin to prepare them for the future. Sadly, this is a time when some mothers abdicate their second watch. They are happy they can have some time to themselves and send their children off to the public school to be taught a socialist agenda. They think they are discharging their responsibility, but they are handing them over to the enemy's camp. Our state schools are increasingly becoming institutions to indoctrinate our children with progressive ideology, alternative lifestyles, the gay agenda, Muslim propaganda, and now they are promoting transgenderism. But no Bible. And no prayer.

If we are God-fearing, Bible-believing parents, we will take responsibility for what they teach our children for so many hours each day. There may have been a time years ago when you could get away with it (I was a teacher myself), but you can no longer trust the system. We are not faithful watchdogs of our children unless we are in the classroom every day to hear what they teach our children.

The ages of five to twelve years are a powerful time in our children's lives as we lay a foundation of truth in their lives. It is a time of great responsibility as we establish them strongly in the truth of God's Word and teach them discernment between good and evil. In every subject we teach, we show them the ways of God because God is in every subject. God is in everything. God is the originator of all knowledge and wisdom. Apart from Him and His Word everything else is vain.

Proverbs 2:6: *"The LORD giveth wisdom: out of his mouth cometh knowledge and understanding."* Why would we send our children to a place where they will constantly be deceived rather than receive wisdom and understanding?

1 Corinthians 1:25: *"The foolishness of God is wiser than men."*

Colossians 2:3: *"In whom (Christ Jesus) are hid all the treasures of wisdom and knowledge."*

God's Word shows us that the home is a beautiful place to teach our children (Deuteronomy 6:6-9 and 11:18-21). Micah 2:9 talks about women and children who were cast out of the homes they love.

The Amplified Version says: *"From her children you take away My splendor and blessing forever (by putting them among the pagans, away from Me)."* God doesn't want His children to be taught by pagans. He wants them to live in His presence and taught by godly parents.

YOU ARE THEIR BEST TRAINER

Begin discipling your children while they are young. Do you remember when Jesus' parents took him up to the Passover in Jerusalem? After a day's journey on the way home, they realized he was missing. Back they went to Jerusalem. On the third day they found him. Where was he? *"In the temple, sitting in the midst of the doctors, both hearing them, and asking them questions. And all that heard him were astonished at his understanding and answers"* (Luke 2:46). And he was only twelve years old, but he was taught daily in His home and was familiar with the teachings of the Old Testament.

Today, many young children are very ignorant of God's Word. This should not be the testimony of your children. This second watch is a never-to-be-gotten-again opportunity to get your children memorizing the Scriptures. Recently I stayed at a home where some very young children could recite chapters of the Bible.

Josephus, the historian says that Samuel would have only been 11 years old when God spoke to him and gave him, as a young child, His prophetic word to carry to the prophet Eli (Samuel 1). God did not think he was too young for this responsibility.

YOU ARE THEIR BEST ENCOURAGER

Even in this second watch, you keep stirring your children on to maturity (Psalm 144:12).

This second watch is such a fun time with your children as you watch their blossoming personalities and see the beginning of the gifts God has uniquely and divinely placed in them. Encourage them in their talents and give them opportunity to develop them.

Encourage them to be who God created them to be. In this deceived transgender world, train your boys to be manly and your daughters to be feminine. This is the time to affirm to them that God created them in His image and their sex is determined at the time of conception.

Males produce two types of sperm, one carrying the X chromosome and the other the Y chromosome. Females only produce eggs with the X chromosome. Therefore, if a male X chromosome sperm fuses with an egg, the embryo will be an XX (a girl). If it is a Y sperm, it will be an XY (a boy). Teach them the truth and teach them the distinction between the sexes.

Timothy Paul Jones writes: "The clothes that our children wear do not merely cover the nakedness of their flesh; they shape and reflect the contours of our children's souls."

Make your family meal tables exciting times for your children. Bring subjects and questions to talk about at the table. Make your face-to face table gatherings times of positivity and learning rather than nothingness.

And in this second watch, teach them responsibility and the value of work. Don't allow any entitlement attitude. You are already training them for their future marriage and life. Make sure you are establishing the right habits now.

Embrace your SECOND WATCH. You are preparing your children for the THIRD WATCH.

PRAYER:

"Thank You, Father, for the joy of parenting these children. These years are such a fun time together. Help me to make their lives happy and enjoyable but also help me to establish godly habits that will prepare them for life. Amen."

AFFIRMATION:

Each day is a new and exciting day as I parent my growing children.

42

THE THIRD WATCH
Part 1

"Blessed are those servants, whom the lord when he cometh shall find
watching . . . And if he shall come in the second watch, or come
in the third watch, and find them so, blessed are those servants"
(LUKE 12:37, 38).

THIRD WATCH (13 – 18 YEARS)

You've got teenagers. Wow! This is an exciting and challenging time of motherhood. Your children want to flex their muscles. They have moments of maturity, but still, lots of immaturity. It's a time to inspire maturity, responsibility, and earnestness as they prepare more diligently for life.

It's certainly not a time to vacate mothering. We need to be on hand for our teens as much as for our little ones. This is one of the great blessings of parents who are open to the blessing of children. They don't stop at two children (unless God does not give them more). What a blessing for older children to have younger brothers and sisters and hopefully a baby in the family. They learn firsthand the art of parenting and the blessing of children. They are preparing for the great task of establishing their own family unit. Their hearts, which are sometimes lured to rebellion, keep soft and tender with little toddlers and babies around them.

I think about the family God chose for His Only Son, Jesus Christ. Many would think He needed a two-child family where He could have his own bedroom and everything He could ever need. But no, God chose a poor family.

Matthew 13:55, 56 tells us about his four brothers (that's five boys in the family) and *"his sisters, are they not **all** with us?"* "Sisters" is plural, which means there were at least two. However, in the context it looks as though there could have been more. What if there were four or five sisters? Jesus lived in a poor family of at least seven children but perhaps ten or more.

It's a temptation when there are only two or three older young people in the home (and they all grow up) to wonder what to do with your life. A baby keeps you in the home and keeps you there for your older children. This is such a powerful blessing. Teenagers need a mother in the home to watch over their lives. We no longer need to care for their physical bodies (except cooking for them!), but they need powerful spiritual watching with our "beady" natural eyes and our "acute" prayerful eyes.

It's a time to carefully guard their friendships. One of the greatest influences on teens is their peers. Their friends determine their lifestyle. When mother is in the home, she has opportunity to invite godly friends to come for dinner or a party with her teens. She can guide her children to good friendships who will have a godly influence on their lives.

We raised our teens on Proverbs 13:20: *"He that walketh with wise men shall be wise; but a companion of fools shall be destroyed."* Sadly, many wonderful Christian parents watch their young people get into drugs and a sinful lifestyle. Invariably, it is because of the friends they have made. And usually in the public school!

TIME FOR DILIGENT WATCHING

Jeremiah 51:12 says: *"Make the watch strong."* I believe we must make our watch stronger on this watch than any other time in our mothering. When our children were little, we gave ourselves physically to care for them night and day. Now, we give ourselves to watch and pray. You can't effectively mother your children through the third watch unless you are a praying mother.

Ask your husband to pray with you each day for your children. There is power in agreeing prayer states Matthew 18:19: *"If **two of you shall agree** on earth as touching any thing that they shall ask, it shall be done for them of my Father which is in heaven."*

What did Jesus say to His disciples? Matthew 26:40, 41: *"Could ye not watch with me one hour? Watch and pray, that ye enter not into temptation."*

Habakkuk 2:1 (NET): *"I will stand at my watch post; I will remain stationed on the city wall."* (Or personally, I will remain stationed at the post of my home).

Luke 12:39: *"And this know, that if the goodman of the house had known what hour the thief would come, he would have watched, and not have suf-fered his house to be broken through."*

Embrace your THIRD WATCH.

PRAYER:

"Dear Father God, I thank You for reminding me of the powerful mothering that is needed in this third watch. Help me to be disciplined in prayer. Help me to take up my powerful mantle of mothering in this vulnerable time of my children's lives. Amen."

AFFIRMATION:

My teens cannot get away from my watchful eyes or my daily pas-sionate prayers.

THE THIRD WATCH
Part 2

"That our sons may be as plants grown up in their youth; that our daughters may be as corner stones, polished after the similitude of a palace"
(PSALM 144:12).

The above Scripture gives an amazing description of God's plan for our young people. It's important to understand God's plan in a society that promotes prolonged adolescence.

Our sons are to be ***"grown up"*** in their youth! We train them to take life seriously, take responsibility, and act more maturely! We teach them to begin preparing to provide a home for the wife God will give them and to provide for a family. They haven't time to fritter away these valuable years.

Young's Literal Translation says: *"Our sons are as plants, **becoming great in their youth**."* They don't have to wait until they are older to become great. They can become great while in their youth. The word "great" is *gadal* and means "to make large in body, mind, and honor, to exceed, to be excellent, magnificent."

YOU ARE RAISING ROYALTY
Our Sons are Princes

We want them to act like **princes**. Psalm 45:16 says: *"Instead of thy fathers shall be thy children, whom thou mayest make princes in all the earth."* What a glorious mandate for raising sons.

These young men are ready for marriage and embracing a family when God brings the right wife to them. Today, many men in their late twenties are still balking at marriage and leaving many beautiful daughters waiting and longing to be married and raise a family. The Bible picture is the opposite.

Malachi 2:15 speaks of *"the wife of his youth."* Read also Proverbs 5:18

and Isaiah 54:4, 6.

Proverbs 2:17 and Joel 1:8 speak of *"the husband of her youth."*

Psalm 127:4 speaks of *"the children of the youth."*

The word "youth" in these passages is *nu'uwr* meaning "the state of juvenility." That can mean late teens, not late twenties!

Young men can influence society even in their youth. Paul speaks to Timothy in 1 Timothy 4:12: *"Let no man despise thy youth; but be thou an **example** of the believers, in word, in conversation, in charity in spirit, in faith, in purity."* Timothy would have only been 18 – 20 years of age when he began working with Paul (1 Corinthians 16:10, 11).

Our Daughters are Princesses

The Bible describes our daughters in the context of a palace. They are royalty. They are princesses. Are we training them to live this way?

Psalm 144:12 (WEB): *"Our daughters like pillars carved to adorn a palace."*

Psalm 144:12 (NLT): *"May our daughters be like graceful pillars, carved to beautify a palace."*

At first thought, we wonder why the Bible describes our daughters as pillars. Shouldn't it be our sons? Pillars are strong—strong enough to bear the weight of a building. And a palace is not a shack, but a huge building.

God wants our daughters to be strong too. We must raise them to be strong physically, ready for childbearing and the great responsibility and weight of raising a family. We raise them to be strong in purity, strong in their convictions, strong in truth, and strong to commit to the plan God has chosen for them as women.

I love to think of our daughters as the four Ps:

They are **princesses**, revealing their royal status.

They are **polished**, trained, and ready to face their destiny.

They are **pillars**, ready and able to bear the weight of raising a family.

And they are carved and sculptured for the beauty of a **palace**. Pillars are not only strong, but the pillars of a palace are decorated and a beautiful feature of the palace.

Let's remind our daughters that they are royalty. They belong to a royal kingdom, the greatest kingdom of all kingdoms. They belong to the King of kings and Lord of lords. They do not act like the ordinary young person today. They are set apart as royalty.

Encourage them to speak like daughters of the King of kings. To walk like a princess. To learn to sit, act, and react like a princess. To dress beautifully. We encourage them to embrace their femininity and glory in their womanhood. We want them to fulfill the purpose for which God created them. Because He created them female, they bring the greatest glory to God in embracing their femininity. Therefore, in a genderless society, we encourage our daughters to lift high their banner of beautiful femininity.

Don't forget to tell your daughters about the four Ps. And remind them that it's not just a pretty face that is beautiful. That is superficial beauty. Every daughter is beautiful when she smiles. When she is polite. When she is thankful and grateful. When she understands etiquette. When she puts others before herself. And when she is godly.

PRAYER:

"Dear Father God, please anoint me by the power of Your Holy Spirit to raise sons and daughters to be princes and princesses in all the earth, showing to the world that they belong to the kingdom of Heaven. Amen."

AFFIRMATION:

I am raising young people for the glory of God and the glory of the nation.

44

THE THIRD WATCH
Part 3

*"Have not I commanded thee? Be strong and of a
good courage; be not afraid, neither be thou dismayed:
for the LORD thy God is with thee whithersoever thou goest"*
(Joshua 1:9).

Although the ages of 13 – 18 years of age are considered the time of adolescence, we must remember that they should be years of training and inspiring them to maturity and adulthood. I know you don't want them to "hang out" and live like many teenagers today with no vision or goal except to please themselves and live for entertainment and social media.

At the age of 13 years for sons, and 12 years for daughters, the Jewish people organize a Bar Mitzvah or Bat Mitzvah for their sons and daughters, encouraging them from childhood to adulthood. The word "teenager" is not in the Bible or in the 1828 Webster's dictionary.

As we read the Bible, we see many examples of young people who lived disciplined and courageous lives in their youth. They were not bound by their youth but were ready for any exploit. Let's look at a few examples:

At 17 years of age **Joseph** was drastically torn from his family and sold as a slave in Egypt. But he stood strong in his faith in a foreign land that denied his God. He was faithful in every situation that happened to him, even in prison. He never gave up. He continued to walk in integrity. And eventually God made him second-in-command to Pharaoh.

Most Bible commentators say that **David** could have been no more than 17 years of age when he killed the giant Goliath. Saul called him *"but a youth"* (1 Samuel 17:33). The word he used was *na'ar* meaning "the age of infancy to adolescence, young."

Let's read again young David's words to the giant. How wonderful to see such bravery, courage, and stalwart faith in God in such a young man:

"You come to me with a sword, with a spear, and with a javelin. But I come to you in the name of the LORD of hosts, the God of the armies of Israel, whom you have defied. This day, the LORD will deliver you into my hand, and I will strike you and take your head from you. And this day I will give the carcasses of the camp of the Philistines to the birds of the air and the wild beasts of the earth, that all the earth may know that there is a God in Israel. Then all this assembly shall know that the LORD does not save with sword and spear; for the battle is the LORD'S and he will give you into our hands" (1 Samuel 17:45-47 NKJV).

David's son, **Solomon**, would have been about 20 years when he began his reign over all Israel. Josephus puts his age at only 14 years. His father, David called him *"young and tender"* (1 Chronicles 22:5) when he was about to become king. And yet he became the greatest king in the then-known world.

We often think of wise old King Solomon, but he was only young at the beginning of his reign when God asked him what he would like God to give to him. We know that he asked for a hearing heart and wisdom to judge God's people (2 Chronicles 1:6-13).

Josiah became king at only eight years of age. But at 16 years of age (still a teenager) he began to seek God with all his heart. 2 Chronicles 34:3 says: *"In the eighth year of his reign, while he was yet young (16 years), he began to seek after the God of David his father; and in the twelfth year (20 years) he began to purge Judah and Jerusalem from the high places, and the groves, and the carved images, and the molten images."* He became a reformer and brought about the greatest revival in Judah at this young age. Read the whole of chapter 34.

1 Kings 11:28 tells us about **Jeroboam** who was *"a mighty man of valor: and Solomon seeing the young man that he was industrious, he made him ruler over all the charge of the house of Joseph."* He was also a young man and yet because he was industrious, Solomon made him a ruler.

1 Chronicles 12:28 talks about **Zadok**, *"a young man mighty of valor."* The word is *na'ar*, meaning an adolescent.

Bible commentators report that **Daniel** and his three friends were about 11 – 15 years of age when they were captured from Jerusalem and taken to Babylon. They were chosen, along with others, to be trained in the way of Babylonian life and to be brainwashed with Babylonian deception and false gods. Yet these young men stood true to God and never wavered.

It's interesting that we can still read in the Bible about Daniel and his friends, Shadrach, Meshach, and Abednego and how they stood true to God against the Babylonian kings. And yet we don't hear a thing about the rest of the young men. Did they cave to the Babylonian pressure?

What about the **disciples**? Did you know that they were not older men, but mostly teenagers, ranging from 13 – 20 years? In this time of history most young people finished their education at 13 – 15 years of age and they were well-educated. Some could recite the whole Torah. They would then disciple with a rabbi or become involved in the family business. Rabbis (at the age of 30) gathered young men around them to teach them before the young men took on the responsibility of providing for home and family.

Luke 9:6 tells us that these young disciples *"went through the towns, preaching the gospel, and healing everywhere."*

Do the stories of these young people challenge you? Let's raise young men who are not flitting their lives away but are prepared to stand true to God and His truth in this deceived age.

Proverbs 20:29: *"The glory of young men is their strength."*

1 John 2:14: *"I have written unto you, young men, because ye are strong, and the word of God abideth in you, and ye have overcome the wicked one."*

PRAYER:

"Thank you, Father, for inspiring me to raise my sons to be young men who are brave and courageous and who will stand for truth in the face of persecution and ridicule. Amen."

AFFIRMATION:

I am raising Bible-believing, Jesus-loving, God-fearing, devil-destroying, evil-resisting, righteous-living, truth-adhering, and very courageous sons and daughters.

45

THE FOURTH WATCH

"Older women likewise are to be reverent in behavior . . . They are to teach what is good, and so train the young women to love their husbands and children, to be self-controlled, pure, working at home, kind, and submissive to their own husbands, that the word of God may not be reviled"
(TITUS 2:3-5 ESV).

Motherhood has its seasons. At last, we are getting to the FOURTH WATCH which is the season when our children leave the nest. Many mothers flake out at this watch. They think they have finished with this "motherhood thing" and can get on with other things in life.

Of course, we find time to do many other things in this season of life, but we never discard motherhood. Motherhood is who we are. It is who God created us to be. We do other things, but we ARE mothers. Physically and innately. It will never change until we meet Jesus face to face.

This fourth watch should be a time for enlarging motherhood, rather than lessening. Sadly, because of society's trend many women are left bereft at this season. I often meet fellow older couples when traveling back and forth to Above Rubies retreats. I feel sad when I hear they only raised two children and now these children are at colleges in other states with no thought of getting married. These older couples are longing for grandchildren, but there are none in sight. Even when their children get married, they often do not want children! They have been conditioned with the wrong mindset.

As our children leave our nest, it becomes a time for increasing our families. Family is a living and growing thing. It should never stagnate but continually grow. Grandchildren coming. Then great-grandchildren coming.

Apart from enjoying grandchildren and great-grandchildren, God has given the older women a responsibility. A divine mandate. A biblical command. We are commanded to encourage, train, and teach the young mothers. We teach and show them by example how to be great wives and mothers. We show them *how* to love their husbands. We inspire them how to embrace motherhood and keep their homes in order.

If we are not faithful to fulfil this mandate, we fail the next generation. There are very few older mothers taking up this mantle. Consequently, we have myriads of young women who have left their homes and gone AWOL! Did I say AWOL (Absent Without Official Leave)? Yes. Motherhood is the home army that God talks about in Psalm 68:11, 12.

Mothers are needed in their homes to raise their children. When mothers leave their homes, the enemy has his opportunity to get hold of the minds and souls of the children. Unless we are with our children, we don't know how they are being mothered (at day care) or what they are being taught at school.

Most older mothers are out at work and therefore not showing the younger generation the role of motherhood. The younger generation has no example.

THE DOUBLE PORTION WATCH

But many will reply: "But there's nothing to do at home now." Dear mother on the fourth watch, God doesn't take away your motherhood career just because your children have grown! You are entering a greater realm of motherhood—the double portion watch!

There is a world of afflicted and hurting people waiting to be loved, encouraged, and ministered to. Ask God who He wants you to reach out to. Ask Him who He wants you to gather into your home to love and nurture. Now that your children have grown, you have more time to minister to the broken-hearted and to uplift and strengthen the downcast and disillusioned.

Your home can overflow with people as you show hospitality, and you'll never have a bored moment again. In fact, as you get a vision to pour out your nurturing anointing to bless and comfort and inspire people around your table, you'll hardly have enough time to minister to every mother and family that God puts upon your heart.

Rise up, older mothers. You don't have time to waste your life earning a bit of extra pocket money. You have a world of young mothers who need help; single mothers who need uplifting and strengthening; young singles who need inspiring in the ways of God instead of the ways of the world;

older people who are lonely and have no one to care for them; children who need caring for; those who are sick and in prison; and the hurting, troubled, and brokenhearted all around you (Matthew 25:31-46). You have a full-time ministry awaiting you.

God has given you a home! Don't vacate it. Your home is the greatest place in the entire world to serve God. Ask Him who He wants you to invite into your home for a meal. Ask a family over to supper to encourage and bless them. Ask a young mother and her children to your home for lunch or take her on a picnic. Open your home in hospitality. Open your doors wide.

Start proactively encouraging your children to get married. Encourage them to have children. That's what the Bible tells us to do (Jeremiah 29:6).

The fourth watch is the last watch of the night, although it's really the early hours of the morning. This is the time that Jesus loved to spend with his Father (Mark 1:35). It's a powerful time to wait on God—to pray like you've never prayed before. No excuses. No little children around to disturb you! Pray for your family. Pray for the coming generations. Pray for your nation. Pray for the world.

This is the time when Jacob wrestled with God and met Him face to face (Genesis 32:22-31).

This is the time when God delivered the Israelites from slavery in Egypt (Exodus 14:24-31).

This is the time when Jesus came walking on the water to bring His disciples *"good cheer"* in the midst of the storm (Matthew 14:25-33).

This is when Peter walked on the water (Matthew 14:29).

This is when the angels appeared to the shepherds to announce the birth of the Savior of the world (Luke 2:8-14).

This is when Jesus rose from the dead (Matthew 28:1).

This is when Mary Magdalene discovered Jesus had risen from the dead (John 20:1).

This is a time for deliverance and miracles! This is a time for you to allow the Holy Spirit to move through you to touch many lives. This is the time to minister "good cheer" to all God sends you to.

1 Thessalonians 5:6: *"Let us not sleep as do others; but let us watch and be sober."*

PRAYER:

"Dear Father, please help me to take on my responsibility as an older mother. You gave me the responsibility to train my own children for motherhood. And there are so many other young mothers around me. Many are discouraged, lonely, and overwhelmed. Show me how I can encourage them and lead them into Your truth and Your ways. Amen."

AFFIRMATION:

I'm in the Fourth Watch and I will not give up until I reach the finishing line!

46

WHAT'S YOUR CHOICE?

*"I call heaven and earth to record this day against you,
that I have set before you life and death, blessing and cursing:
therefore **choose life**, that both thou and thy seed may live"*
(DEUTERONOMY 30:19).

We face life and death issues every day. Because we belong to a kingdom of life, we must get into the habit of choosing life in every situation. But to choose life, we must have God's understanding of life. We often make decisions with our humanistic thinking. I believe it is imperative to know what God thinks about life from the beginning to the end.

What about the beginning of life? We believe that life begins at conception. However, I see in the Scriptures that God goes even beyond conception. One of the many words that He uses to describe children is the Hebrew word *zera*. This word describes the sperm but also people—babies, toddlers, teens, and adults. God sees them all the same. He sees that the life begins with the sperm. There would be no babies or no adults if there were no sperm!

Compare Leviticus 15:16-18 which uses *zera* for sperm and Genesis 46:6-7 (among many other Scriptures) that uses zera for people: *"They came into Egypt, Jacob, and all his seed (zera) with him: his sons, and his sons' sons with him, his daughters, and his son's daughters, and all his seed (zera) brought he with him into Egypt."* This speaks of three generations of different ages.

I am always amazed at God's revelation in Hebrews 7:9, 10 where it says: *"Levi also, who receiveth tithes, paid tithes in Abraham. For he was yet in the loins of his father, when Melchisedec met him."* Levi was four generations down from Abraham, not even a twinkle in Abraham's eye, but God says he was literally in the loins of Abraham and paid tithes to Melchisedec when Abraham paid tithes. God sees the seed of life that continues in each continuing generation. What a tragedy that so much life is cut off before it is even conceived!

What about the end of life? It is prevalent today to encourage people into the arms of Jesus when they are nearing the end. I have heard pastors and counselors say, "The Lord is waiting for you. You can now go to the arms of Jesus. We release you to go." A pastor said this to my father as he neared his last moments. I thought it sounded very spiritual at the time.

It was not until sometime later that the Holy Spirit convicted me that, although it sounded very spiritual, it is far from right! No one, no matter who they are, has any authority to tell a person it is time to leave this earth. This kind of thinking slowly leads us toward euthanasia. A person will give their last breath when they are ready, without anyone's help. Even when they are unconscious or in a coma, they can still be aware of their loved ones around them. Maybe they want to linger on and savor the presence of family members as long as they can. They do not need autosuggestion from anyone.

It is a divine privilege to breathe our last when we are ready, not when someone else thinks we are ready. Jesus gave up His own spirit. Luke 23:46 says: *"And when Jesus had cried with a loud voice, he said, Father into thy hands I commend my spirit: and having said thus, he gave up the ghost."*

We are living in a culture of death, masterminded by Satan who wants to destruct. He comes to rob, kill, and destroy (John 10:10). He wants to rob life from this world before conception and after conception. He wants to snuff people's lives out before it is their time to go.

In this culture, we must stand out like beacon lights, promoting life! Never being deceived by society around us! Never giving in! Never compromising! There is no middle ground. We either belong to the kingdom of God which promotes life or the kingdom of Satan which chooses death. One brings blessing, the other cursing. If we do not choose life, we are contrary to God's kingdom.

Philippians 2:15-16 says: *"That ye may be blameless and harmless, the sons of God, without rebuke, in the midst of a crooked and perverse nation, among whom ye shine as lights in the world; holding forth the word of* **life***."*

Make it a habit to choose life in every situation, even when you open your mouth to speak! Embrace life. Give life. Love life. Stand up for life. Speak life. Make decisions for life. Choose life that you and your descendants will live!

PRAYER:

"Dear Father, please save me from being subtly deceived by the culture of death in which I live. Help me to always stand for life. Amen."

AFFIRMATION:

I'm lighting up, standing up, and speaking up for life!

BETTER IS THE END

"Better is the end of a thing than the beginning thereof"
(ECCLESIASTES 7:8).

It's easy to embark on a new vision or project with a "hiss and a roar." But as time goes on, our enthusiasm wanes. Sometimes we peter out altogether. I understand this in the ministry of Above Rubies which I began over 44 years ago (as I write this devotion). The vision was so heavy upon my heart that I felt compelled to do it. I didn't realize at the time that it is perspiration that keeps something going. Someone once said that a vision is usually "One percent inspiration and 99 percent perspiration." True. It doesn't happen without daily plodding and faithfulness.

It's the same with the greatest institutions of life—marriage and family. God ordained these powerful foundations before church, before government, and before schools. Because they are God ordained, we don't stop half-way through. We dare not stop before the finishing line. It's all the way to the end.

Ecclesiastes 7:8 reminds us that it's not so much how we start, but how we end.

Perhaps you didn't get a good start to your marriage. Or even with motherhood. You came into motherhood unprepared and not knowing what you were doing. Don't despair. I know you are learning as you go. You are mothering better with each baby God gives you. You grow stronger as you mother. Remember, it's not so much the beginning but the end that counts.

You start weak in mothering, but you grow stronger.

You start a failure, but you end a victor.

You start by being overwhelmed each day, but you end up an overcomer.

With each new baby, you become wiser and stronger.

This was my own experience. With every baby I learned more of the art of mothering, the art of breastfeeding, and the art of homemaking. We must gradually learn and hone these wonderful arts.

Hebrews 11:34 gives this testimony of the great heroes of faith: *"Out of weakness were made strong, waxed valiant in the fight, turned to flight the armies of the aliens."* These great heroes didn't begin strong. They began in weakness but as they faced the struggles and the fight against the enemy, they became stronger and more valiant.

Philippians 1:6: *"Being confident of this very thing, that He which hath begun a good work in you will perform it until the day of Jesus Christ."*

FINISH STRONG

Revelation 2:25, 26 encourages us: *"But that which ye have already hold fast till I come. And he that overcometh, and keepeth my works **unto the end,** to him will I give power over the nations."*

Keep pressing on. Keep seeking God for the way He wants you to be a wife and mother. Always keep learning. There is so much more to learn. And keep fighting the fight of faith. Keep on until the end. Let's read about the following examples:

JESUS finished His work. He confessed in John 4:34: *"My meat is to do the will of him that sent me, and to **finish** his work."*

He said again in John 17:4: *"I have **finished** the work which thou gavest me to do."* Will you follow His example?

PAUL also made these same confessions. Acts 20:24: *"But none of these things move me* (the fact that he was going to face prison and afflictions), *neither count I my life dear unto myself, so that I might **finish** my course with joy, and the ministry which I have received of the Lord Jesus."*

What is the ministry you have received from God? If He has graciously given you children, this is your greatest ministry at hand—to nurture and train them. And it's not only when our children are young, but mothering extends to the end of our days. We are always a mother. When our children grow up and leave the nest, we become an older mother to younger mothers,

Paul confesses again in 2 Timothy 4:7: *"I have **fought** a good fight, I have **finished** my course, I have **kept** the faith."* Let's look at the three things Paul did in this Scripture:

HE FOUGHT THE GOOD FIGHT

We are certainly in a fight for families in our nations today. Because the family is God's idea, the enemy is out to destroy it. Because motherhood is

God's ultimate plan for women, the devil hates it and wants to destroy it.

Feminism, humanism, the media, and public education have brainwashed many women to think that motherhood is insignificant and unworthy of their time. Because we know this is deception, we fight against the tide. We will not give in. We will fight a good fight. We fight on the side of life. We embrace our calling because we know it comes from God. We will not only embrace motherhood with all our hearts but fight against the deceptions in our society. We fight to destroy the works of the enemy.

Nehemiah 4:14: *"Be not ye afraid of them: remember the Lord, which is great and terrible (awesome), and **fight** for your brethren, your sons, and your daughters, your wives, and your houses."*

HE FINISHED THE RACE

We will not give up until we finish our fourth watch!

HE WAS FAITHFUL TO THE END

The NLT says: *"I have remained faithful."* Paul remained faithful through hardships, discouragement, imprisonments, beatings, stonings, shipwrecks, dangers, robbings, weariness, painfulness, hunger, thirst, destitution, plus the care of all the churches. Surely, we can remain faithful through the few trials we face.

Don't give up on your marriage. Don't give up on mothering. Don't give up homeschooling.

And never forget, there will be a reward. 2 Timothy 4:8 continues: *"Henceforth there is laid up for me a crown of righteousness, which the Lord, the righteous judge, shall give me at that day, and not to me only, but unto all them also that love his appearing."*

PRAYER:

"Thank You, Father, for wooing me on to the end. I don't want to stop in the race halfway. I want to be faithful to the end. Please help me each day to be faithful. Faithful in the little things, the mundane things, and the ordinary things, for this enables me to be faithful in the big things. Amen."

AFFIRMATION:

I'm not giving up. I'm going all the way to the end.

48

OUR FIRST RESPONSE

"And God blessed them, and God said unto them . . . "
(Genesis 1:28).

The first thing God did after creating Adam and Eve was to bless them. That was God's first response. He created us in His likeness and therefore we should have this same desire to bless people too. We can bless in different ways:

1. WE BLESS PEOPLE BY WHAT WE SAY

God blessed and *"**said** unto them . . ."* What do you say when you open your mouth? Is your first response to bless? To bless your husband. To bless your children. To bless the people you meet. It is a God-like habit we need to cultivate. We should think about things to say that will encourage, inspire, and bless—and then say them. Words of blessing are exhilarating words that gladden a person's heart. They are exhorting words that spark vision and revelation that release people to do great things. They inspire people to be what God created them to be.

The word for "bless" in the Hebrew is *eulogeo* from *eu* which means "good" and *logos* which means "word, speech." If you are a "blessing person" you will constantly speak blessing words.

2. WE BLESS PEOPLE BY HOW WE PRAY

We invoke blessings when we pray. Pray prayers of blessings over your husband, your children, and others. Pray and bless those who persecute you and say evil things about you (Matthew 5:44).

The Lord commanded Moses and his sons to speak blessing over all the children of Israel. Here is the blessing He gave them to bless. You can bless your children and others with this blessing from Numbers 6:24-26:

"The LORD bless thee, and keep thee:
The LORD make his face shine upon thee, and be gracious to thee:

The LORD lift up his countenance upon thee, and give thee peace."

3. WE BLESS PEOPLE BY WHAT WE DO

Actions speak louder than words. 1 John 3:17-18 says: *"But whoso hath this world's good, and seeth his brother have need, and shutteth up his bowels of compassion from him, how dwelleth the love of God in him? My little children, let us not love in word, neither in tongue; but in deed and in truth."*

4. WE BLESS PEOPLE BY OUR AFFIRMATION OF TRUTH

We must always keep the Scripture in context and the context of God's blessing in today's Scripture is the blessing of children.

Genesis 1:28: *"And God blessed them, and God said unto them, Be fruitful, and multiply, and replenish the earth, and subdue it: and have dominion . . ."* To embrace children and be fruitful was the first blessing God gave to the man and woman He created.

Conception comes by God blessing us. If we are in touch with God, we will think of children as a blessing. No matter what the circumstances, a child is always a blessing. This is what God says, so we either believe God or we don't.

This should be our first response when we conceive a baby: "How awesome! God is blessing me. Praise His wonderful name!"

This should also be our response when we hear the news of someone else having a baby: "God is blessing you. Isn't that wonderful? We rejoice with you."

Psalm 107:41-43: *"Yet setteth he the poor on high from affliction, and maketh him families like a flock. The righteous shall see it, and rejoice, and all iniquity shall stop her mouth. Whoso is wise, and will observe these things, even they shall understand the lovingkindness of the LORD."*

This is the attitude those who are wise and righteous have when they hear God is blessing a family with another baby.

PRAYER:

"Dear Father, You are a God of blessing. You have blessed me with life, salvation, and every good gift. Please help me to be a blessing too. Help me to speak words of blessing to my family. Help me to make this a habit of my life so it is the first response to come from my lips. Amen."

AFFIRMATION:

God has blessed me and therefore I will bless others.

49

A STOREHOUSE
OF TREASURE

*"And the LORD God took the man, and put him
into the garden of Eden to dress it and to keep it"*
(GENESIS 2:15).

Do you like to enjoy pleasures in your life? I'm sure you do. Well, guess what? God wants you to enjoy pleasures too. He wants to fill your life and your home with pleasures and delights. When God created the first home for Adam and Eve, He called it Eden which means "pleasure, delicate, delight." He wants your home to be a delight too.

The Knox version translates it correctly: *"God had planted a **garden of delight**, in which he now placed the man he had formed."*

Everything God did in the beginning He did as a pattern for the future of mankind. God made the first home a place of delight and this is His intention for all future homes.

It is true that God put Adam in the garden to work. This is the pattern of life. Work and pleasure. We work hard in our homes to keep them in running order. But God also wants them to be places of joy and pleasure.

The following should be a top priority in our thinking:

How can I make my home a more delightful place to live?

How can I bring more enjoyment into our marriage relationship?

How can I bring more pleasure into the lives of each of my children?

How can I make my home a treasure house?

Proverbs 15:6 says: *"In the house of the righteous is much treasure."* I believe this treasure is more than beautiful furnishings and wealth. I believe it is the true treasures of love, joy, peace, harmony, and the richness of fellowship. I have walked into homes with beautiful décor and felt unmoved. I have dined in humble homes where the atmosphere was rich with love and the joy of fellowship.

Isaiah 51:3 says: *"For the LORD shall comfort Zion . . . he will make her wilderness like Eden, and her desert like the garden of the LORD; joy and gladness shall be found therein, thanksgiving, and the voice of melody."*

Maybe it's like a wilderness in your home. It doesn't have to stay like that. If you let Him, God wants to help you make your home a place of joy and gladness.

He wants you to fill it with thankfulness instead of complaining and songs of praise instead of grumbling. He wants you to take care of the relationships in your home too—with your husband and your children. Eden also has the meaning of "delicate." Relationships can easily be broken or damaged. A few hurtful or negative words or a mean look and the relationship is weakened. We must handle each one delicately, considerately, and with loving care.

What about children? I think they are the greatest treasures we can have in our homes. They are eternal treasures. They are the treasures we won't leave behind. We can take them with us into eternity. Isn't it unbelievable that many families have more TVs in their homes than children? This is in Christian homes too!

The CJB translation of Proverbs 15:6 says: *"The home of the righteous is a **storehouse of treasure**."* What do you have stored up in your home? Are there lots of "things"? Or is it filled with children and the delights of joy, thanksgivings, and praises?

PRAYER:

"Lord God, You had a plan for the first home and You have a plan for my home. Please fill my home with Your presence because I want it to be an Eden home. Help me to see that one of my greatest roles is to bring pleasure and delight to everyone in my home. Amen."

AFFIRMATION:

I am no longer a pleasure seeker; I am a pleasure giver!

MIRACLES IN YOUR HOME

"I will praise thee; for I am fearfully and wonderfully made: marvelous are thy works; and that my soul knoweth right well"
(PSALM 139:14).

You know that God is a miracle-working God. You believe it. You are in awe at how God stretched forth His mighty right arm to deliver the Israelites from the clutches of Egypt and how He brought them through the Red Sea on dry land. Yet you sometimes wonder why God doesn't do any personal miracles for you.

You don't have to wonder any longer! You already have miracles in your home. You are looking at them all day long! You are a miracle. Your husband is a miracle. Each one of your precious children are miracles, created by God's miracle working power.

David was certainly writing under the inspiration of God when he wrote that we are *"fearfully and wonderfully made: marvelous are thy works; and that my soul knoweth right well"* (Psalm 139:14). He uses two amazing words in this Scripture.

"Wonderfully" is the Hebrew word *palah* meaning "to distinguish, put a difference between, separated, and set apart." God reveals to us in this Scripture how He makes every new person in the world unique. Every new baby is an unrepeatable miracle. There has never been a human being like this one in the history of the world and there will never be another child like this one in the future. Each one is set apart to be someone special and to fulfill a destiny that no one else can fulfill. Now that's amazing! That's awesome!

"Marvelous" is the Hebrew word, *pala*. It means "extraordinary, wonderful, miraculous, astonishing, difficult, and beyond the bounds of human powers or expectations."

Look at each one of your children. Each one is uniquely special. Start thanking God for these miracles in your home! Look upon them as miracles. Each one is irreplaceable. Each one has different gifts and callings and a different personality from you! That's why some children don't seem to "fit" the family strain. God created them differently!

Allow them to be the distinctive miracle God created them to be. That's why you cannot stereotype parenting. You must call upon God for wisdom for each individual child.

Of course, you will still see family traits coming through. That's another miracle.

My daughter Pearl is not like me. She looks like my mother and has a very similar personality to her—and yet she is uniquely Pearl. Pearl's daughter, Meadow has strong traits of my personality, and yet she is distinctively Meadow! I am amazed at the different giftings in our children. They are continually doing things that are different to the bent that Colin or I have. They have gifts far beyond ours. They didn't get them from us; they got them from God. This keeps life from getting boring! It enlarges our thinking and our coasts! It causes us give honor to God that He is the Creator!

What about your husband? God created him exactly in the mold He planned for him! Can you stop trying to make him like you want him to be? Instead, see him as a God-planned miracle too?

Charles Spurgeon says: "We need not go to the ends of the earth for marvels, nor even across our own threshold; they abound in our own bodies." He also writes: "If we are marvelously wrought upon even before we are born, what shall we say of the Lord's dealings with us after we leave His secret workshop, and He directs our pathways through the pilgrimage of life?"

It is interesting to note that David did not talk about his parents when he wrote about his creation in Psalm 139. He ascribed it all to God. No matter who the parents, each new baby is a new miracle, created by God Himself. Even if a child is born of incest or prostitution, it does not change the fact that they are a special miracle, masterminded and fashioned by God for His glory and praise. They are a separate entity from their birth parents.

S. D. Gordon writes: "The new-born babe is a fresh act of God. He is the latest revelation of God's creative handiwork."

Surely, we must exclaim again with the Psalmist: *"Know ye that the LORD He is God: it is He who has made us, and not we ourselves; we are his people, and the sheep of his pasture"* (Psalm 100:3).

PRAYER:

"Dear Father, I am sorry that I have taken my husband and children for granted. I acknowledge that they are miracles of Your creation. Lord God, I thank You for the miracles in my home. Help me to always see them as miracles. Amen."

AFFIRMATION:

I am so blessed. My home is filled with miracles!

GOD WANTS TO WALK IN YOUR HOME

"These things saith he that holdeth the seven stars in his right hand, who walketh in the midst of the seven golden candlesticks"
(REVELATION 2:1).

The seven golden candlesticks referred to in the above Scripture are the seven churches of Asia who were to be shining lights to the darkness around. God also wants to walk in the midst of our churches today. He wants to walk in the midst of our homes. He wants to fill our homes with His presence so we can be a light in our neighborhoods.

Would you like Jesus Christ, the Son of God, to walk in your home? If He walked around in your home, do you think it would make a difference to what is going on? Do you think it would make a difference to what you say? How would it affect the arguing, the complaining, and the bickering? Would you change what you watch and listen to? How would it affect the atmosphere of your home?

I love the words that many families used to hang on the wall of their homes:

> Christ is the head of this home,
> The unseen guest at every meal,
> The silent listener to every conversation.

Jesus wants to be in your midst. Matthew 18:20 says: *"For where two or three are gathered together in my name, there am I in the midst of them."* Why don't you start the day by honoring His name and inviting Him to come into every room of your home. Honor His name throughout the day. Call upon His name. Do everything and say everything in the name of the Lord Jesus as it commands us in Colossians 3:17 and He will fill your home with His presence.

I love the beautiful Scripture in Zephaniah 3:17: *"The LORD thy God in the midst of thee is mighty; he will save, he will rejoice over thee with joy; he will rest in his love, he will joy over thee with singing."* What happens when Jesus comes to your home?

He lives with you. He delivers you. He comes to your rescue. He is your Warrior who is mighty to save. How wonderful that He is always available to come to your rescue.

He rejoices over you with joy. He takes great delight in you. When Jesus is in the midst, there will be rejoicing instead of gloom and despair.

He quietens you. The word for "rest" in this Scripture is *charash* which means "to hold one's peace." That's amazing. When Jesus is in the midst, He will help you to hold your tongue and be silent. He will help you to be quiet instead of lashing out or reacting negatively.

The NET gives a different rendering: *"With his love, he will calm all your fears."* Don't you love that? Not only some of your fears, but **all** your fears.

He sings over you. Isn't it wonderful to know that when Jesus is in your midst that He sings over you with joyful songs? He takes delight in you. He rejoices over you to do you good. (Deuteronomy 30:9 and Jeremiah 32:41). And because He sings over you, He wants you to sing joyful songs over your children too.

Isaiah 65:19: *"I will . . . joy in my people."* Because God takes joy in us, His people, He wants you to take joy in your children.

Instead of worrying over every detail, relax and enjoy your children.

PRAYER:

"My Lord God, I thank You that You want to walk in the midst of my home. I invite you to come into every room. I invite you to be the Head of our home. Amen."

AFFIRMATION:

I am walking with Jesus, and He is walking with me in my home.

52

THE BIGGER PICTURE

"Who is she that looketh forth as the morning, fair as the moon,
clear as the sun, and terrible as an army with banners?"
(SONG OF SONGS 6:10).

Are you feeling exhausted, worried, frazzled, and overwhelmed? During your daily tasks, it is easy to forget the bigger picture and the divine task to which God has commissioned you.

You are not involved in some insignificant career. You have the highest calling in the nation. You may have been involved in a career at some stage and of course you had to be faithful to your employer. But you now have a far more important task. You are employed by a heavenly employer, the King of all kings and the Lord of all lords. You are now responsible to Him.

The following are a few reminders of the magnitude of your great commission.

1. YOU ARE THE REVEALER OF GOD'S MATERNAL HEART

In all the activities of keeping your home, never lose sight of your highest purpose—to walk in the anointing of your maternal instinct. This is who you are. You are a maternal being. You are created to ooze with nurturing. This is the greatest need of your children. This is the greatest need of this sin-sick, hurting world.

It doesn't matter if you do not finish every project and curriculum you have planned for your children, but it does matter that your children live in an atmosphere of nurture and love. Embrace your maternalness. Pour it out upon your family and all you meet. In doing this you will walk in the anointing and glory of womanhood.

2. YOU ARE A NATION SHAPER

More than anyone else, mothers determine the destiny of the nation. You may feel a little worthless in your home while many of your neighbors drive off to work each morning. They may think you are wasting your life, but they have no idea of what you are doing! They don't realize you are shaping lives. You are polishing and sharpening "arrows." You are getting children ready to fulfill God's divine purposes for their lives. There will come a day when they come out of your home to rock this nation—and even the world!

Look out, world! Get out of the way, Satan. There is a mother in this home who knows who she is and knows her calling. You can't trifle with this woman. She is like an awesome army with banners (Song of Songs 6:4, 10)!

3. YOU ARE A LEGACY MAKER

Not only do you determine the destiny of this nation, but you influence the generations to come. Ruth became the great-grandmother of King David, and I am sure she had the privilege of holding him in her arms.

Did you ever read about Hudson Taylor who founded the China Inland Mission? His godly generation started with his great-grandfather who lived in the time of John Wesley. This godly line passed on from one generation to the next and there are now more than nine generations of preachers in the Taylor family.

What mighty children will be born in your following generations as you strongly impress God's ways into the hearts of your children?

4. YOU ARE AN ETERNITY FILLER

Motherhood is an eternal career. Every precious baby you receive from the hand of God is another eternal soul that will live forever. There is absolutely nothing more powerful and more eternal that you could do in this life than bring an eternal soul into this world! You will leave everything in this world behind, except your redeemed soul, the redeemed souls of your children, and others you lead to Jesus.

5. YOU ARE A HOME NESTER

Don't let this humanistic society deceive you to think that your home is a boring place. On the contrary, it is a place of divine appointment for you. It is a sacred place. God chose the home as the place where He wants His children nurtured and raised. Before God gives us children, He first puts us in a home.

Psalm 113:9: *"He maketh the barren woman to keep house, and to be a joyful mother of children."* Our humanistic society provides daycares for children, but these are poor substitutes for the home. A little boy was asked why he didn't like daycare. "Because I didn't have a mommy," he replied. Embrace your home. Thank God for it. Know that it is where God wants you to be to fulfill your great commission.

6. YOU ARE THE BEST TEACHER OF YOUR CHILDREN

There is no one who can teach your children better than you can. Proverbs 6:20-22 says: *"Forsake not the law of thy mother: Bind them continually upon thine heart, and tie them about thy neck. When thou goest, it shall lead thee; when thou sleepest, it shall keep thee; and when thou awakest, it shall talk with thee."*

Abraham Lincoln stated: "The greatest lessons I ever learned were at my mother's knees.

George Washington confessed: "All that I am I owe to my mother. I attribute all my success in life to the moral, intellectual, and physical education I received from her."

John Wesley said: "I learned more about Christianity from my mother than from all the theologians of England."

Dear mother, God has chosen you to be the mother of your children. No one can do it as well as you can. And God is behind you all the way.

PRAYER:

"Dear Father, thank You for the great calling and career You have given to me. I embrace it with all my heart. Help me to fulfil it with all my heart and soul. Amen."

AFFIRMATION:

I am influencing the world as I embrace motherhood and raise mighty arrows for God's kingdom.

53

DEDICATING YOUR CHILDREN
Part 1

*"Train up a child in the way he should go:
and when he is old, he will not depart from it"*
(PROVERBS 22:6).

The Jewish people celebrate Hanukkah to remember how the brave Maccabees gained back the temple in Jerusalem after it had been taken over by Antiochus Epiphanes. The temple was in a state of disrepair. They found only enough oil for one day to relight the Golden Lampstand, but tradition tells us that the light kept burning for eight days while they made God's recipe for the oil for the lamps. That's why Hanukkah is celebrated for eight days. After cleansing out the temple they rededicated it to God. That's why it is also called the Feast of Dedication which Jesus went up to Jerusalem to celebrate.

Interestingly, it is the same word the Bible uses for training children in Proverbs 22:6. The Hebrew verb *chanakh* means "to teach, to dedicate, to consecrate to a sacred purpose." Apart from Proverbs 22:6, the following are other examples where chanakh it is used:

1. Dedication of a house (Deuteronomy 20:5).

2. Dedication of the altar of Moses' tabernacle (Numbers 7:10, 11, 84, 88).

3. Dedication of Solomon's temple. (1 Kings 8:63 and 2 Chronicles 7:4-9).

4. Dedication of Zerubbabel's temple (Ezra 6: 16-18).

5. Dedication of the walls of Jerusalem (Nehemiah 12:27.)

6. Dedication of Nebuchadnezzar's image (Daniel 3:2-3).

7. Dedication and cleansing of the temple in 165 BC. This is recorded in the Apocrypha in 1 Maccabees 4:54: *"It was dedicated anew, with singing of hymns, and music of harp, zither and cymbals."*

This certainly gives us a new light on the meaning of training our children, doesn't it? When we train our children, we are consecrating them to a sacred purpose. We are setting them apart for God's service and the purpose He destined for them. Each of our children is born with a destiny that God planned for them before the foundation of this world. We do not train them according to our ideas. We do not train them by society's standards. Our whole purpose is to dedicate them to the purposes of God.

How did they dedicate in the Old Testament?

1. WITH PURITY

Ezra 6:20 tells us that the priests and Levites who were involved in dedicating the temple *"were purified together, all of them were pure."*

They also dedicated the people. Verse 21 tells us: *"And all the children of Israel, which were come again out of captivity, and all such as had separated themselves unto them from the filthiness of the heathen of the land, to seek the LORD God of Israel, did eat."*

When they dedicated the walls in Nehemiah's time *"the priests and the Levites purified themselves, and purified the people, and the gates, and the wall"* (Nehemiah 12:30).

To train children, we must first dedicate ourselves to God. They dedicated each temple in the Old Testament. God no longer has a temple of wood and stone. He now has temples of flesh and blood. I am a temple of the living God. You are a temple of God to be pure and holy for His dwelling. Your children are temples waiting to be dedicated to His purposes.

As mothers, we must keep our hearts pure from all contamination of sin, rebellion, bitterness, and anger. If there is iniquity and rebellion in our hearts, it will cause rebellion in our children's hearts (Exodus 20:5).

We must be purified mothers to raise purified children!

2. WITH SACRIFICE

They always sacrificed offerings at the dedication of the temple. At the dedication of Solomon's temple, he personally offered up 22,000 oxen and 120,000 sheep. In our currency today this would be worth at least $9,550,000.00! And this was apart from the rest of the offerings of the children of Israel (1 Kings 8:63).

It takes sacrifice to train children to be set apart for God's service. It takes forgetting our own agenda and laying down our own lives. But it is for God, and it comes with His reward. *"For whosoever will save his life shall lose it; but whosoever shall lose his life for my sake, and the gospels, the same shall save it"* (Mark 8:35).

The blood was shed in every sacrifice in the Old Testament. They all pointed to Christ who became the ultimate sacrifice for our sins. It is only through the power of the blood of Jesus that we keep pure and cleansed from the contamination that blights our lives and our children's lives.

3. WITH PRAYER

When Solomon's temple was completed after seven years of labor, he dedicated it to God with prayer (2 Chronicles 6:14-42). We cannot successfully set apart our children for God without much prayer. One of the most important aspects of parenting, and yet the least observed, is prayer. Do you find parenting difficult? Prayer is your answer. Are you having difficulties with one of your children? Prayer is your answer. Are you concerned about the direction of your children? Prayer is your answer.

If you don't pray for your children, who will?

PRAYER:

"Dear Father God, help me to keep my mind and heart pure before You so that I can raise pure and holy children. Cleanse me with Your precious blood from all my sin. Amen."

AFFIRMATION:

I am set apart for God's purpose and I am raising children to be set apart for God.

DEDICATING YOUR CHILDREN
Part 2

"Also that day they offered great sacrifices, and rejoiced: for God had made them rejoice with great joy: the wives also and the children rejoiced: so that the joy of Jerusalem was heard even afar off"
(NEHEMIAH 12:43).

We continue to learn about dedicating our children.

4. WITH JOY AND GLADNESS

Training our children is a solemn responsibility, but God wants us to do it with joy.

In Ezra's time they *"kept the dedication of this house of God with joy . . . for the LORD made them joyful"* (Ezra 6:16, 22).

In Nehemiah's time they celebrated the dedication *"with gladness, both with thanksgivings, and with singing, with cymbals, psalteries, and with harps."* (Nehemiah 12:27, 42, 43).

At the dedication of Solomon's temple there was *"one sound to be heard in praising and thanking the LORD"* (2 Chronicles 5:13).

In the same way that God rejoices and sings over us, His children, so we should rejoice over our children (Zephaniah 3:17). We should take great joy in training our children to be separated to the Lord. We should rejoice in the privilege of co-working with God to fulfill this great task (Psalm 113:9).

God wants our homes to be homes of joy. In Isaiah 32:13 He calls them *"the houses of joy."* Joy is the atmosphere in which He wants us to train our children. He wants you to be joyful and your children to be happy and joyful.

Isaiah 51:3 gives a description of Zion: *"For the LORD shall comfort Zion*

*. . . joy and gladness shall be found therein, **thanksgiving, and the voice of melody.***" This should also be the atmosphere of our homes. Do you notice we should have sets of twins in our homes?

The first twins are *"joy and gladness."* The MLB translation says that *"joy and gladness shall abound in her."* It's not enough to have a bit of joy from time to time. Our homes should **abound** with joy and gladness. This is the kind of atmosphere that draws our children to hanker after God, to love His will, and to desire to fulfill His purposes.

The second set of twins are *"thanksgiving and the voice of melody."* The NLT translates them: *"Lovely songs of thanksgiving will fill the air."* Does thanksgiving fill the atmosphere of your home? Are your children filled with thanksgiving and songs of praises? If you have a thankful spirit, your children will be thankful. If you are filled with the praises of the Lord, your children will have the spirit of praise. You set the tone, mother.

The Bible talks about a third set of twins for our homes. Psalm 118:15 says: *"The voice of **rejoicing and salvation** is in the tabernacles of the righteous: the right hand of the LORD doeth valiantly."* Other translations call them ***"joy and victory."***

What is the song of joy and victory? *"The right hand of the LORD doeth valiantly."* Our confession and our song should proclaim that God is in control! His right arm does valiantly! We believe that He will work deliverance for us. The homes of the righteous should be temples of praise. Name your doors Praise! Call your walls Salvation. Did you know that your walls carry the words and songs that fill your home?

Isaiah 60:18 says: *"Thou shalt call thy walls Salvation, and thy gates Praise."* Another set of twins!

Cast out the evil twins of gloom and despair, negativity and unbelief, and self-pity and bitterness. Instead, welcome in joy and gladness, thankfulness and song, joy and victory, and salvation and praise.

PRAYER:
"Oh God, please help me to raise my children with joy. Help me to fill my home with thanksgiving all day long. Amen."

AFFIRMATION:
Joy and thanksgiving—welcome to my home!

55

FALSE PEACE

"Peace I leave with you, my peace I give unto you: not as the world giveth, give I unto you. Let not your heart be troubled, neither let it be afraid"
(JOHN 14:27).

Each one of us desires peace. Peace of mind. Peace in our marriages. Peace in our homes. "Peace at any cost," we cry out. But what kind of peace are we looking for? Is it God's idea of peace or ours?

"I feel God's peace in my heart," says a wife who is leaving her husband. Perhaps her marriage has been a battlefield of wills and constant stress. What relief to get out of the situation! But is this God's peace? No, the good feeling is a relief from the battle.

"I feel such peace now," exclaims a mother who has just had a tubal ligation. Is this really the peace of God? No, it's relief! This mother no longer has to put up with the pressure of family and friends to stop having children. Stress between her and her husband is alleviated. She no longer has to worry about having any more babies. No more sleepless nights. No more bother! Relief! Yes, but a false sense of peace.

The true peace of God does not counteract His commandments or basic design for our lives. We cannot have God's peace when we willingly interfere with the way that He divinely created us. It is playing God.

"We feel peace about our decision," a couple acknowledge as they leave their church. Maybe their church has been going through difficulties and strife. The easiest way out is to leave! This seems to be normal behavior today. If there are problems in the marriage, walk out. If things aren't going "my way" in the church, walk out! And then they feel a sense of relief that feels like peace.

But God's peace, the peace that passes all understanding, is not relief from stress. It doesn't walk out on the battle. It doesn't take the easy way out. It finds God's grace and rest in the circumstances.

When our daughter, Evangeline, was pregnant with her seventh baby and hemorrhaging for many weeks and she and her baby's life were at stake, she lived in a state of peace. I must confess that we were in a state of concern, but her confidence was in God who is the God of peace. Later in her pregnancy God came into her room and miraculously healed her, but she lived in peace and rest even when she did not have her healing.

It is not necessarily God's peace just because we have a good feeling. We experience God's peace when we walk according to God's divine laws and His commandments. Isaiah 48:18 says: *"O that thou hadst hearkened to my commandments! then had thy peace been as a river."* Our feeling of peace is false if it doesn't line up with God's Word.

I love the words in Psalm 85:10: *"Righteousness and peace have kissed each other."* Another set of twins. We will not experience true peace without righteousness.

It is easy to bring God down to our level of thinking. We are prone to walk humanistically and this is where a false peace can deceive us. God speaks to us in Psalm 50:21 (ESV) and says: *"You thought that I was one like yourself. But now I rebuke you, and lay the charge before you."* God is not like us. He is God. We cannot bring Him down to our level. We can't make Him fit into our circumstances. We've got to live on His terms.

May God help each one of us, including me, to discern what is true peace.

PRAYER:
"Dear Father, God of truth and peace, please help me to discern Your peace in my life. Save me from falling into false peace because of getting my own way. Help me to discern between relief and peace. Thank You, Father. Amen."

AFFIRMATION:
I will balance my peace alongside God's commandments.

56

IT WAS NOT SO
IN THE BEGINNING

"But from the beginning it was not so"
(MATTHEW 19:8).

We now live in the 21st century, over 6,000 years since God created man. Are we still meant to be living by God's original plan that He gave us at the very beginning of creation?

We hear people say, "Oh yes, I know that's in the Bible, but it's not relevant to our society today." This kind of statement totally undermines the validity of the Bible. God's Word is timeless. The Psalmist proclaims in Psalm 111:7, 8: *"All his commandments are sure. They **stand fast for ever and ever.**"* That means they don't go out of date. God designed and refined these eternal laws to work for all generations.

I like this quote by Charles Henry Mackintosh (1820 – 1896). "We cannot listen for a moment to men, however profound in their reading and thinking, who dare to treat God's book as though it were man's book and speak of those pages that were penned by the All wise, Almighty, and Eternal God, as though they were the production of a shallow and short-sighted mortal."

Let's check to see if we are still walking in God's original intention in just two basic areas.

In Matthew 19:7-9 (ESV), the Pharisees challenge Jesus that Moses allowed for divorce. What was Jesus' reply? *"Because of your hardness of heart Moses allowed you to divorce your wives, but from the beginning it was not so."* Divorce has become part of our society, as much amongst those who say they are Christians, as those in the secular world, but it is not God's original plan.

Why do many marriages fall apart? Because we try to do it our way! We think we have a better way than God. God created male and female with total equality. But God also created the husband to be the head of the home. 1 Corinthians 11:3 says: *"I would have you know, that the head of every man is Christ; and the head of the woman is the man; and the head of Christ is God."* I know that there are cruel and controlling men who hurt women, but that is far from God's heart. God never planned for a man to demean his wife but to protect her. He is not to imprison her but to liberate her to be who God created her to be.

The husband's mandate from God is to cover his wife by caring for her needs—physically, emotionally, and spiritually. He covers her by caressing her with the same kind of love with which Christ loved the church. He provides for her so she does not have to leave her nest and her little ones to the mercy of others. He protects her from the deceptions of this world so she can fulfil her destiny in the home. She basks in the privilege of submitting to this glorious covering.

Many women are more submitted to their employer at work than they are to their husbands at home. They must fit in and run to the dictates of their employer rather than the desires of their husband.

"But I can earn more than my husband," you reply. It doesn't matter whether you make three times as much as him. That's not the issue. God didn't create two Adams. He created an Adam and an Eve, each to fulfill a different task. We see God's plan for the husband to be the head of the home even in the order of creation. God created the man first, then He created the woman to be his co-helper. He created her an *ezer kenegdo,* a life-saving helper to counterbalance her husband. She needs him, but he can't function without her.

Why does God hate divorce? Because it hurts the godly seed. You can read about this in Malachi 2:14-16. A child cannot avoid suffering hurt in his or her soul when parents' divorce.

What about the message God gave to the first wedded couple? What was it? Let's read it again: *"Be fruitful, and multiply, and replenish the earth, and subdue it: and have dominion over . . . every living thing that moveth upon the earth."* (Genesis 1:28.) These were the very first words that man ever heard from the mouth of God! Wow! They must be important! But do we take any notice of God's original plan? Oh no! We'd rather do anything than obey God's very first command. We'd rather go to Siberia and "serve the Lord" than have another baby! Many are so emphatic about it that they get "sterilized" to make sure their reproductive cycle, which God so amazingly designed, can no longer function!

But it wasn't so at the beginning! God's people filled the land. When the Israelites were in Egypt, they continued to be fruitful, even in the face of hard bondage and persecution. They became *"more and mightier"* than the Egyptians (Exodus 1:7-12)!

When a husband and wife fulfill the specific tasks that God planned for them, they will accomplish far more than both trying to do the same job. When both partners seek to do Adam's job, the wife cannot fulfill her true anointing of embracing and nurturing children. And the opposite can be true. I have seen husbands who have been badgered into doing half the wife's work and therefore they are hindered from accomplishing the task of providing adequately for the home.

This is the big question. Do we live our lives according to the thinking of society today, or according to what God stated at the very beginning? Read again what Jesus said in Mathew 19:4-6 (ESV): *"Have you not read that he who created them from the beginning made them male and female, and said, 'Therefore a man shall leave his father and his mother and hold fast to his wife, and the two shall become one flesh'? So they are no longer two but one flesh. What therefore God has joined together, let not man separate."*

PRAYER:

"Dear Father, help me to understand Your ways. Forgive me for walking away from Your original mandate. Lord God, I want to live my life by Your mandate, not by the customs of this age. Give me strength and anointing to live in Your light in the midst of darkness and deception around me. Help me to stand strong and not give into the trends of society around me. Help me to walk the "narrow way" rather than joining the throngs on the broad way that leads to destruction. I thank You that You will lead me, Father. Amen."

AFFIRMATION

God's perfect will for my life will never contradict His original commandments.

57

ARE YOU ASKING THE RIGHT QUESTIONS?

"You should keep asking each other, 'What is the LORD'S answer?'
or 'What is the LORD saying?'"
(JEREMIAH 23:35 NLT).

Years ago, a dear friend came to stay with us for a couple of weeks and on her arrival wanted to catch up with all the family news. Our daughter, Serene, had just lost a baby through miscarriage and shared her pain of the loss with her.

This older lady didn't give the normal reply, "Oh you poor dear. It must be so hard for you." Instead, she asked her, "And what did you learn through it, Serene?" Serene told me later that this lady's question really provoked her to think more about what she learned from this experience and of all God taught her.

It was a growth question. Too often we ask negative questions of ourselves and even of others.

"Why should I have to go through this experience?"

"Why has this happened to me?"

"What have I done to deserve this?"

"Why do I have to live in this cramped house, I deserve a better one?"

These negative questions come from a root of self-pity or a misunderstanding of the nature of our God.

When the children of Israel came into the wilderness, God miraculously and daily provided them with manna. But they soon got tired of it and longed for the food they ate in Egypt. Numbers 11:4 tells us how they wept tears as they cried out: *"Who will give us flesh to eat?"* God was displeased with their complaining question. He said He would answer their cry and send them flesh, not just for one day, but for a whole month, so much so that it would come out their nostrils! But He sent judgment upon them at the same time. Complaining displeases God because it undermines His faithfulness.

Don't you think it would be a good idea to get into the habit of changing our questions to a positive level? Instead, we could ask, "Lord God, what are you trying to show me in this situation?" "Lord, in what way do you want to change me and enlarge my understanding of You." Not one of us can avoid going through difficult times in our lives. However, if we sulk and groan in these circumstances, we'll never grow.

We mature through adversity. Maybe God wants to expose something in our lives that is not pleasing to Him. Maybe He is stirring up our nest to lead us in a different direction. This is often the only way God can get us to change. Maybe we have been trusting in our own abilities and possessions and this situation will cause us to seek His face and learn to trust Him.

It is not easy to go through hard times, but it is always for our good. David wrote Psalm 4 while he was going through one of the most heart-wrenching times of his life. His very own son, Absalom, had risen up against him and was seeking to take his crown and kingdom from him. I am sure there could be nothing more grieving than being betrayed by your own son. But as he was fleeing for his life from Absalom, he wrote the words: *"Thou hast enlarged me when I was in distress"* (Psalm 4:1). Read also Psalm 18:19; 31:8; and 118:5.

The Psalmist also confesses in Psalm 119:67: *"Before I was afflicted I went astray: but now have I kept thy word."*

Psalm 119:71: *"It is good for me that I have been afflicted."*

Psalm 119:75: *"Thou in faithfulness hast afflicted me."*

Many years ago, I remember reading in one of Watchman Nee's books about a woman who noticed another lady crying profusely. She went up to her and instead of the usual, "What's the matter, dear?" she asked her, "Who are you crying for?" Was she crying for herself or were her tears for another? Often, we use all our tears upon ourselves so that we have no emotions left to pour out in intercession and care for others.

May God help us to change our questions to those that will help to bring us into growth, rather than leave us in the rut or the pit of despair. God loves us too much to leave us where we are. He is not content with letting us stay the same. He wants to lead us on. He wants to change us into the likeness of Christ, from one degree of glory to another. If God did not allow difficulties to come to our lives, we'd stagnate instead of grow.

Let's ask this question continually, "Lord, what are you saying to me? I am listening as I read your precious Word. I want to hear you speak into my heart. What are you telling me through these circumstances I am going through?"

PRAYER:

"Oh, dear Father, I pray that You will lift my eyes off myself and how things affect me. Lift my eyes to see what You are doing in my life. Help me to hear what You are saying to me. Help me to see what You are doing. I know that Your ways are higher than my ways and Your thoughts are higher than my thoughts. Please, lift me up to Your ways and thoughts for I want to move on with You. I don't want to stay in the ditch of despair. I don't want to crouch in complaining corner. I want to lift my eyes, my soul, and my hands, and praise You in the midst of my affliction. Thank you, Lord. Amen."

AFFIRMATION:

*"But to act
That tomorrow find us further than today."
~ Henry Wadsworth Longfellow*

58

COME UP, MOTHER!

"But God, who is rich in mercy, for his great love wherewith he loved us, even when we were dead in sins, hath quickened us (made us alive) together with Christ, and hath raised us up together, and made us sit together in heavenly places in Christ Jesus"
(EPHESIANS 2:4-6).

God comes down to bring us up! Isn't that wonderful? And yes, it is biblical. When God saw His people in bondage in Egypt, He said to them: *"I am come down . . . to bring them up"* (Exodus 3:8).

God always leads us upwards and onwards. The devil leads us downwards and ultimately to destruction. The Bible speaks of going "down" to Egypt (which typifies the flesh and the world, e.g., Isaiah 30:1-2 and 31:1) and going "up" to Jerusalem or Zion (which speaks of the ways of the Lord, e.g., Isaiah 2:3). Even when you are in the north of Israel, people still speak of going "up" to Jerusalem. It is interesting that the Hebrew word for Jews immigrating to Israel is *aliyah* which means "going up."

God lifts us up when we are bowed down. He holds us up when we are about to fall. He causes us to mount up with eagle's wings when we are weary (Isaiah 40:31)..

God also raises motherhood to a great height. In Ezekiel 19:10-11 God gives an allegory about motherhood and says that it is *"exalted"* above everything other tree round about. The Hebrew is *gabah* and means "to soar, to mount up, to raise up to a great height." The devil deceives you to think that motherhood is an inferior role and that you could accomplish more out in a career. God wants you to know that He has lifted motherhood to the highest status of all careers. He wants to lift you up to walk in the fullness of your role—to embrace it, to rejoice in it, to give your life to it, and to realize its powerful influence.

But wait, here is the greatest revelation of all. God wants to lift you up to where Christ is! And where is Christ? He sits at the right hand of the Father *"far above all principality, and power, and might, and dominion . . . and hath put all things under his feet."* (Ephesians 1:21, 22).

Jesus, who was equal with God, came down to the lowest when He submitted to the cruel death on the cross for our sins and was buried in the grave. But praise God, He rose again and ascended to heaven. But the most astounding revelation is that when Jesus died, we died with Him; when He was buried, we were buried with Him; when He rose from the grave, we rose with Him; and when He ascended, we ascended with Him and are now seated in heavenly places in Christ Jesus (Romans 6:3, 4)!

We generally think of Christ living in us. This is true and a glorious truth. But it is also true that we are in Christ, living in Him where He lives. Can I urge you to lift your sights? God has raised you up to this place. You are in Christ as He reigns over all things. By faith, begin to picture yourself in Christ in heavenly places far above all—far above all the pressures and problems that weigh you down.

From what position do you run your home? Groveling under the deception of doubt, depression, and defeat? Weighed down by worries and weariness? Or do you govern your home from the heavenlies? In this heavenly position in Christ, you can look down upon your problems. You can see them as Christ sees them. From this position, you'll walk in victory over the enemy and every subtle evil force that wants to destroy your home. From this position, you will overcome. From this position, you will see clearly and have wisdom to know what to do.

When your children squabble and get on your nerves, instead of blowing your cool, you handle the situation from your truthful position of "in Christ"! Instead of screaming at them, you take your authority in Christ and pray unity and harmony into their lives. (Of course, you'll need to use godly discipline when necessary). When things get on top of you and you feel overwhelmed, you remember that you are above the situation. In fact, you are far above all.

You can stop what you are doing, pray aloud, and release God's peace and rest into your home. Dear mother, there's no need to stay down in the dumps. There's no need to feel a failure and that you can't do it! It's futile to come down from your position in Christ.

Come up, dear mother! Come up to where God has placed you and stay seated in your heavenly place.

PRAYER:

"Oh, dear Father, I am totally amazed at Your love for me and the exceeding greatness of your salvation. You not only saved me from my sin, but You have lifted me up to live in Christ in the heavenlies. It is hard for me to understand but by faith I receive Your truth. I thank You that this is where I am in Christ. Please help me to constantly live in this heavenly place. Help me to govern my home from this conquering position. Help me to remember that in Christ, I have all power over the enemy and that I am far above all his insidious attacks. Thank you, Lord Jesus. Amen."

AFFIRMATION:

In Christ I am far above all!
Confess this powerful statement aloud many times during the day.

FURTHER STUDY:
GOD LIFTS UP YOUR HEAD

Psalm 3:3; 28:9; and 69:29.

GOD LIFTS YOU UP OUT OF THE DUNGHILL

Psalm 113:7.

GOD LIFTS YOU UP FROM THE GATES OF DEATH

Psalm 9:13 and 71:20.

GOD LIFTS YOU UP ABOVE THOSE WHO PERSECUTE YOU

Psalm 18:48; 27:6; and 30:1.

GOD LIFTS YOU UP UPON A ROCK

Psalm 27:5 and 40:2

GOD HOLDS YOU UP

Psalm 17:5; 18:35; 71:6; 91:11-12; 94:18; and 145:14.

ARE YOU AN ALIEN?
Part 1

"Beloved, I urge you as aliens and strangers to abstain from
fleshly lusts, which wage war against the soul"
(1 PETER 2:11 NASB).

How would you like to be called an alien? Well, that's exactly what we used to be called. We come from away down in the bottom of the world in New Zealand. When we first came to America, we applied for and eventually received Green Cards. We felt blessed to live in this great country and enjoy all the benefits. However, on our Green Cards were the words, "Resident Alien." Although we could legally live here, we were still called aliens! We eventually applied for citizenship and are now privileged to be American citizens.

We couldn't get too upset about being aliens however, because isn't that what we are meant to be? The Bible says that we are to live like "aliens and strangers" in this world. What is an alien? It's someone who belongs to another country. Our true citizenship is in Heaven! That is our real home!

Do we live according to this truth, or do we live as if this earth was our real home?

In the faith chapter of Hebrews 11, it tells us about men and women who lived like *"strangers and pilgrims"* in this earth. As we read about them, we begin to see the characteristics of aliens. Let's see if we line up, shall we?

1. ALIENS LIVE BY FAITH

"By faith Abel . . . By faith Enoch . . . By faith Noah . . . By faith Abraham . . . By faith Sarah . . . By faith Isaac . . . By faith Jacob . . . By faith Joseph . . . By faith Moses . . ." and so it continues down the chapter.

The heroes and heroines of the Bible were not dictated to by their circumstances. They lived by faith. They trusted God when it looked impossible. They put their faith in what they could not see.

Hebrews 11: 9 (JBP) says of Abraham: *"It was **faith** that kept him journeying like a foreigner through the land of promise."* Our journey through this world is a faith journey. It is only faith that pleases God. Are you going through a time in your life where you feel stripped of everything? Don't despair. You are in a place when you can exercise faith. Faith should be our normal lifestyle.

Hebrews 11:6: *"But without faith it is impossible to please him: for he that cometh to God must believe that he is, and that he is a rewarder of them that diligently seek him."*

2. ALIENS PLEASE GOD

Hebrews 11:5: *"By faith Enoch was translated that he should not see death; and was not found, because God had translated him: for before his translation he had this testimony, that **he pleased God.**"*

What an epitaph to have over our lives, "She pleased God." That's my desire and I am sure it is yours too. Aliens are more interested in pleasing God than pleasing the world. Alien mothers are more interesting in pleasing God and doing what He wants them to do than following the trend of society around them. They stand up for God's truth, even if the rest of the world is going a different direction. They confess: *"Let God be true, but every man a liar"* (Romans 3:4). Alien mothers raise their children by faith. They lean on God and trust Him in the difficulties and challenges they face each day.

3. ALIENS HAVE A DIVINE CALLING

Hebrews 11:8: *"By faith Abraham, when he was **called** to go out into a place which he should after receive for an inheritance, obeyed."*

God called Abraham out of one kingdom into another kingdom. We are called out of the kingdom of darkness into the kingdom of God. We don't belong to the kingdom of this world. We owe our allegiance to God's kingdom. We didn't just land in this kingdom—God Himself called us.

Deuteronomy 6:23 says: *"He brought us out . . .that He might bring us in."* God brought the children of Israel out of Egypt with a mighty deliverance to bring them into the Promised Land.

4. ALIENS OBEY GOD RATHER THAN MAN

Hebrews 11:8: *"By faith Abraham **obeyed** when he was called . . ."*

Abraham obeyed God's call to him even though he didn't understand it or know his final destination.

If we are truly living as a pilgrim, we will be obedient to God's ways, even if they are contrary to the ways of this world in which we live. When the apostles were on trial for preaching about Jesus, the priests strictly commanded them not to teach in His name, but Peter and John answered: *"Whether it be right in the sight of God to hearken unto you more than unto God, judge ye. For we cannot but speak the things which we have seen and heard"* Acts 4:19-20.

Another time they were on trial, Peter and the other apostles answered: *"We ought to obey God rather than men"* (Acts 5:29). They gave their allegiance to God, their highest authority.

PRAYER:

"Dear Father God, You have said that I cannot please You without faith. Please increase my faith. Ignite faith in my heart. Help me to live by faith instead of trusting in the resources of this world. Help me to constantly remember that I am an alien in this world. Amen."

AFFIRMATION:

I am a pilgrim, a foreigner, a stranger, a sojourner, a refugee, a nomad, a passing traveler, a temporary resident, a transient, an exile, and an alien in this world!

60

ARE YOU AN ALIEN?
Part 2

"I am a stranger in the earth"
(PSALM 119:19).

We continue looking at the characteristics of an alien.

5. ALIENS DO NOT HAVE AN ITINERARY

Hebrews 11:8 (ESV): *"And he (Abraham) went out, not knowing where he was going."*

Of course, we plan our day. We plan commitments for the future, but our trust should always be in the sovereignty of God. Our daily motto should be from James 4:15: *"If the Lord will, we shall live, and do this or that."* Or 1 Corinthians 16:7: *"If the Lord permits."*

When I was growing up in New Zealand, many of the folk in our church would say D.V. after any plans they made. For example, "We plan to join you for Christmas, D.V." Or "We are planning a weekend seminar on 'How to Know the Will of God, D.V.'"

D.V. is short for two Latin words, *Deo volente*, meaning, "God being willing."

If things don't turn out the way we planned, we should not be upset. God is greater than our plans. In fact, His plans are better than ours.

Psalm 37:5: *"Commit thy way unto the LORD; trust also in him; and he shall bring it to pass."*

Isaiah 55:8-9: *"For my thoughts are not your thoughts, neither are your ways my ways, saith the LORD. For as the heavens are higher than the earth, so are my ways higher than your ways, and my thoughts than your thoughts."*

6. ALIENS LOOK UPON THE WORLD AS A FOREIGN COUNTRY

Hebrews 11:9: *"By faith he sojourned in the land of promise, as in a strange* country."

The word "strange" in the Greek is *allotrios* and means "belonging to other people, not one's own." This is how aliens view the world. They have no kinship with it. They realize it belongs to another race.

Do you look at this world as a "strange" place? Or have you settled into the lifestyle of this world system?

7. ALIENS LIVE LIKE TEMPORARY CITIZENS

Hebrews 11:9 (AMPC): *"By faith he dwelt as a **temporary resident** in the land . . ."*

Moses called his first-born son, Gershom, which means "temporary visitor, stranger, alien" because this was his experience. Gershom was born to him while he was a stranger in the desert.

Aliens don't get entrenched in this world. The J. B. Phillip's translation of Romans 12:2 always challenges me: *"Don't let the world around you squeeze you into its own mold . . ."*

Alien mothers don't accumulate too much junk. They realize that this life is temporary, and they will one day leave everything behind. They don't live like they are going to be here forever.

6. ALIENS LOOK UPON THEIR HOMES AS TENTS

Hebrews 9:11 (ESV): *"**Living in tents** with Isaac and Jacob, heirs with him of the same promise."*

Aliens lay up their treasures in heaven, rather than on this earth. (Matthew 5:19-21). We do not build for this world, but for our eternal kingdom.

We should look upon our homes as temporary arks to protect and save our children in the midst of this sinful world. This is what Noah did. Hebrews 11:7 says: *"By faith Noah, being warned of God of things not seen as yet, moved with fear, prepared an ark to the saving of his house; by the which he condemned the world, and became heir of the righteousness which is by faith."*

There were three arks mentioned in the Bible. The first was Noah's ark, which was an ark of protection against the judgment of God. We are called to build an ark of protection for our families in this crooked and deceived generation. We should put more time into building a protecting ark for our children's souls than building a great edifice that will one day pass away. The structure of our homes will pass away, but our children's souls will live forever.

The second ark was the one Jochabed made for her baby Moses. What faith it took to place her baby in this ark and trust God to protect him. It was also a protecting ark and as she launched it out in faith, God demonstrated his deliverance (Hebrews 11:23).

The third ark was the Ark of the Covenant in the tabernacle which housed the presence of God. It is more important to fill our homes with the presence of God than to fill them with beautiful décor and material things that will not last. We influence this world and eternity far more by filling our homes with children than with TV's and expensive décor and furniture.

PRAYER:

"Dear Father, help me to live my life in the light of eternity. Save me from developing a kinship with this world. Help me to remember that I am a temporary resident here, raising temporary residents for eternity. Amen."

AFFIRMATION:

I'm holding lightly to the things of earth but clinging tightly to the things of Heaven.

61

ARE YOU AN ALIEN?
Part 3

*"Looking for that blessed hope, and the glorious appearing
of the great God and our Savior Jesus Christ"*
(TITUS 2:13).

Let's look at the dictionary meaning of alien. It means "owing political allegiance to another country, derived from another place, not one's own, strange." Remember, this is who we are on this earth.

8. ALIENS LOOK FOR ANOTHER CITY

Hebrews 11:10: *"For he **looked for a city** which hath foundations, whose builder and maker is God."*

Hebrews 11:16: *"But now they desire a better country, that is a heavenly: wherefore God is not ashamed to be called their God: for he hath prepared for them a city."*

Aliens have their sights on another world, their heavenly city.

My husband and I often travel to different countries to speak about marriage and family. Because we are New Zealanders by birth and still have family living in that country, each time we touch down in Auckland, we exclaim, "We're home!"

We lived in Australia for ten years and have family members living there also, so when we land in Brisbane, Queensland, we declare, "We're home!"

Now we are US citizens, and our earthly home is in Tennessee, USA. All our children and grandchildren live here and therefore when we land in USA, we are very glad to be back home again! We feel we have three homes on this earth, but none of them are our real homes. Our true home is the heavenly city.

9. ALIENS EXPERIENCE MIRACLES

Hebrews 11:11, 2: *"Through faith also Sarah herself received strength to conceive seed, and was delivered of a child when she was past age, because she judged him faithful who had promised."* Read also verses 29 and 30. Although Abraham and Sarah lived as strangers in Canaan, they experienced great miracles during their sojourning.

10. ALIENS KNOW THEIR GREATEST PROMISES ARE FOR THE NEXT LIFE

Hebrews 11:13: *"Not having received the promises, but having seen them afar off, and were persuaded of them, and embraced them . . ."* Read also verses 35 – 40.

The Living Bible says it clearly: *"These men of faith I have mentioned died without ever receiving all that God had promised them; but they saw it all awaiting them on ahead and were glad, for they agree that this earth was not their real home but that they* **were just strangers visiting down here.**"

Aliens are more concerned about the eternal promises than what they receive in this life. They know that this life is only a vapor that will soon disappear, but the eternal kingdom is forever and ever. They put their hope in this kingdom.

11. ALIENS KEEP BELIEVING WHEN THEY SEE NO VISIBLE ANSWER

Hebrews 11:13: *"These all died in faith, not having received the promises, but having seen them afar off, and were* **persuaded** *of them, and* **embraced** *them, and confessed that they were strangers and pilgrims on the earth."*

How often have you prayed and prayed and yet not received the answer? Maybe you have prayed for a loved one to be healed and instead they passed away. You felt God let you down. Dear one, the outcome of your prayers is not your responsibility. God determines what happens. He knows what is best. Our responsibility is to walk in faith. We continue in faith even when we don't see any change. We continue in faith even if the person dies! We never give up believing!

Our faith goes beyond this life. We embrace God's promises. We are persuaded (convinced) of them even if we don't see their fulfilment on earth.

The account of Shadrach, Meshach, and Abednego challenges me.

These young men were cast into the fiery furnace because they would not worship the image. But they would not bow down. They would give their allegiance to no other than the King of kings.

Read their bold confession before the king in Daniel 3:16-17: *"O Nebuchadnezzar, we are not careful to answer thee in this matter. If it be so, our God whom we serve is able to deliver us from the burring fiery furnace, and he will deliver us out of thine hand, O king.* **But if not**, *be it known unto thee, O king, that we will not serve thy gods, nor worship the golden image which thou hast set up."*

These men exercised faith. They believed God would deliver them. But their trust was not in faith itself, but in God. They were ready to burn in the fire if God did not deliver them. Their trust was totally in God, no matter what the outcome.

Oh, that our faith would mature to the place where our faith and trust in God is so complete that our eyes are upon the Deliverer even more than the deliverance!

PRAYER:

"Father God, help me to trust You completely. Help me to trust You, rather than the outcome. Help me to embrace the promises even when I don't see them fulfilled in this life. Amen."

AFFIRMATION:

It is not wrong to question our faith, but it is wrong to question God's faithfulness.

62

ARE YOU AN ALIEN?
Part 4

"Pass the time of your sojourning here in fear"
(1 PETER 1:17).

God does not leave us ignorant that we are strangers and pilgrims on this earth. We learn more today.

13. ALIENS CONFESS THEY ARE STRANGERS AND PILGRIMS

Hebrews 11:13, 14: *"They . . . **confessed** that they were strangers and pilgrims on the earth. For they that say such things **declare plainly** that they seek a country."*

Aliens tell everyone they belong to a heavenly country. They are not ashamed but confess it openly. Aliens do not sit on the fence. They know what they believe, where they come from, and where they are going.

The word confessed is *homologeo*. It means to say the same thing God says even if we don't see it or feel it. It means sticking to the truth no matter what.

David confessed this truth in 1 Chronicles 29:15: *"For we are strangers before thee, and sojourners, as were all our fathers: our days on the earth are as a shadow, and there is none abiding."* He confesses it again in Psalm 39:12.

Make this your daily confession. It will keep you on track and keep you from getting bogged down with the vain things of this world which you will one day leave behind.

14. ALIENS DO NOT ENTERTAIN THE THOUGHT OF GOING BACK TO THE WORLD

Hebrews 11:15 (TLB): *"If they had wanted to, they could have gone back to the good things of this world. But they didn't want to. They were living for heaven."*

Hebrews 11:27: *"By faith he **forsook Egypt** . . ."*

When God brought the children of Israel out of the bondage of Egypt, He purposed that they would never go back there again!

Deuteronomy 17:16 (TLB): *"For the LORD has told you, '**Never return to Egypt again.**'"* Also read Isaiah 30:1-2; 31:1; and 36:6.

Egypt speaks of the spirit of the world, and we no longer belong in that country. Jesus died to set us free from our sins and to *"deliver us from this present evil world, according to the will of God and our Father"* (Galatians 1:4).

Are you totally freed from the spirit of this world? Or do you allow Egypt to come into your heart and into your home? Watch out for signs of Egypt. Stamp on them and oust them from your home. God has delivered you from the spirit of Egypt so why go back to bondage?

15. ALIENS WOULD RATHER BEAR THE REPROACH OF CHRIST THAN ENJOY THE SHORT-LIVED PLEASURES OF THIS WORLD

Hebrews 11:24-26: *"By faith Moses, when he was come to years, refused to be called the son of Pharaoh's daughter; **choosing rather to suffer affliction with the people of God**, than to enjoy the pleasures of sin for a season; Esteeming the reproach of Christ greater riches than the treasures of Egypt: for he had respect unto the recompense of the reward."*

The things of this world do not lure aliens. They would rather do the will of God.

They know the truth of 1 John 2:15-17: *"Love not the world, neither the things that are in the world. If any man love the world, the love of the Father is not in him. For all that is in the world, the lust of the flesh, and the lust of the eyes, and the pride of life, is not of the Father, but is of the world. And the world passeth away, and the lust thereof: but he that doeth the will of God abideth forever."*

James 4:4: *"Know ye not that the friendship of the world is enmity with God? Whosoever therefore will be a friend of the world is the enemy of God."* Perhaps those who are friends with the world should doubt whether they are truly pilgrims on the way to the heavenly city.

16. ALIENS HAVE GRACE TO ENDURE

Hebrews 11:27: *"Moses . . . **endured**, as seeing him who is invisible."* This Greek word is *kartereo* and means "to be strong and steadfast as you endure."

Hebrews 11:26 (MLB): *"For he fixed his eye on the final recompense."*

Aliens can endure tribulations because they see beyond the trial. They see what God is doing in them through their suffering and testing. They know that God is refining them. They know that God is working something beautiful in them that will last for eternity. They can endure because their eyes are upon Christ, rather than their circumstances (2 Corinthians 4:16-18).

Do you find it hard to endure your present circumstances? Look up to your Savior, Jesus Christ. Take your eyes off the visible and turn them to the invisible Christ. This is your secret.

PRAYER:

"My Lord God, please help me to keep my eyes on You. Teach me to take my eyes off the visible and turn them to the invisible. Help me to realize that the eternal realm is far more real and lasting than this world. Amen."

AFFIRMATION:

The things of this world grow strangely dim when I turn my eyes to Jesus.

63

YOUR HEAVENLY TOWER

"The LORD is my rock, and my fortress, and my deliverer;
my God, my strength, in whom I will trust; my buckler,
and the horn of my salvation, and my high tower"
(Psalm 18:2).

As a nation, we still grieve the unnecessary deaths of over 3,000 lives which were taken from us on 9/11/01, not just numbers, but mothers, fathers, brothers, and sisters who continue to be sorrowfully missed. Our twin towers of the World Trade Center could not withstand the attack of the enemy.

When we think of towers in the Bible, we immediately think of the tower of Babel where God intervened in the project before it was finished. Historians say that it was about seven stories and 300 feet high when God scattered the people and confounded the language (Genesis 11-9).

We read in Judges 9:46-47 about the tower of Shechem (which was meant to be a stronghold) that burned to the ground and about a thousand men and women burned to death.

In Luke 13:1-5 Jesus talks about the tower of Siloam that fell and toppled to the ground and 18 people were killed.

Man-made towers cannot survive enemy strikes. They cannot give everlasting protection. But praise God, we have a tower that can withstand all enemy attacks.

I want to remind you today that you have a High Tower. It is your God, and He waits to be your refuge. However, He can only be your High Tower when you come into Him, when you totally put your trust in Him.

Perhaps you have things going on in your home and in your marriage that weigh you down. You can hardly think straight. God waits to receive you in His safe tower. He will lift your head. He will cover you. Your situation may not change, but as you abide in the High Tower, He will lift you up above your problems. Instead of groveling in the pit, you can live your life from the heavenlies and look down upon your troubles.

The Shinarites tried to build a tower that would reach to the heavens. They never made it! But you can live in a tower that reaches to the heavens. In fact, it's a tower that is situated in the heavenlies! How about that?

In 2 Corinthians 10:5 it says: *"Casting down imaginations, and every high thing that exalts itself against the knowledge of God, and bringing into captivity every thought to the obedience of Christ."*

What are the "high" things we must bring down? All thoughts that take higher place than the knowledge of God. Do your thoughts loom bigger in your mind than God Himself? Are you plagued with thoughts of fear, dread, anger, worry, despair, self-pity, bitterness and so on? What is higher in your mind? Your thoughts that hold you captive or the peace of God? If negative thoughts consume your mind, cast them down. Plead the blood of Jesus and tear them down in the name of Jesus. Let your burdens go and run to your High Tower.

Here are some other wonderful promises for you.

Psalm 61:2, 3: *"From the end of the earth will I cry unto thee, when my heart is overwhelmed: lead me to the rock that is higher than I. For thou hast been a shelter for me, and a **strong tower** from the enemy."*

Psalm 144:2: *"My goodness, and my fortress, my **high tower**, and my deliverer; my shield, and he in whom I trust, who subdueth the people under me."*

Proverbs 18:10: *"The name of the LORD is a **strong tower**: the righteous runneth into it, and is safe."*

Resist your own "high" thoughts. Put your trust in the Lord and live in your heavenly tower. Will you run into your Strong Tower today?

PRAYER:

"Dearest Father, I thank You that You are my Strong and High Tower. I can run into You and be safe. I want You to be the highest place in my mind. In the name of Jesus, I cast down all negative and fearful thoughts and put my trust in You. I lean on You. You are my safeguard and the safeguard of my mind. Thank You, Lord. Amen."

AFFIRMATION:

There's turmoil all around me but I'm living in my heavenly Tower.

64

LET THE WORLD
SEE YOUR JOY

*"Let your light so shine before men, that they may see your good works,
and glorify your Father which is in heaven"*
(MATTHEW 5:16).

Years ago, when our daughter, Evangeline, was raising her young children she went to Wal-Mart with her five little ones. A lady came up to her and said, "I have to tell you that you are incredible mother. Here's $10.00!"

Evangeline continued her shopping in Wal-Mart, but about ten minutes later this same lady came up to her again and said, "I'm not done. I must tell you that you are a wonderful mother. Here's another $10.00!"

Wherever we go, people are watching. We are either a light, shining God's path before them or we show a blurred picture. I believe the greatest testimony a mother can give to the world is to be a joyful and contented mother of children.

Psalm 113:9 talks of *"the joyful mother of children."* When you go out with your children, lift your head high, put a smile on your face, and be proud to be a mother. You have the most important career in the nation. God Himself is your Employer and you are determining the future of this nation.

Be a light in the midst of a society that does not embrace children. Don't be intimidated. Show your love for your children as you speak sweetly and patiently to them. And if God has blessed you with several children, be proud to show off your "blessings" from the Lord. You are showing to the world what our God is like. He loves children. He is the giver of life.

If people make negative remarks when they see all your children piling out of your van, put on a bigger smile than ever. If they ask, "Are all these yours?" beam with joy and answer, "Oh yes, we love children, don't you?"

Jesus did not reject children. He welcomed the children to come to Him.

Mark 9:36, 37: *"And he took a child, and set him in the midst of them: and when he had taken him in his arms, he said unto them, Whosoever shall receive one of such children in my name, receiveth me: and whosoever shall receive me, receiveth not me, but him that sent me."*

There is no more beautiful picture than to see a serene and happy mother with well-trained children in tow. There can be no argument from those who don't embrace children.

We should not only be happy about our own children, but also take notice of all children. When you see a mother with a baby, encourage her and tell her how beautiful her baby is.

I think of my husband's father. He fathered nine of his own children, but he loved all children. And he loved babies. He could not go down the street without stopping every mother with children. In those days, the mothers walked their babies in prams. He would look into the pram and ooh and aah at the baby and delightfully talk to the children.

He went to be with the Lord many years ago, but one Christmas our daughter, Serene, painted a picture of him for my husband. Underneath she wrote the caption: "Jack Hedley Campbell – Lover of children." What a great testimony to have over his life.

Let your light shine. Let everyone see that you are a *"joyful mother of children."*

PRAYER:

"Dear Father, please help me to be a shining mother—shining the light of Your joy in my home and shining with the light of Your joy and glory when I go to the supermarket with my children. Amen."

AFFIRMATION:

Why should I not be happy? God has blessed me with eternal treasures!

65

ARE YOU ON THE SIDE OF TRUTH?
Part 1

"Judgement is turned away backward, and justice standeth afar off: for truth is fallen in the street, and equity cannot enter."
(ISAIAH 59:14).

Let's get the facts straight. Our God is a God of truth. It is impossible for Him to lie. One writer says: "Truth is not truth unless it meets God's definition of truth." Conversely, the devil is a liar. He is *"the father of lies"* (John 8:44).

There is no middle road. We are either on the side of truth or we believe the devil's lies. We are either in God's kingdom which is a kingdom of absolute truths, or we are in the devil's kingdom of lies and distorted truth. The devil makes his deceptions look good, plausible, and wise, but they are still lies. The worst lies look like the truth.

Charles Spurgeon wrote: "Discernment is not a matter of simply telling the difference between right and wrong; rather it is telling the difference between right and almost right."

Because God is truth, He wants us to live in truth. We must saturate ourselves with truth. We must be proactive about truth. If we don't proactively go after truth, we can be deceived. If we think we'll know the truth without studying the truth, we can be misled.

Our God is *"abundant in truth,"* and therefore we should be abundant in truth also (Exodus 34:6).

God releases His blessings on a nation that is founded and governed by truth but lies and corruption destroy. Isaiah 59:14, 15 (NLT) discloses what's happening in our nation now: *"Our courts oppose the righteous, and justice is nowhere to be found. Truth stumbles in the streets, and honesty has been outlawed. Yes, truth is gone, and anyone who renounces evil is attacked."*

It's time for truth to be restored. It's time for parents who love truth and want truth established in our nation to raise children who are grounded in truth, who are filled with truth, and who know how to speak the truth.

It's time to stand up against the deception, corruption, and tyranny. It's hard to believe that so-called intelligent people can believe their own lies. Romans 1:28 tells us that when they don't want God in their minds and hearts, He gives them over to a *"reprobate mind"* (a mind void of judgment and abhorred by God and man). 2 Thessalonians 2:11 tells us that He sends them a *"strong delusion."*

I am giving you 50 biblical verbs about truth. Each point stands on its own, but please forgive me if I get writing on some of the points! Do you think you could make each one part of your lives? Don't keep them to yourselves but share them with your children as you raise them to be filled with truth and become truth speakers in the land. The following points will be a great Bible study for you and your family.

I believe we should be . . .

1. TRUTH ACKNOWLEDGERS

Titus 1:1: *"Paul, a servant of God . . . according to the faith of God's elect, and the **acknowledging of the truth** which is after godliness."* Also read 2 Timothy 2:25.

2. TRUTH ANSWERERS

Proverbs 22:20, 21: *"Have not I written to thee excellent things in counsels and knowledge, That I might make thee know the certainty of the words of truth; that thou mightiest **answer the words of truth** to them that send unto thee?"*

1 Peter 3:15: *"Sanctify the Lord God in your hearts; and **be ready always to give an answer** to every man that asketh you a reason of the hope that is in you with meekness and fear."*

We must know the truth to be able to answer the questions of our children, and all we associate with, for it is mothers who primarily pass truth on to the next generation. Also read Colossians 4:6.

3. TRUTH BEARERS

As Jesus stood before Pilate ready to be delivered to death He said:

*"For this cause came I into the world, that I should **bear witness unto the truth.** Every one that is of the truth heareth my voice"* (John 18:37).

Paul confessed: *"I **bear in my body** the marks of the Lord Jesus"* (Galatians 6:17 and 2 Corinthians 4:10). He suffered stripes, beatings, and stonings for speaking the truth of the Gospel.

4. TRUTH BELIEVERS

We are saved through *"belief of the truth"* (2 Thessalonians 2:13). We come to Christ by believing the truth. We continue walking in Christ by believing the truth. We come to understand more of God as we read His truth and believe it. We don't doubt it. We don't question it. We believe it because it is God's infallible Word written by the One who cannot lie.

The psalmist states in Psalm 119:66: *"I have **believed** thy commandments."* We are either believers or unbelievers. There is no in between. Doubting is still unbelief.

Mark 9:23: *"If thou canst believe, all things are possible to him that believeth."* Read also Mark 11:23, 24.

PRAYER:

"I thank You, Father, that You are the God of Truth. I trust You wholly. I trust Your word. Heaven and earth will pass away, but Your living Word abides forever. Please help me to never deviate from Your truth. Amen."

AFFIRMATION:

When I stick with truth, I am safe; when I deviate from truth, I am on a shaky path.

FURTHER STUDY: Go to page 311.

66

ARE YOU ON THE SIDE OF TRUTH?
Part 2

*"And shalt return unto the LORD thy God, and shalt obey
his voice according to all that I command thee this day,
thou and thy children, with all thine heart, and with all thy soul"*
(DEUTERONOMY 30:2).

5. TRUTH BUYERS

Proverbs 23:23: *"Buy the truth and sell it not."* When we get hold of the truth, we don't give it away. Nor do we sell it! We will not be tempted by the bribery of deception.

6. TRUTH CHOOSERS

The Psalmist states in 119:30: *"I have **chosen** the way of truth: thy judgments have I laid before me."* Again in 119:173: *"I have **chosen** thy precepts."*

We constantly face choices, but we do not need to vacillate when making decisions. The right decision is always the way of truth (which is what God states in His Word on the subject), no matter what everyone else is doing and no matter what the cost.

7. TRUTH COMMANDERS

God lifted up Abraham as an example of godly fatherhood and said of him: *"For I know him, that **he will command his children** and his household after him, and they shall keep the way of the LORD to do justice and judgment"* (Genesis 18:19).

Deuteronomy 32:46: *"Set your hearts unto all the words which I testify among you this day, which ye shall **command your children** to observe to do, all the words of this law."*

We don't allow our children to find their own way. We command our children in the truth. God does not give suggestions, but commands. He lovingly commands but expects obedience. As we parent in the likeness of God's heart, we don't bark commands at our children but affectionately command them in the right way—and we also expect obedience.

8. TRUTH CONFESSORS

Romans 10:9, 10: *"That if thou shalt **confess with thy mouth** the Lord Jesus, and shalt believe in thine heart that God hath raised him from the dead, thou shalt be saved. For with the heart man believeth unto righteousness; and with the mouth confession is made unto salvation."*

We are saved by believing in our hearts and confessing with our mouths. We cannot say we are truly saved unless we confess with our mouths that Jesus is Lord. This is the way we come into God's family. This is the way we continue to walk in God's kingdom. As God continues to reveal truths to us through His Word, we not only believe them, but confess them aloud!

The psalmist declared in Psalm 116:10: *"I believed, therefore have I spoken."*

That's not only in the Old Testament. It's repeated in the New Testament in 2 Corinthians 4:13: *"I believed, and therefore have I spoken; we also believe, and therefore speak."* If we truly believe, we will confess. When we confess, the truth becomes stronger in our hearts and lives.

Matthew 10:32, 33: *"Whosoever therefore shall **confess me before men,** him will I confess also before my Father which is in heaven. But whosoever shall deny me before men, him will I also deny before my Father which is in heaven."* Also read Luke 12:8; Romans 14:11; and Philippians 2:11.

1 Timothy 6:12 (NKJV): *"Fight the good fight of faith, lay hold on eternal life, to which you were also called, and have **confessed the good confession** in the presence of many witnesses."*

Hebrews 4:14 (NKJV): *"Let us **hold fast our confession."***

Hebrews 10:23 (NKJV): *"Let us **hold fast the confession** of our hope without wavering, for he who promised is faithful."*

The word confession in the Greek is the word *homologeo* meaning "to confess the same truth God says in His Word." We don't speak a different language than the Bible. Our words line up with God's truth.

9. TRUTH CONTENDERS

Jude 1:3: *"It was needful for me to write unto you, and exhort you that* *ye should **earnestly contend** for the faith which was once delivered unto the saints."*

To earnestly contend for the faith means "to strive for, to fight for." When folks speak things that are contrary to the Bible or promote false doctrine, we earnestly argue for the truth. We fight for the truth, but we don't do it in a combative spirit. We answer with love, grace, and earnestness.

Ephesians 4:15 exhorts us to *"speak the truth in love."* We never compromise the truth, but we lovingly speak it. We don't show love to people when we leave them in deception. Jesus came to this earth *"full of grace and truth"* (John 1:14, 17). He spoke gracious words, but never compromised the truth.

PRAYER:
"Dear Father in Heaven, please help me to be a confessor of Your truths. You gave me a mouth to speak for You and to confess Your salvation. Save me from being silent when I have opportunity to confess. Amen."

AFFIRMATION:
I believe and I confess that Jesus Christ is my Savior and Lord.

67

ARE YOU ON THE SIDE OF TRUTH?

Part 3

"I will delight myself in thy statutes: I will not forget thy word"
(PSALM 119:16).

More truth points to meditate upon and talk about with your children.

10. TRUTH CONTINUERS

Jesus spoke to those who believed in Him in John 8:31, 32: *"If ye **continue** in my word, then are ye my disciples indeed; and ye shall know the truth and the truth shall make you free."*

It's not enough to accept and believe the truth of the glorious Gospel. We must continue in it. The word continue is *meno* and means "to stay, abide, dwell, remain." We don't deviate from God's Word. We live in it, dwell in it, and remain in it. To do that we need to read it continually. We are only His disciples when we continue in the truth.

John 15:7: *"If ye abide (meno) in me, and **my words abide** (meno) **in you**, ye shall ask what ye will, and it shall be done unto you."* Do God's words live in you? Are they part of the essence of your being?

Galatians 2:5: *"That the truth of the gospel might **continue** with you."*

11. TRUTH DECLARERS

We are to show forth God's truth in our conduct and speech.

a) We are to declare God's truth in the congregation of God's people: Psalm 40:10: *"I have not hid thy righteousness within my heart; I have declared thy faithfulness and thy salvation: I have not concealed thy lovingkindness and thy truth from the **great congregation**."* Read also Psalm 22:22, 25 and 66:16.

b) We are to declare God's truth to the heathen and to those who don't know Him. Psalm 86:3: *"Declare his glory among the **heathen**, his wonders among all people."* Also read 1 Chronicles 16:24.

c) We are to declare His truth in the gates of the city. Psalm 9:14: *"That I may show forth all thy praise in the **gates** of the daughter of Zion."*

d) We are to declare God's truth to the following generation. Psalm 48:13: *"Tell it to the **generation following**."* Dear parents, your table is your pulpit where you daily impart God's words and ways to the next generation. Also read Exodus 10:2; Psalm 44:1; 79:13; 78:4-7; Isaiah 59:21; and Joel 1:3.

12. TRUTH DELIGHTERS

Do you delight in God's truth? Ten times in Psalm 119 the psalmist declares that He delights in God's truth. Read these Scriptures and constantly declare that you delight in His truth: Psalm 119:16, 24, 35, 47, 48, 70, 77, 92, 143, and 174.

13. TRUTH DELIVERERS

Proverbs 14:25: *"A true witness delivereth souls."* Don't be afraid to tell the truth to a needy soul. Your witness could deliver them from destruction.

When someone you know is being judged unfairly, and you know the truth, don't be afraid to stand up and speak the truth. You could deliver your friend.

14. TRUTH DISCERNERS

Do you constantly pray for discernment? I do. I don't want to be deceived. I want to discern between what is really truth and what only looks like truth. They can look very similar. The only way we truly discern truth is to become totally familiar with the Book of Truth, God's living Word. Federal agents do not learn to recognize counterfeit money by studying the counterfeits. They study the genuine. They become so familiar with the original that it enables them to discern the counterfeit.

Similarly, the more we entrench ourselves in God's Word, the more we discern what is deception. It may look like and sound like truth, but we will have that check from the Holy Spirit that there is something off key.

God's Word is powerful. It not only discerns deception, but it is *"a **dis-***

cerner of the thoughts and intents of the heart" (Hebrews 4:12).

Malachi 3:18: *"Then shall ye return, and **discern** between the righteous and the wicked, between him that serveth God and him that serveth him not."* Do you notice that it is when we return to God and His Word that we'll know discernment? Also read Jeremiah 15:19; Ezekiel 22:26; and 44:23.

15. TRUTH DISPLAYERS

Psalm 60:4: *"Thou hast given a banner to them that fear thee, that it may be **displayed** because of the truth. Selah."* Our lives are banners displaying God's truth.

PRAYER:

"Oh God of Truth, I thank You for Your living Word. It is the delight of my heart. I thank You for teaching me Your truths each new day. Amen."

AFFIRMATION:

I choose the truth. I will contend for it. I will continue in it. And I will declare it."

FURTHER STUDY:
NO. 11. TRUTH DECLARERS

1 Chronicles 16:24; Psalm 9:1; 26:7; 22:22; 48:13; 71:15; 73:28; 79:13; 96:3; 107:22; 118:17; 119:13; 145:6; Isaiah 43:21; and Jeremiah 51:10.

68

ARE YOU ON THE SIDE OF TRUTH?

Part 4

*"Pay close attention to what you hear. The closer you listen,
the more understanding you will be given—and you will receive
even more. To those who listen to my teaching more understanding
will be given. But for those who are not listening, even what little
understanding they have will be taken away from them"*
(MARK 4:24, 25) NLT).

Isn't it amazing how much the Bible says about truth? Well, it shouldn't be amazing because God is Truth.

16. TRUTH GIRDERS

Ephesians 6:14: *"Stand therefore, having your **loins girt about with truth**."* When speaking about the armor, God begins with truth, and He starts at the loins! Many translations of the Bible translate it: *"The belt of truth buckled around your waist."* However, when I check this Scripture in the Strong's Concordance, I see that the original word is "loins," not waist. There is no mention of waist! It is the Greek word *osphus* and literally means "the loins, procreative power." We don't have procreative power in our waists.

In Bible days, men often wore long robes and when they began to work, they tucked up their robes in their belt, so their clothes did not impede their actions. Of course, they would hold up the garment with a belt around the waist. I can see where they get that. But why do they eliminate the word "loins" altogether? I can't see what benefit there is in having truth around your waist!

Can you imagine a warrior going out to war with only a belt? No, he wore protective covering around his loins. His strength and procreative power were in his loins, and he guarded them well.

However, there is a powerful truth in this Scripture, and I think this must be why God starts with the loins. The devil has deceived God's people regarding their loins more than any other area. He has convinced men to stop their procreative power through vasectomies. He has deceived mothers to stop childbearing through tubal ligation and other birth control methods so readily available today.

The devil, who hates every plan of God, has successfully hindered God's very first commandment *"to be fruitful."* He is the deceiver who comes to *"steal, kill and destroy"* through birth control, sterilization, and abortion. God is the giver of life, but Satan is the eliminator of life.

Do you see how God wants us to have the armor of truth around our loins? Can you believe how many translations have missed this?

17. TRUTH GUSHERS

Am I getting carried away? No, I'm giving it to you straight from the Word of God. David pours out his heart in Psalm 145:7 saying: *"They shall* **abundantly utter** *the memory of thy great goodness, and shall sing of thy righteousness."* The Hebrew word *naba* for "abundantly utter" means "to gush forth, belch out, to flow, to pour out, to send forth."

Have you been so excited and enriched as you receive revelation from the Scriptures? Sometimes I've wanted to stand up on my chair and raise my hands to God in worship. This Scripture informs us that we are not "over the top" and "super-spiritual" when we are so full that we can't wait to share God's truth to others. This should be natural for those who seek and live in the truth.

Proverbs 18:4 says: *"The words of a man's mouth are as deep waters, and the wellspring of wisdom as a* **flowing** *(naba) brook."* When we are filled with the wisdom of God's truth, it should flow from our lips.

18. TRUTH HEARERS

It's so easy to hear and yet not hear, isn't it? We must first hear to be grounded and rooted in truth. No wonder Jesus constantly said: *"He that hath ears to hear, let him hear"* (Matthew 11:15; 13:9; Mark 4:9, 23; 7:16; Revelation 2:7, 11, 17, 29; 3:6, 13, 22;13:9; and 22:17). Wow, He repeated this a lot of times!

We must listen not only with our outer ears but our inner ears. I love the line of the hymn that says: "Hearing His voice in every line, making each faithful saying mine."

Jesus also said: *"Every one that is of the truth heareth my voice"* (John 18:37).

19. TRUTH HEEDERS

Deuteronomy 11:16: *"**Take heed to yourselves**, that your heart be not deceived, and ye turn aside, and serve other gods, and worship them."*

Psalm 119:9: *"Wherewithal shall a young man cleanse his way? by **taking heed** thereto according to thy word."*

20. TRUTH INCLINERS

Psalm 78:1: *"Incline your ears to the words of my mouth."* Read also Proverbs 4:20.

Psalm 119:36: *"Incline my heart unto thy testimonies."*

Psalm 119:112: *"I have inclined mine heart to perform they statues always, even unto the end."*

The word incline means "to stretch out, to extend, bow down." It's not enough to casually listen to truth. We must stretch out our spiritual ears to hear. Do you try to do this? This is how we get truth right down into our very beings.

PRAYER:

"Dear God, I want to be one who hears Your truth. I want to keep my ear listening close to Your voice instead of the voices of this world. Please keep me in Your truth. Amen."

AFFIRMATION:

"I don't want to miss one word You speak
'Cause everything You say is life to me!"
~ Chris McClarney

FURTHER STUDY:
NO. 21: TRUTH HEARERS

Deuteronomy 6:4 (Mark 12:29-31); Psalm 81:13-16; Proverbs 8:34; Isaiah 48:18; Matthew 7:24-27 (Luke 6:47-49); Matthew 13:15-23 (Mark 4:13-20 and Luke 8:11-15); John 5:24; 8:47; and Mark 4:24, 25.

69

ARE YOU ON THE SIDE OF TRUTH?
Part 5

*"O that there were such an heart in them, that they
would fear me, and keep all my commandments always,
that it might be well with them, and with their children forever!"*
(DEUTERONOMY 5:29).

21. TRUTH KEEPERS

We read so many Scriptures about keeping the truth. The Hebrew word is *shamar* and means "to guard, protect, watch over, take heed, observe." To guard that we don't forget God's truth, we must attend to it daily and never let it go.

Deuteronomy 5:29 reminds us to keep God's truth *"always,"* not only when it suits us.

Deuteronomy 6:17; 11:22; and Psalm 119:4 remind us to keep God's truth *"diligently."*

Deuteronomy 7:9 reminds us to keep God's truth *"to a thousand generations."* We must be faithful to pass it on from one generation to the next.

Psalm 119:33 reminds us to keep God's truth *"unto the end."*

Psalm 119:34 and 69 remind us to keep God's truth with *"my whole heart."*

Psalm 119:44 reminds us to keep God's truth *"continually, forever and ever."*

Psalm 119:63 and 115 remind us to be *"a companion"* of those who keep God's truth. We make friends with those who keep God's truth.

I love Isaiah 26:2: *"Open ye the gates, that **the righteous nation which keepeth the truth** may enter in."* It is the nation the keeps truth that receives God's blessings. And this is a nation which is comprised of families that keep His truths. Oh, how we need to be praying for our nation today.

22. TRUTH KNOWERS

Many Christians love to quote the familiar Scripture in John 8:32: *"Ye shall know the truth, and the truth shall make you free."* However, we don't experience real freedom until we know the truth. It's not enough to hear it at church. We must get to **know** it personally and then we walk in the freedom God intends for us.

Proverbs 22:20, 21: *"Have not I written to thee excellent things in counsels and knowledge, That I might make thee* **know the certainty of the words of truth***; that thou mightiest answer the words of truth to them that send unto thee?"* Read also Psalm 119:79; Isaiah 38:19; John 8:32; 1 Timothy 2:3, 4; and 1 John 5:20.

23. TRUTH LEARNERS

Deuteronomy 5:1: *"Hear, O Israel, the statutes and judgments which I speak in your ears this day, that ye may* **learn them***, and keep, and do them."*

Psalm 119:7: *"I will praise thee with uprightness of heart, when I shall have* **learned** *thy righteous judgments."*

Psalm 119:71: *"It is good for me that I have been afflicted; that I might* **learn thy statutes.***"*

Psalm 119:73: *"Thy hands have made me and fashioned me: give me understanding, that I may* **learn thy commandments***."*

24. TRUTH LOVERS

Psalm 119:127: *"I love thy commandments above gold; yea,* **above fine gold***."*

Ten times the psalmist expresses His love for God's truth: Psalm 119:47, 48, 97, 113, 119, 127, 140, 159, 163, and 167. Look up these wonderful Scriptures and affirm your love for God's Word as you speak them out loud.

Do we really love them as much as gold and riches? Do we spend as much time searching God's Word as acquiring possessions?

What is the sign of being in love? To spend every moment with the one we love. Therefore, if we genuinely love the truth, we will constantly and diligently search for God's truth in His Word. Charles Spurgeon writes: "If you do not love the Bible, you certainly do not love the God who gave it to us."

Psalm 119:167 is the psalmist's testimony: *"My soul hath kept thy testimonies; and* **I love them exceedingly.***"* Is this your testimony too?

Zechariah 8:19: *"**Love the truth** and peace."*

25. TRUTH MEDITATORS

Eight times the psalmist talks about meditating in God's Word in Psalm 119:15, 23, 27, 48, 78, 97, 99, and 148. The word is *siyach* and means "to ponder, meditate, commune, and muse, but it also means to declare, speak, and to talk." Bible meditation is not silent. Speak out and tell people about the truths on which you are meditating.

Psalm 77:12: *"I will meditate also of all thy work, and talk of thy doings."*

26. TRUTH OBEYERS

Truth is ineffective unless we obey it. James 1:22 states: *"Be ye doers of the word, and not hearers only deceiving your own selves."*

And of course, we know the words of Jesus in Matthew 7:24: *"Therefore whosoever heareth these sayings of mine, and doeth them, I will liken him unto a wise man, which built his house upon a rock."*

Jesus again asks the question in Luke 6:46: *"And why call ye me, Lord, Lord, and do not the things which I say?"*

Read also Psalm 119:166; Matthew 7:21-23, 24-27; Luke 6:46-49; Galatians 3:1; 5:7; James 1:22-25; 1 Peter 1:22; and 1 John 3:7, 18.

PRAYER:

"Oh God of Truth, I want truth to be part of my life too. Help me to be a learner and meditator of Your truth so that I am ready to teach my children Your truth. I want to penetrate it into their very beings so they will never be pulled away by the deceptions of this world. Amen."

AFFIRMATION:

I love God's Word exceedingly. It is my daily delight.

FURTHER STUDY: Go to page 312.

70

ARE YOU ON THE SIDE OF TRUTH?

Part 6

"The Lord gave the command; a great company of women brought the good news: 'The kings of the armies flee—they flee!' She who stays at home divides the spoil"
(PSALM 68:11, 12 HCSB).

Isn't it amazing how much God speaks about truth in His Word? I would encourage you to not only read the Scriptures but to confess with your mouth that you stand on the side of truth. Take each one of these pointers and say them aloud. When you speak the words aloud, they become so much more part of you. For example:

I am a truth chooser.

I am a truth confessor.

I am a truth a declarer.

I am a truth delighter.

I am a truth keeper.

I am a truth lover. And so on.

27. TRUTH PENETRATORS

Deuteronomy 6:6, 7 (AMPC) tells us specifically how to teach God's truth to our children: *"And these words which I am commanding you this day shall be (first) in your (own) minds and hearts; (then) you shall whet and sharpen them so as to **make them penetrate**, and teach and impress them diligently upon the (minds and) hearts of your children, and shall talk of them when you sit in your house and when you walk by the way, and when you lie down and when you rise up."*

28. TRUTH PERSUADERS

Paul not only shared the truth but persuaded (with convincing arguments) his hearers. To make the truth known, we must first know it. We must be ready to combat the arguments people throw at us. Make apologetics an important subject in your homeschool curriculum.

Acts 19:8: Paul *"went into the synagogue, and spake boldly for the space of three months, **disputing and persuading** the things concerning the kingdom of God."* Read also Acts 13:43; 18:4; 28:23; and 2 Corinthians 5:11.

29. TRUTH PREACHERS

Every believer is called to preach. Some will be public preachers, but all of us must preach the truth of the Gospel to people we meet in our day to day lives, or wherever we go.

Romans 10:14: *"How then shall they call on him in whom they have not believed? and how shall they believe in him of whom they have not heard? and how shall they hear without a preacher?"*

1 Corinthians 9:16: *"For though I preach the gospel, I have nothing to glory of: for necessity is laid upon me; yea, woe is unto me, if I preach not the gospel!"* Notice the exclamation mark!

2 Timothy 4:2: *"Preach the word; be instant in season, out of season; reprove, rebuke, exhort with all longsuffering and doctrine."* As a mother in your home, you are a preacher to your children, always ready, in season and out of season, to drop words of truth into your children's hearts. Read 1 Peter 3:15.

30. TRUTH PROCLAIMERS

Psalm 68:11 (NASB): *"The Lord gives the command; the women who proclaim the good tidings are a great host."* These are the homemaking mothers (v. 12) who proclaim God's deliverance and good tidings. The KJV uses the word publish and it means "to bring good tidings."

31. TRUTH REJOICERS

The psalmist proclaims in Psalm 119:111 that God's words are *"the rejoicing of my heart."* Do you rejoice in the truth? Even when it challenges you? Even when it hurts?

Read Psalm 119:14, 162, Psalm 19:8; and 1 Corinthians 13:6.

32. TRUTH REMEMBERERS

We must not forget the truth. It must always be part of us.

2 Kings 17:38: *"The covenant that I have made with you ye **shall not forget**."* Also read Deuteronomy 4:9, 23; Proverbs 3:1; and 4:20-21).

Psalm 119:16: ***"I will not forget thy word."***

Psalm 119:93: *"I will **never forget** thy precepts: for with them thou hast quickened me."*

Psalm 119: 176: *"**I do not forget** thy commandments."* (vs. 109, 141, 153, and 176).

Isaiah 59:21: *"As for me, this is my covenant with them, saith the LORD; My Spirit that is upon thee, and my words which I have put in thy mouth, **shall not depart out of thy mouth**, nor out of the mouth of thy seed, nor out of the mouth of thy seed's seed, saith the LORD, from henceforth and forever."*

God has given a mandate to parents to not only get God's Word into the hearts of their children but into their mouths. When they have it in their mouths, they won't forget it. How much of God's Word do your children have in their mouths? Can they recite many passages of Scripture?

PRAYER:

Dear God and Father, I don't want truth to only reside in my brain. I want it to become part of my life. I want to reveal Your truth in my life, to my family, and to all I meet. Please fill me and overflow me with Your truth. Amen."

AFFIRMATION:

God's truth is the rejoicing of my heart.

FURTHER STUDY: Go to page 312.

71

ARE YOU ON THE SIDE OF TRUTH?
Part 7

"Search the Scriptures; for in them ye think ye have eternal life:
and they are they which.testify of me."
(JOHN 5:39).

33. TRUTH REVEALERS

2 Corinthians 4:2, 3: *"Not walking in craftiness, nor handling the word of God deceitfully, but by manifestation of the truth commending ourselves to every man's conscience in the sight of God. But if our gospel be hid, it is hid to them that are lost."*

Does your life reveal God's truth, to your family and to those with whom you associate? Do you manifest His truth through your conduct, through what you say, and what you write? "The World's Bible" by Annie Johnson Flint says:

"We are the only Bible this careless world will read,
We are the sinner's Gospel; we are the scoffer's creed."

34. TRUTH RUNNERS

Psalm 119:32: *"I will run the way of thy commandments."*

The Hebrew word for run is *ruts* and is often translated "post" in the Bible. It's the original word for postman. In Bible days, the runners or "the post" as they called them, ran from one city to the other to deliver the messages. These men did not walk, they ran swiftly! You could not be a postman unless you were fast!

This is the kind of attitude we should have toward God's truth. We run to receive it. We run to give it. Not necessarily literal running, but always eager and ready to deliver the good tidings.

35. TRUTH SEARCHERS

Jeremiah 29:13: *"And ye shall seek me, and find me, when ye shall **search for me with all your heart**."*

Proverbs 2:3-5: *"Yea, if thou criest after knowledge, and liftest up thy voice for understanding; If thou seekest her as silver, and **searchest for her as for hid treasures**; Then shalt thou understand the fear of the LORD, and find the knowledge of God."*

Acts 17:11 tells us about the people in Berea who *"received the word with all readiness of mind, and **searched the Scriptures daily**, whether those things were so."* After hearing Paul preach, they didn't immediately accept his word but searched the Scriptures to see if it was true. We should not be ignorant or gullible, believing everything we hear. If we are searching for truth, we will often be concerned about something we hear. Therefore, we dig into the Scriptures and diligently search for the truth. We don't find the truth of a subject in only one Scripture. We must be diligent to search God's Word from Genesis to Revelation to get the whole truth.

Jesus said in John 5:39: *"Search the Scriptures; for in them ye think ye have eternal life: and they are they which testify of me."*

What Scriptures was Jesus talking about? The Old Testament! Yes, the Old Testament also reveals Jesus. When Jesus talked with the two disciples on the way to Emmaus Luke 24:27 says: *"And beginning at Moses and all the prophets, he expounded unto them in all the Scriptures the things concerning himself."*

When Philip found Jesus, he said to Nathanael: *"We have found him, of whom Moses in the law, and the prophets, did write, Jesus of Nazareth, the son of Joseph"* (John 1:45). Do you also search the Old Testament? Do you understand the typology of the tabernacle in the wilderness? Every offering, sacrifice, and every piece of furniture all pointed to Christ. Many Christians today know nothing of this teaching and therefore fail to understand the fullness of their great salvation.

May God save us from being shallow in the truth. True disciples diligently and daily search the Scriptures.

36. TRUTH SEEKERS

Psalm 27:8: *"When thou saidst, Seek ye my face; my heart said unto thee, **Thy face, LORD, will I seek**."* The Hebrew for face is *paniym* which is always a plural word. That's why the bread upon the Table of Shewbread was called "The Bread of Faces." The bread upon the table spoke of God in all His different attributes and of Christ *"in whom are hid **all** the treasures of wisdom and knowledge"* (Colossians 2:3).

Psalm 119:2: *"Blessed are they that keep his testimonies, and that **seek him with the whole heart.**"* Also read 2 Chronicles 7:14; Psalm 119:10, 45, 94; Jeremiah 5:1 and 29:13.

Proverbs 8:17: *"I love them that love me; and those that **seek me early** shall find me."* I believe that means early in life and early in the day. The Israelites had to collect the mana early in the day for when the sun rose it melted. If we don't get our spiritual mana early in the day, we usually don't get it! Life gets too busy.

Hebrews 11:6: *"But without faith it is impossible to please him: for he that cometh to God must believe that he is, and that he is a rewarder of them that **diligently seek him.**"*

PRAYER:

Dear Father, I love Your Word and I want to run to it every morning. I long to feed on Your truth. Please teach me and feed me as I search for Your truth. Amen.

AFFIRMATION:

I am not satisfied with hearsay. I will be a seeker and a searcher after truth.

72

ARE YOU ON THE SIDE OF TRUTH?

Part 8

"And now Lord, behold their threatenings: and grant unto thy servants, that with all boldness they may speak thy word"
(ACTS 4:29).

37. TRUTH SINGERS

The Bible tells us to not only speak the truth but sing the truth.

The psalmist says: *"Your statues have been my songs in the house where I live"* (Psalm 119:54 NET).

Psalm 119:172 (BSB) says: *"My tongue sings Your word, for all Your commandments are righteous."*

The Passion translation says: *"As I journey through life, I put all your statues to music; they become the theme of my joyous songs."*

It is certainly easier to memorize the Scriptures when we sing them isn't it? I loved the era of "Scripture in Song." God touched a New Zealand couple, Dave and Dale Garrett, to put Scriptures to music. For many years, churches all over the world sang and worshipped God through the Scriptures. My husband knows so many Scriptures in song that when he comes to read a Scripture for which he knows the tune, either preaching or at Family Devotions, he begins to sing. It's a great way to receive the Scriptures into our hearts.

We go over to the New Testament where we read of the lifestyle God wants us to live: *"Be filled with the Spirit; Speaking to yourselves in psalms and hymns and spiritual songs, singing and making melody in your heart to the Lord; Giving thanks always for all things unto God and the Father in the name of our Lord Jesus Christ"* (Ephesians 5:18-20).

38. TRUTH SPEAKERS

Proverbs 8:6-8: *"Hear; for I will speak of excellent things; and the opening of my lips shall be right things. For my **mouth shall speak truth**; and wickedness is an abomination to my lips. All the words of my mouth are in righteousness; there is nothing forward or perverse in them."*

Malachi 2:6: *"The law of **truth was in his mouth**, and iniquity was not found in his lips: he walked with me in peace and equity, and did turn many away from iniquity."*

2 Corinthians 7:14: *"We spake all things to you in **truth.** "*

Ephesians 4:15, 25: *"**Speaking the truth** in love . . . Wherefore putting away lying, **speak every man** truth with his neighbor: for we are members one of another."*

LIES OUT, TRUTH IN! That's a good motto for your family life. You could write it out in big letters and pin it up in your kitchen. Children are prone to tell lies and it can become a habit. Eradicate this habit from their lives when they are young. You will do them a great favor. Teach them Psalm 51:6 where it says: *"Behold, thou desirest **truth in the inward parts.**"* Teach them to have truth deep inside them and then they will automatically speak the truth.

Become a TRUTH-SPEAKING FAMILY. Before you speak to others of truth and all the treasures of wisdom and knowledge, you must first speak truth to you children.

Deuteronomy 11:19 (NET) says: *"Teach them to your children and **speak of them** as you sit in your house, as you walk along the road, as you lie down, and as you get up."*

As you speak God's truth into their lives, you prepare them to be truth speakers. Yes, mothers, this is our great vision, to raise our children to be truth speakers. Psalm 127:5 says: *"Happy is the man that hath his quiver full of them (full of children): they shall not be ashamed, but **they shall speak with the enemies in the gate.**"* In this hour of great deception, we are preparing and training children to be truth speakers in their sphere of influence, in the gates of their cities, and even the land!

39. TRUTH SPREADERS

We spread seeds of truth to our children throughout the day. We spread seeds of truth to people we meet in the supermarket and wherever we go. Some may fall in stony places, but others will bring forth much fruit. We have the responsibility to sow; it is God's responsibility to bring forth the harvest.

Read Matthew 13:1-23 (Mark 4:1-20 and Luke 8:4-15); John 4:36, 37; and 1 Corinthians 3:8, 9.

40. TRUTH STANDERS

Ephesians 6:13, 14: *"Wherefore take unto you the whole armor of God that ye may be able to withstand in the evil day, and having done all, to stand. Stand therefore . . ."*

Jeremiah 9:3 talks about those who *"are not valiant for the truth upon the earth."* May God anoint us to raise children that are so strong in the truth, that no matter how much they are buffeted and ridiculed, they will continue standing true to God's Word. Can you say Amen with me?

PRAYER:

Dear Father, it is so easy to be shady about the truth. Help me to always speak the truth, even when it means I must expose myself and my sin. Help me to be a truth-speaker. Please help me never to stay silent when I should speak up for truth. Help us to be a truth-speaking family. Amen."

AFFIRMATION:

I am making truth the banner over our family.

FURTHER STUDY: Go to page 313.

73

ARE YOU ON THE SIDE OF TRUTH?
Part 9

"And they overcame him by the blood of the Lamb, and by the word of their testimony, and they loved not their lives unto the death"
(REVELATION 12:11).

41. TRUTH STICKERS

Psalm 119:31: *"I have stuck unto thy testimonies."* Let's be stickers to God's truth.

2 Thessalonians 2:15 (NLT): ***"Stand firm and keep a strong grip** on the teaching we passed on to you."*

2 Timothy 1:13 (NKJV): ***"Hold fast** the pattern of sound words, which you have heard of me, in faith and love which is in Christ Jesus."* There are some who begin walking in God's truth, but when things get tough or don't go their way, they give up. They don't hang on to the truth in faith. Let's be those who never deviate.

Mark 4:16, 17 tells us what happens to the seed of God's Word that falls on stony ground who: *"When they have heard the word, immediately receive it with gladness; And have not root in themselves, and so endure but for a time: afterward, when affliction or persecution ariseth **for the word's sake**, immediately they are offended."* Instead of trusting God's Word and His promises, they give in to the easy road.

42. TRUTH STUDIERS

2 Timothy 2:15: ***"Study** to show thyself approved unto God, a workman that needeth not to be shamed, **rightly dividing the word of truth."***

This Scripture is not talking about a casual reading of the Bible, but thoroughly studying it to truly know what it says. Many are content to read the Bible but don't take time to study it. There's far more than what we read on the surface. There are layers and layers of revelation to receive as you diligently and daily study and meditate.

The psalmist said in Psalm 119:94 (CSB): *"I have **studied** your precepts."*

Did you notice that we study to be "Approved Unto God"? Maybe, one of the greatest degrees you should encourage your children to go for is the A.U.G (**A**pproved **U**nto **G**od) through diligent study of the Word.

Charles Spurgeon writes: "Bible study is the metal that forges a Christian."

43. TRUTH TEACHERS

God gives the mandate to teach His truth to every believer. Let's remind ourselves again of The Great Commission in Matthew 28:18-20: *"All power is given unto me in heaven and in earth. **Go ye therefore, and teach** all nations, baptizing them in the name of the Father, and the of the Son, and of the Holy Ghost; **Teaching them to observe all things** whatsoever I have commanded you: and, lo, I am with you always, even unto the end of the world."*

There is much debate today about whether women should be preachers and teachers. Of course, we should! But that doesn't necessarily mean we will be a public evangelists or teachers in the church. God has given older women a specific and powerful call to teach His ways to the younger women. He even itemizes the subjects He wants them to reach. Read them again in Titus 2:3-5. If older mothers were faithful to this mandate, we would change the world!

As mothers are faithful to teach and disciple the children God gives them, they will send forth mighty warriors to bring God's truth and justice again to the land. This is God's plan, and He hasn't changed it!

Deuteronomy 4:8, 9 (HCSB): *"What great nation has righteous statutes and ordinances like this entire law? . . . **Teach them to your children and your grandchildren."***

Deuteronomy 6:6, 7: *"Thou shalt **teach them diligently unto thy children,** and shalt talk of them when thou sittest in thine house, and when thou walkest by the way, and when thou liest down, and when thou risest up."*

Proverbs 6:20-22 (NASB): *"My son . . . do not forsake the **teaching of your mother,** bind them continually on your heart; tie them around your neck. When you walk about, they will guide you; when you sleep, they will watch over you; and when you awake, they will talk to you."*

Colossians 1:27, 28: *"Christ in you, the hope of glory: Whom we preach,* *warning every man, and **teaching every man** in all wisdom; that we may present every man perfect in Christ Jesus."* This was Paul's vision. Dear mothers, it should also be our vision for our children. God has given us the responsibility to teach them and get them ready to present them to Him with great joy on that Day when we meet Him face to face. Also read 1 Thessalonians 2:19.

44. TRUTH TESTIFIERS

Acts 20:24 sums up Paul's life: *"But none of these things move me, neither count I my life dear unto myself, so that I might finish my course with joy, and the ministry, which I have received of the Lord Jesus, **to testify the gospel of the grace of God."***

The word testify in this Scripture is *diamarturomai* and means "to protest, urge earnestly, repeatedly, hortatively, to charge and exhort." Paul didn't "beat around the bush," mince words, or compromise. He spoke the truth with passion. This is the way we are to testify to the truth of the Gospel.

In 1 John 4:14 John shares: *"And we have seen and do **testify** that the Father sent the Son to be the Savior of the world."* This time it is the Greek word *martureo* meaning "to be a witness, to give honest evidence and testimony." It is used 89 times in the New Testament which is full of examples of testifying to the truth of Jesus and His Word.

The Holy Spirit is called the *"Spirit of truth"* and John 15:26 tell us that He testifies of Jesus. Therefore, if the Holy Spirit dwells in us, that's what we'll be doing!

Are you a truth testifier?

45. TRUTH THINKERS

Philippians 4:8: *"Whatsoever things are **true** . . . think on these things."* We must fill and flood our minds with truth.

46. TRUTH TREMBLERS

I think here are very few who tremble at God's Word today. The Bible is not a normal book. We cannot read it is an ordinary book. We must read it with fear and trembling as we acknowledge that every word comes from our holy and awesome God. There are times when I have literally trembled at what I am reading.

God states clearly in Isaiah 66:3: *"To this man will I look, even to him that is poor and of a contrite spirit, and **trembleth** at my word."* He goes on to say in verse 5: *"Hear the word of the LORD, ye that **tremble** at his word."* I believe God speaks to those who tremble at His Word. Often, we do not hear from God because we take Him and His Word far too lightly.

Read how the people trembled when they heard the words of God in Ezra's time: Ezra 9:4 and 10:3.

Psalm 119:161: *"My heart **standeth in awe** of thy word."*

PRAYER:

"Dear Father, please save me from ever taking Your precious Word lightly. Help me to see it as it is, Your powerful and eternal Word. Teach me what it means to tremble at Your Word. Amen."

AFFIRMATION:

I will be a truth teacher to my children, always guiding them to seek after God's truth.

74

ARE YOU ON THE SIDE OF TRUTH?
Part 10

We come to our last study about truth. You will need to pour over all these wonderful Scriptures again to really get them into your heart. May God mightily bless you as you seek after truth and seek to encourage your children to also be truth seekers and searchers.

47. TRUTH UNDERSTANDERS

We must be believers who take time to understand the truth of God's words to us. Without understanding we cannot effectively pass on the truth. Read the following Scriptures: Psalm 119:27, 34, 73, 99, 100, 104, 125, 130, 144, 169; Proverbs 15:14; and Daniel 9:13.

48. TRUTH WALKERS

What was David's testimony? *"I have **walked** in thy truth"* (Psalm 26:3).

Psalm 119:1 reminds us that those *"who **walk** in the law of the LORD"* will be blessed. Also read 1 Kings 2:1-4; 3:6; 9:4; and Psalm 86:11.

It's not enough to speak, teach, and testify to the truth through our lips. The truth of His words should flow through our conduct and way of life. It's not enough to talk God's truth; we've got to walk God's truth.

49. TRUTH WRITERS

There is a wonderful word used in the Old Testament, *caphar*, that means to not only "show forth, declare, and tell," but to "write God's truth." This word is translated *"scribe"* 50 times in the Old Testament. We must speak the truth and **write** the truth. Use any social media you are part of to write words of truth. You are welcome to use any writings of mine on your social media (as long as you mention their source).

You can write cards with Scriptures and inspiring words to give to those God puts on your heart. You can write books.

I think it is good to write what God says to you through His Word. I like to do this each day. If I don't, I forget, and I want to remember the truth God gives to me. I have kept a journal for years of what God speaks to me each day in His word. I began as a teenager when I read Jeremiah 30:2: *"Write thee all the words that I have spoken unto thee in a book."* And I am still doing it up until this day.

50. TRUTH YEARNERS

Psalm 42:1 (NET): *"As a deer longs (pants) for streams of water, so **I long for you, O God!**"*

Psalm 119:20: *"My soul breaketh for **the longing** that it hath unto thy judgements at all times."* Is this your testimony too?

Psalm 119:40: *"Behold, I have **longed after thy precepts**."*

Psalm 119:131 (NET): *"I open my mouth and pant, because **I long for your commands**."* Do you pant after truth? Do you long for it? Do you for thirst for it? I wake in the morning, and I am desperate for water and food for my soul. I must get the Word the moment I wake. To really know truth, we must pant for it.

What about the New Testament? 1 Peter 2:2 tells us that a young believer cannot grow unless they *"desire the sincere milk of the word."* To desire means "to yearn, to intensely crave, to long after."

Well, I have reached our 50 points! And I will stop! But there are more, so I will mention 25 more here for you. We must also be . . .

truth accepters,

truth adherers,

truth binders (Proverbs 3:3),

truth comforters (Psalm 119: 50, 52, 76, 82),

truth embracers (Acts 7:51),

truth exhorters (Romans 12:8; 1 Thessalonians 2:1; 4:1; 5:14; 1 Timothy 2:1; 4:13; 2 Timothy 4;2; Titus 2:15; Hebrews 10:25; 12:5; and 13:22),

truth exercisers (Hebrews 5:14),

truth finders (Psalm 119:162),

truth followers (Ephesians 6:1 and Hebrews 13:7),

truth guarders,

truth instructors (Luke 1; Acts 128:25; 2 Timothy 2:25; 2 Timothy 3:16),
truth heralders,
truth liberators (Isaiah 42:7 and 61:1),
truth lighters (Psalm 119:105, 130),
truth lookers (James 1:25),
truth openers (Luke 24:32),
truth pleaders (Isaiah 59:4),
truth praisers (Psalm 56:4, 119:48, 164, 171, 175),
truth readers (Nehemiah 8:8 and 1 Timothy 4:13),
truth receivers (John 1:12; Acts 17:11; and James 1:21),
truth respecters (Psalm 119:6, 15, 117),
truth sharers,
truth strengtheners (Psalm 119:28),
truth treasurers (Psalm 119:11, 162), and
truth verifiers.

May you become a truth-grounded, truth-established, truth valiant, and truth-speaking family.

PRAYER:

"Dear Father God, I want to be faithful to teach my children Your truth and Your ways. Help me to be diligent in seeking Your truth so I will know the truth to impart to them. Amen."

AFFIRMATION:

I am doing everything in my power to make the truth known—teaching my children, testifying to all I meet, and writing the words of truth on all media platforms possible."

FURTHER STUDY:

No. 45. TRUTH TESTIFIERS

Diamarturomai Scriptures:
Luke 16:28; Acts 2:40; 10:42; 28:25; 10:42; 18:5; 20:21, 24; 23:11; 28:23; 1 Timothy 5:21; 2 Timothy 2:14; 4:1-3; and 1 Thessalonians 4:6.

No. 48. TRUTH WALKERS

Psalm 86:11; 119:1, 3, 35, 45; 1 Kings 2:4; 3:6; 2 Kings 20:3; Isaiah 38:3; 2 John 1:4; and 3 John 1:3, 4.

75

A HIGHER PLANE

"But if you are led by the Spirit, you are not under the law"
(GALATIANS 5:18).

The Ten Commandments are banned from our schools and public places. How grieving. These commandments are God's laws for society. They protect the nation and make it a secure place to live.

But although they are good, God has now provided something even better! He has given us a higher law.

A "**better**" law (Hebrews 7:22 and 8:6)!

Moses' law was glorious; this new law is "**even more glorious**" (2 Corinthians 3:7-10)! Moses' law could not save us; this new law can save to the uttermost, even the guttermost (Hebrews 7:25)!

How does this happen?

1. THE LAW OF LOVE

James 2:8: *"If ye fulfill the royal law according to the Scripture, Thou shalt love thy neighbor as thyself, ye do well."*

The Bible calls the law of love the **royal law**, firstly because it is a royal command, given by the King of Kings and Lord of lords. Secondly, it is the most important of commandments in the old law. A lawyer once came to Jesus and asked him which was the greatest commandment. Jesus answered: *"Thou shalt love the Lord thy God with all thy heart, and with all thy soul, and with all thy mind. This is the first and great commandment. And the second is like unto it, Thou shalt love thy neighbor as thyself. On these two commandments hang all the law and the prophets"* (Matthew 22:37-40).

2. THE LAW OF THE SPIRIT OF LIFE IN CHRIST JESUS

Romans 8:2: *"For the law of the Spirit of life in Christ Jesus has made me free from the law of sin and death."*

We keep Moses' law by the strength of the flesh, but we keep the new covenant by the power of the Spirit. I like Way's translation of Galatians 5:18, a translation of the Bible published in 1901. It says: *"But if you definitely surrender yourselves to the Spirit's guidance, you are then not under the Law, but on* **a higher plane.***"* This is the higher plane on which God wants us to live. To be led by the Spirit rather than the feelings and passions of the flesh. To walk in the Spirit rather than the flesh (Romans 8:1-14).

3. THE LAW OF CHRIST

Galatians 6:2: *"Bear ye one another's burdens, and so fulfill the law of Christ."*

Christ's law is not to think of myself, but to think of others and bear the burdens of their failings. This can only happen as the Holy Spirit has His way in me. It is a law of love. Not my natural love, but the agape love of Christ in me. Way's translation says: *"Ever bear each other's burdens; fulfill in this way Messiah's Law of Love. If any of you thinks himself too big for such condescension . . . he is the victim of self-delusion."*

4. THE LAW OF LIBERTY

James 2:12, 13: *"So speak ye, and so do, as they that shall be judged by the law of liberty. For he shall have judgment without mercy, that hath showed no mercy; and mercy rejoices against judgment."*

Moses' law showed no mercy, but the new covenant is filled with mercy. To be merciful is to live by the law of freedom; to be unmerciful is to be in bondage (2 Corinthians 3:17).

5. THE LAW OF RIGHTEOUSNESS

Romans 9:30-32 talks about the law of righteousness which we can only experience by faith.

We could never attain true righteousness and holiness by the Law of Moses. But in Christ, in the new covenant, we can walk in righteousness without even trying. It is not our own righteousness, but the righteousness of Christ Himself. Instead of trying to be holy, we are holy through Christ living His life in us and through us.

Second Corinthians 5:21 explains this new law: *"For he hath made him to be sin for us, who knew no sin; that we might be made the righteousness of God in him."*

Jesus Himself is our righteousness and holiness. We see this again in 1

Corinthians 1:30, 31: *"But of him are ye in Christ Jesus, who of God is made unto us wisdom, and righteousness, and sanctification, and redemption."*

6. THE LAW OF FAITH

We had to keep the old law by works. We keep the new law by faith. Faith and faith alone. Read Romans 3:27, 28; Galatians 2:20; 3:11, 12; and Ephesians 2:8, 9).

PRAYER:

"Dearest Jesus, I thank you with all my heart for the new law You gave to us. I no longer have to strive to do what I cannot do in my own flesh. I thank You that I can embrace Your holy, joyful, victorious, glorious life that now dwells in me. I can walk in the power of Your life instead of my own feelings and flesh. Amen."

AFFIRMATION:

I'm no longer striving in the flesh but living according to the power of the Holy Spirit in me.

76

JESUS PRAYS FOR YOU
Part 1

"I pray for them: I pray not for the world, but for them which thou hast given me; for they are thine"
(JOHN 17:9).

In John chapter 17 we read the prayer that Jesus prayed for His disciples and for those who would one day believe in Him. That means you. Isn't it amazing that Jesus prayed for us away back when he was here on earth? Because this prayer is the heart of Jesus for His own children, we can also pray these prayers for ourselves, and for our own children, knowing that they are in the perfect will of God. Read the whole of John chapter 17 again when you get a moment. In the meantime, we'll look at some of the specific things that Jesus prayed for us.

1. THAT YOU WILL BE UNITED AS ONE

John 17:11, 21, 22b, and 23: *"That they may be one, as we are."*

Wow! What a prayer. What a vision. Oh, to experience the same kind of oneness with one another that Jesus had with his Father. We can't expect this to happen in the body of Christ until we experience it in our own marriage and family. When husbands and wives walk in oneness, and families live in harmony together, we'll begin to see this happen in the church of God.

Join with Jesus and keep praying it into being until you experience it.

2. THAT YOU WILL BE KEPT FROM EVIL

John 17:15, 16. *"I pray not that thou shouldest take them out of the world, but that thou shouldest keep them from the evil. They are not of the world, even as I am not of the world."*

When we come to Jesus, He does not want to let us go (John 10:28-30). He keeps us by His power (1 Peter 1:5). Join with Jesus in praying this prayer for your children. Pray that He will keep them from the lures of the world. Pray that He will keep them from the lust of the flesh, the lust of the eyes, and the pride of the life (1 John 2:15-17). Pray that He will keep them from the deceptions of the enemy. Pray that they will keep close to the Lord.

We don't separate ourselves, or our children, from the world to do this. We train them to be strong in the Lord and His truth so they can stand against the spirit of the world. God's desire is for us to live in this world, untouched by its lures, evils, and temptations. He wants us to touch the world with His love and salvation but be untouched by the temptations of its evil ways.

3. THAT YOU WILL LIVE IN HIS JOY

John 17:13: *"That they might have my joy fulfilled in themselves."*

Jesus' joy was not determined by his outward circumstances but on His relationship with His Father. He was filled with joy because he kept His eyes on the final goal. He endured the cross *"for the joy that was set before him"* (Hebrews 12:2).

The joy Jesus wants us to experience is not based on happiness. It is not dependent on our circumstances. It is an inward joy. We have it in us because He lives in us, and He is joy. His joy is not here today and gone tomorrow. It is constant! It is always in us because He abides in us. Jesus said in John 15:11: *"These things have I spoken unto you, that **my joy might remain in you**, and that your joy might be full."* It's a joy that does not go away, no matter what happens in our lives.

Don't let outside pressures rob Jesus' joy from your life. Continually confess the joy of the Lord in your soul. Keep the joy flowing.

PRAYER:

"Dear Lord Jesus, I thank You for praying for me. I thank You that right now You are interceding for me at the right hand of the Father. I yield myself to You that your desires for me will be worked out in my life and in my home. Thank You, Lord Jesus. Amen."

AFFIRMATION:

Sometimes I feel joy, sometimes I feel pain,
But the joy of the Lord will forever remain!

77

JESUS PRAYS FOR YOU
Part 2

*"Neither pray I for these alone, but for them also
which shall believe on me through their word"*
(JOHN 17:20).

Today we complete the seven specific things that Jesus prayed for us.

4. THAT YOU WILL BE SANCTIFIED

John 17:17: *"Sanctify them through thy truth: thy word is truth."*

The word sanctify means "to make holy, purify, consecrate." How can we keep pure and holy in this world? Jesus tells us the answer in His prayer. God's Word keeps us holy. Read it. Memorize it. Think about it. Confess it aloud. Talk about it.

Do you want your children to be sanctified? Feed them the Word of God. Read it to them daily. Encourage them to memorize it too. The following are two important Scriptures for your children to memorize on this subject. It amazes me that most Christian young people and adults don't know these Scriptures. Make sure your children know them.

Psalm 119:9: *"Wherewithal shall a young man cleanse his way? by taking heed thereto according to thy word."*

Psalm 119:11: *"Thy word have I hid in mine heart, that I might not sin against thee."*

5. THAT YOU WILL EXPERIENCE HIS GLORY

John 17:22: *"And the glory which thou gavest me I have given them."*

Can you believe this statement? It is amazing. When Simeon saw the baby Jesus, He spoke prophetically as he proclaimed: *"For mine eyes have seen thy salvation, Which thou hast prepared before the face of all people; A light to lighten the Gentiles, and the glory of thy people Israel"* (Luke 2:30-

32). Jesus was the light and glory of God on earth.

Now that Jesus has returned to the heavenly realm, He still wants His light and glory to be revealed in this sin-sick world. He has now chosen His redeemed people to be His light and glory. *"Christ in you, the hope of glory"* (Colossians 1:27). Yes, He wants you to show forth His light and glory from your life.

Unless you shine your light, people will stay in darkness.

"Arise, shine; for thy light is come, and the glory of the Lord is risen upon thee" (Isaiah 60:1).

Jesus was not a flickering light, but a great light. He wants you to shine brightly too. Remember that Jesus prayed this prayer for you and is still praying it at the right hand of the Father (Romans 8:34; Hebrews 7:25; 9:24; and 1 John 2:1).

6. THAT YOU WILL BEHOLD HIS GLORY

John 17:24: *"Father, I will that they also, whom thou hast given me, be with me where I am; that they may behold my glory, which thou hast given me: for thou lovedst me before the foundation of the world."*

Jesus longs for you to live in the eternal realm with Him and behold the glory that He shares with the Father. This is why He came to earth to redeem us. What a redemption! What a hope!

This is also the prayer that we pray for our children, isn't it? That they will be born again, receive eternal life, and come to know Christ intimately. Our most important task as parents is to prepare our children for the eternal world.

7. THAT HIS FATHER'S LOVE WILL BE IN YOU

John 17:26: *"That the love wherewith thou hast loved me may be in them, and I in them."*

What kind of love does Jesus want us to have for one another? The love that the Father has for His only begotten Son! Oh, to experience this kind of love in our lives. Oh, to have this love in our families. Oh, for this kind of love in the body of Christ.

It is sacrificial love. Love that does not think of itself. Love that does not demand its own way. Love that delights to serve. Love that pours itself out for the other person.

This is the love that keeps a marriage together. This is the love that binds a family together. This is the love that brings true revival to the body of Christ.

We can't experience this love in the natural. It is only as we lay down our lives, take up the cross, and allow the Holy Spirit to fill our lives.

PRAYER:

"Come, Oh, Lord, and overflow me with Your love. My love runs out so easily, but I thank You that in Your heart there is a well of love that is inexhaustible. I draw from Your everlasting well. Fill me to overflowing. I want Your love to spill out to everyone in my home—and everyone I meet. Amen."

AFFIRMATION:

The Word of God will keep me from sin, or sin will keep me from the Word of God.

78

WHAT IS PRECIOUS TO GOD?
And is it Precious to You?
Part 1

"If thou take forth the precious from the vile, thou shalt be as my mouth"
(JEREMIAH 15:19).

God wants us to separate the things that are precious in His sight from the things that are worthless and vile. God does not live in a gray area, and He doesn't want us too either. He doesn't want our minds to be clouded and dulled by the thinking of this world so that we can no longer discern the difference between what is precious and what is vile.

God cannot stand lukewarmness. He would rather we were hot or cold. I'm sure you remember that it says in Revelation 3:16 that if we are *"luke-warm"* He will *"spew us out of His mouth."* That's strong language.

In Ezekiel 44:23 God tells his priests to *"teach my people the difference between the holy and profane, and cause them to discern between the unclean and the clean."* Also read Leviticus 10:10 and Ezekiel 22:26.

Sometimes the precious things of God get submerged under the busyness of our hectic lives. They get clouded and jaded because the deceptions and mindset of this world overpower us. They get forgotten in the maze of everything else that clamors for our attention.

How would you like to do some digging for the precious things? Let's see if we can dig them out from all the worthless junk that has crowded our lives. Once you've dug them out again, keep them separate. Make them preeminent. Don't let them get lost again under the big junk pile of worthless and unnecessary garbage that fills our lives.

What are the precious things of God? Everything that is pure and holy. All that is good and wholesome. All the beautiful things mentioned in Philippians 4:8, the things that are true, honest, just, pure, lovely, of good report, virtuous, and praiseworthy.

However, there are certain things that God specifically states are precious to Him. Let's look at some of these, shall we?

1. JESUS CHRIST, THE SON OF GOD

Isaiah 28:16: *"Behold, I lay in Zion for a foundation a stone, a tried stone, **a precious corner stone**, a sure foundation."*

The New Testament reiterates this truth. 1 Peter 2:4 says that Jesus is *"chosen of God, and precious."* Also read Colossians 1:15-19.

1 Peter 2:7: *"Unto you therefore which believe he is precious."*

Is Jesus the most precious of all to you? Is He the corner stone on which you build everything else in your life? Does everything in your life pivot from Him? Have you separated Jesus to be the preeminent one, above everything else in your life?

Whisper His name all day long. Speak His name aloud frequently. Lift up the name of Jesus in your home. You only exist because of Him.

2. THE BLOOD OF JESUS CHRIST

1 Peter 1:18, 19: *"Forasmuch as ye know that ye were not redeemed with corruptible things, as silver and gold . . . But with the **precious blood of Christ,** as of a lamb without blemish and without spot."*

The blood of Jesus is very precious. Without the blood of Jesus, we would still be under the guilt of sin. Without the blood of Jesus, we could not enter the presence of the Lord. Without the blood of Jesus, we would still be alienated from the kingdom of God.

Thank Jesus every day that He poured out His blood to wash away your sins. Honor the blood of Jesus. Plead the protection of the blood of Jesus over your family and over your home. Don't lose sight of its preciousness.

3. THE LIVING WORD OF GOD

2 Peter 1:4: *"Whereby are given unto us **exceeding great and precious promises**: that by these ye might be partakers of the divine nature."*

Do you notice that it takes three adjectives to describe God's promises? How precious are they to you? How much time do you take out of each day to read and meditate on them? Are they more precious to you than life? Job says in Job 23:12: *"I have esteemed the words of his mouth more than my necessary food."*

Dear mother, I know that you don't have a lot of time to read the Word of God when you have all your little lambs around you. However, even though you don't have time to have long sessions reading the Word, it is amazing what you can receive here and there throughout the day. Place the Bible on your windowsill above your kitchen sink and open it to the Psalms or Proverbs. Every now and then you can look up and read a Scripture and meditate upon it as you wash the dishes and cook.

Place an open Bible on the table. You can often read a verse as you pass by or sit for a few minutes. Read a few verses when you nurse your baby. Keep a Bible in the bathroom. I have often received wonderful promises from the Lord in these moments.

One older mother shared with me what she used to do when her children were little. "Some mornings I would get up and have so much work to do and I would wonder where to start. Many times, I would feel the Lord say to me: 'Now, Mother, just clean off the table and make it look really neat and pretty. Lay a little cloth in the center of the table. Find a Scripture in the Bible and lay the Bible open on the cloth. Light a candle and put it beside the Bible as a symbol that the Word is a light unto your feet. As you fix your breakfast speak sweetly to the children and refer often to the little candle and the open Bible. Sing sweet songs of joy and as you run by the table, glance often at the promises you have marked in your Bible.' This simple act of faith often organized my day."

Of course, don't forget your Family Devotions together as a family. As you faithfully do this in your home each day, your children will also realize the importance and preciousness of God's Word.

PRAYER:

"Dear Lord Jesus, I want You to be preeminent in my life. I want You to be uppermost in all my thoughts. I want to say Your name over and over again. Lord Jesus, please help me to truly discern between what is holy and what is worthless. Save me from becoming jaded by the thinking patterns of this world. Amen."

AFFIRMATION:

I am sifting through my life—keeping what is precious and throwing out all that is worthless.

79

WHAT IS PRECIOUS TO GOD?
And is it Precious to You?
Part 2

"Let the words of my mouth, and the meditation of my heart, be acceptable in thy sight, O LORD, my strength, and my redeemer"
(PSALM 19:14).

We continue our search for the things that are precious to God.

4. THE TRIAL OF YOUR FAITH

1 Peter 1:7: *"That the trial of your faith, being **much more precious than of gold** that perisheth, though it be tried with fire, might be found unto praise and honor and glory at the appearing of Jesus Christ."* Also read 2 Peter 1:1.

Dear mother, don't be discouraged when your faith is being tested. This is a necessary part of your walk with the Lord. Faith must go through the fire to test if it is real and lasting. We all have our faith tested at certain times. Often these times can seem hard—and so long. But remember, if we allow God to work in us, refine us, and mold us more into the image of Jesus during these times, without resisting and rebelling, we will receive great reward in the eternal kingdom. And it will be very precious to God's heart. Also read 2 Corinthians 4:17-18.

5. A GENTLE AND QUIET SPIRIT

1 Peter 3:4: *"But let it Be the hidden man of the heart, in that which is not corruptible, even the ornament of a meek and quiet spirit, which is in the sight of God of great price."*

The ESV version calls it *"the imperishable beauty of a gentle and quiet spirit, which in God's sight is **VERY precious**."*

Our culture does not consider a gentle and quiet spirit very precious, but this is what God looks for in His female creation. It is *"very precious"* to Him. The Greek word is *poluteles* and means "extremely expensive, very precious, of great price, and very costly." If it is so very precious to God, don't you think it should be precious to us too? Shouldn't we seek after it with all our hearts? Shouldn't we separate it from the callous, hard, independent, and rebellious attitude that is prevalent among women in society today? Let's seek after the precious and beautiful which God calls . . .

"The incorruptible beauty" (NKJV).

"The imperishable quality and unfading charm" (AMP).

"Imperishable jewel" (RSV).

"The ageless beauty" (GNB).

Seek God to help you be gentle in mothering and nurturing your children. Seek God to have a quiet and submissive spirit to your husband whom God has placed as head of your home. The world may laugh at this attitude, but it is very precious to God.

6. GOD'S WISDOM

Proverbs 3:13-15: *"Happy is the man that findeth wisdom . . . She is **more precious than rubies**: and all the things thou canst desire are not to be compared unto her."*

There is worldly wisdom and spiritual wisdom. We must learn to discern between the two. How can you dig for wisdom? You won't find her watching TV and videos. You won't find her reading novels. You won't find her listening to the mindset of this humanistic society.

You will find her seeking after God's heart and His mind. His ways are higher than our ways. His thoughts are higher than our thoughts. We must seek a higher plane. We seek after many things in this world, but God says that nothing can be compared to seeking wisdom.

Proverbs 9:1: *"Wisdom hath builded her house, she hath hewn out her seven pillars."* What are the seven pillars of God's wisdom like? James 3:17 gives us a picture. Let's read it in the Amplified Bible:

1. Pure (morally and spiritually undefiled),
2. Peace-loving (courteous and considerate),
3. Gentle,
4. Reasonable (and willing to listen),
5. Full of compassion and good fruits,
6. Unwavering,
7. Without (self-righteous) hypocrisy (and self-serving guile).

Are these pillars of wisdom flowing through your life as you mother in your home? Do these wisdom attitudes influence your relationship with your husband? Separate these pillars of wisdom from the selfish and independent spirit that often creeps into our hearts. Don't let them get lost in the midst of all that is going on in your life.

7. SPEAKING KNOWLEDGE

Proverbs 20:15: *"There is gold, and a multitude of rubies: but the lips of knowledge are a **precious jewel**."*

May God fill your lips with His wisdom and His word that it will constantly drop from your lips as you daily teach and train your children. Mothers should have lips that drop with wisdom and the knowledge of the Lord. Scriptures that speak about "dropping" words are Job 29:22 and Ezekiel 21:2. The word is *nataph* and means "to ooze, drip, flow, to speak by inspiration." May God's ways and His words literally ooze and drip from our lips.

8. A GOOD NAME

Ecclesiastes 7:1: *"A good name is **better than precious ointment** . . ."* Read also Proverbs 22:1.

It is more important to keep a good name than to compromise. If we give our word, let's keep it, even if it is inconvenient for us. I love the example of David in 1 Samuel 18:30: *"David behaved himself more wisely than all the servants of Saul; so that his name was much set by."* The words "much set by" literally mean "precious, to be prized, valuable."

PRAYER:

"Dear God and Father, please help me to separate vile thoughts from my mind—the negative thoughts of unbelief, discontentment, despair, bitterness, and self-pity. Lord, I want the meditations of my heart to be acceptable in Your sight. I ask You to transform my mind. Fill my mind with precious thoughts—thoughts of faith, hope, love, joy, gratitude, thankfulness, and joy. Amen."

AFFIRMATION:

I want the "unseen woman" of my heart to be kind and gentle.

WHAT IS PRECIOUS TO GOD?
And is it Precious to You?
Part 3

"Wherefore come out from among them,
and be ye separate, saith the Lord, and touch not the unclean thing;
and I will receive you, And will be a Father unto you,
and ye shall be my sons and daughters, saith the Lord Almighty"
(2 CORINTHIANS 6:17-18).

We continue our meditation from the last two days as we seek to dig up the things that are precious to God and separate them from the worthless.

9. GOD'S THOUGHTS TO US

Psalm 139:17-18: *"**How precious also are thy thoughts** unto me, O God! how great is the sum of them! If I should count them, they are more in number than the sand."* Read also Psalm 40:5.

Take time to meditate on God's thoughts. Let them fill your mind. When I was a young teen, I memorized Joshua 1:8 and it has been part of my life ever since: *"This book of the law shall not depart of thy mouth; but thou shalt meditate therein day and night, that thou mayest observe to do according to all that is written therein: for then thou shalt make thy way prosperous, and then thou shalt have good success."*

The word meditate in the Hebrew is *hagah* and it contains three different meanings:

a) to ponder, muse, meditate, imagine

b) to mutter, to murmur

c) to speak the word aloud

As you meditate on God's thoughts to you, murmur them to yourself. But don't keep them to yourself; speak them aloud to others. Bless others with the revelations that God gives to you.

Teach your children how to separate the vile thoughts from their minds and to think precious thoughts.

10. THE VALIANT WOMAN

We all know about the virtuous woman of Proverbs 31. But the word virtuous means more than what we usually think. The Hebrew is *chayil* meaning "virtue, valor, military strength." This woman is not a wimp. She is someone to be reckoned with. She has the strength of a soldier in battle. She has physical strength, but her inward strength is even greater.

I love the picture of the bride given in Song of Songs 6:10: "*Who is she that looketh forth as the morning, fair as the moon, clear as the sun, and terrible (awesome) as an army with banners?*"

She is not strong in independence but strong in the precious qualities that God has given to His female creation. And God pours out His praises upon her. Let's read Proverbs 31:10 in the AMPC version: "*A capable, intelligent, and virtuous woman—who is he who can find her? She is far more precious than jewels and her value is far above rubies or pearls.*"

Her strength of character enables her to submit to her husband instead of jumping up and down and demanding her own way.

Her strength of character guards her mouth instead of spitting out harsh and hurtful words.

Her strength of character enables her to stand strong against temptations of lust. She is strong in morality and purity. She will be true to her husband as long as she lives. She lives "only unto him" as she vowed on her wedding day. She stands true to her marriage vows in the good times and the difficult times, "for better, for worse, in sickness and in health . . ."

Her strength of character enables her to trust God even when life is overwhelming and full of trials. She keeps calm no matter what is happening around her.

Her strength of character causes her to purposely do good to her husband every day of her life (Proverbs 31:12).

Her strength of character saves her from getting sucked into the humanistic mindset of this world. She is not swayed by the crowd and what everyone does. Instead, she searches God's Word to see what God says.

She lives by the eternal principles of God's Word rather than the mindset of current society. She is prepared to do it God's way even if no one else follows!

Her strength of character keeps her from lowering herself to gossip and worthless words. When she speaks, she opens her mouth in kindness (Proverbs 31:26).

Her strength of character saves her from selfishness and thinking only of her own needs. Her heart is big and open to the needs of others (Proverbs 31:20 and 1 Peter 5:10).

Her strength of character enables her to work hard and not neglect the feeding and clothing of her family (Proverbs 31:14, 15, 21, 27).

Her strength of character causes her to fear the Lord rather than man (Proverbs 31:30).

This woman is very precious. But dear mothers, don't despair if you don't feel that you have arrived. You cannot wave a wand and become a virtuous woman. You grow into it as you go through your trials and your battles. They make you stronger and more *valiant in the fight* (Hebrews 11:34). You grow into it as you seek God, His precious Word, and His wisdom.

PRAYER:

"Dear God, please help me to be strong in godly character. I want to live a life that is precious to You, to my husband, and to my children. Amen."

AFFIRMATION:

I am seeking to be strong in the womanly strengths God has given to me, the strengths that build a strong marriage and family.

81

WHAT IS PRECIOUS TO GOD?
And is it Precious to You?
Part 4

*"Trust ye in the LORD forever: for in the
LORD JEHOVAH is everlasting strength."*
(ISAIAH 26:4).

11. GOD'S PRECIOUS PEOPLE

Lamentations 4:2: *"**The precious sons of Zion**, comparable to fine
gold. . ."*

This is how Jeremiah saw the people of God. Do we look upon God's
redeemed people as precious? Or do we destroy them by gossip and judg-
mental attitudes? Let's ask God to see His people as He sees them.

Psalm 16:2, 3 shows us how David looked at God's people: *"O my soul,
thou hast said unto the LORD, Thou art my Lord: my goodness extendeth not
to thee; But to the saints that are in the earth, and to the excellent, in whom
is all my delight."*

When David was overflowing with love and praise the Lord, he extend-
ed it not only to the Head, but also the body, the saints in whom he de-
lighted. He called them *"the excellent"* which is a powerful word. In the
Hebrew it is *addir* which means "mighty, gallant, great, powerful, glorious,
majestic, splendid, stately, and distinguished." This same Hebrew word describes God in Psalm 8:1. Isn't that amazing? The Bible uses the same word
to describe God and His people!

This may not be how the body of Christ is truly portrayed today. However, it is a picture of the triumphant bride who will emerge in the last days
"not having spot, or wrinkle, or any such thing" (Ephesians 5:27). In the
meantime, instead of judging, let's pray that God will truly be revealed in
each individual believer and consequently in the corporate body of Christ.

12. TRUSTING GOD WHEN HE DOESN'T ANSWER

Jeremiah 15:18, 19: *"Why is my pain perpetual, and my wound incurable, which refuseth to be healed? Wilt thou be altogether unto me as a liar, and as waters that fail? Therefore thus saith the LORD, If thou return, then will I bring thee again, and thou shalt stand before me: and if thou take forth the* **precious** *from the vile, thou shalt be as my mouth: let them return unto thee; but return not thou unto them."*

What is happening in this story? Jeremiah is down in the dumps. He doesn't trust God's promises any longer. God isn't coming through the way he wants him to. God isn't answering his prayers. He feels God has failed him and tells God so!

What is God's reaction to Jeremiah? The Living Bible says: *"The LORD replied, stop this foolishness and talk some sense! Only if you return to trusting me will I let you continue as my spokesman."* God says it is vile to Him when we complain that He fails us. He wants us to separate from our complaining and grumbling spirit and trust Him, even when He does not answer us. Can we trust Him even when we don't see an answer in sight? Can we trust Him when we can't even feel God?

Habakkuk 2:20 says: *"The Lord is in his holy temple: let all the earth keep silence before him."* In other words, God does not have to answer to mankind for what He does. He is God. We can have no arguments or queries against Him. All we must do is trust Him for He knows what He is doing.

Charles Spurgeon writes: "If you cannot trust God for temporals, how dare you trust him for spirituals? Can you trust him for your soul's redemption, and not rely upon him for a few lesser mercies? Is not God enough for thy need, or is his all-sufficiency too narrow for thy wants? Dost thou want another eye beside that of him who sees every secret thing? Is his heart faint? Is his arm weary? If so, seek another God; but if he be infinite, omnipotent, faithful, true, and all-wise, why gaddest thou abroad so much to seek another confidence? Why dost thou rake the earth to find another foundation, when this is strong enough to bear all the weight which thou canst ever build thereon?"

Job 13:15: *"Though he slay me, yet will I trust in him."*

God doesn't have to answer our prayers. He doesn't have to do it the way we want. He is the Sovereign Lord. All we must do is trust Him no matter what. This attitude is most precious to God.

PRAYER:

"Oh God, please forgive me for when I have not believed You. Help me to understand that I can trust You even when I can't see You at work. Help me to separate this vile complaining spirit from me. Amen."

AFFIRMATION:

"'Tis so sweet to trust in Jesus,
Just to take Him at His word;
Just to rest upon His promise;
Just to know, Thus saith the Lord."
~ Louisa M. R. Stead

82

A HAPPY FACE

"The show of their countenance doth witness against them"
(ISAIAH 3:9).

I remember walking one morning with my daughters, Evangeline and Serene. We walk fast but we talk as well. One morning I asked them the question, "How can we have a heavenly atmosphere in our homes?"

"Wear a happy face," Evangeline responded immediately. It was a good answer.

The face we wake up with in the morning determines the atmosphere in our home for the day. Even if you are feeling depressed, it is important to put on a happy face for your children and for your husband.

"But that's not being real," you answer.

I guess that depends on whether you prefer to give into your feelings or live by the power of Christ who lives within you! There are some who think that reality is living according to how you feel. That is deception. True reality is not living according to the dictates of my flesh or my emotions, but by faith, living the life of Christ who lives in me (Galatians 2:20).

You will be amazed at how your actions can change the way you feel. Perhaps you have been up all night with the baby. You feel tired. Put on a happy face anyway. Smile at your husband. Smile at each of your children. You'll begin to feel better right away. Yes, you will. Just try it.

Perhaps you are in a negative mood. Everything is going wrong, and self-pity is taking over. It's already showing on your face! Stop. Look up to the Lord and thank Him for your blessings. Thank Him that He is near you and will never leave you or forsake you.

Now show your happy face to your children. Your gloominess will soon leave. A downcast face will lock you into your tiredness or anxiety. A miserable face will sink you into self-pity, but a happy face will ignite a spark of joy in your heart.

Put on a smile, even if it is the last thing you feel like doing, and you will feel your heavy burden lift.

Proverbs 15:13: *"A merry heart maketh a cheerful countenance."*

The MLB version says: *"A happy heart makes the face look sunny."* Don't you love that?

And I love Proverbs 15:15 in the Living Bible: *"When a man is gloomy, everything seems to go wrong; when he is cheerful, everything seems right!"*

And what about Proverbs 17:22 in the Good News Bible? *"Being cheerful keeps you healthy. It is slow death to be gloomy all the time."* Gloominess not only brings death to you, but to your whole family. It casts a shadow over your home.

It's a good idea to type or write out these Scriptures and pin them up in appropriate places in your home, for yourself, and for your children!

Dear mother, as you look to Jesus, you are changed into His image from glory to glory (2 Corinthians 3:18). In the same way, your children look to you all day long and you influence their lives by your countenance. They become like what they see on your face. What a challenging truth!

The MLB of our above Scripture, Isaiah 3:9 states: *"The expression of their faces witnesses against them."* I know you have heard the expression, "Looks can kill!" The expression on your face brings death or life to your home.

Make a smiling face and a positive attitude part of your life. Make it a habit. Show it by example to your children and teach them to make it a habit in their lives. Don't allow your children to get into moods, be grumpy, or to pout! We never allowed this for one second in our children and they don't battle with any of these attitudes today.

Psalm 34:5 (NLT): *"Those who look to him for help will be radiant with joy; no shadow of shame will darken their faces."*

Put on a happy face and change the atmosphere of your home.

PRAYER:

"Dearest Jesus, I look up to You and behold Your face. I want to be changed into Your image. I want to be changed from glory to glory. Shine the light of Your countenance upon me so that it shines from my face to my children. Help me to remember that there is a higher truth than my feelings. It is the truth of Your life in me, and this is the life I want to live. Thank You, Jesus. Amen."

AFFIRMATION:

Feelings come and feelings go,
Feelings are deceiving.
I'll put a smile upon my face,
That's a lot more pleasing!

83

CONTINUE ON

"Continue in the grace of God"
(ACTS 13:43).

God has given us so many wonderful promises in the Word of God. However, most of them are prefixed or suffixed by a condition. One of the biblical conditions is "to continue," to keep on keeping on. Let's look at them together, shall we?

1. IF YOU CONTINUE IN THE WORDS OF JESUS

Jesus said in John 8:31-32 (NASB): *"If you **continue in My word**, then you are truly My disciples; and you will know the truth, and the truth will set you free."*

I have always loved confessing: *"You will know the truth and the truth will set you free."* However, one day I noticed the true context of these words. We will only know the truth when we walk in obedience to God's Word. We must continue in the Word, or we can be led into deception.

The line by Alexander Pope is true: "A little learning is a dangerous thing." It's not enough to half understand God's principles. We must search after the whole truth. And it's not enough to search after it; we must obey it and walk in it.

James 1:25 (NKJB): *"He who looks into the perfect law of liberty and **continues** in it, and is not a forgetful hearer but a doer of the work, this one will be blessed in what he does."* After realizing this, I wrote in my daily devotional book the following words:

Disobedience leads to deception!

Obedience leads to truth!

Delayed obedience is disobedience!

2. IF YOU CONTINUE IN THE FAITH

In Colossians 1:22, 23 God promises to present you *"holy and unblame-*

*able and unreprovable in His sight: **if ye continue in the faith** grounded and settled, and be not moved away from the hope of the gospel . . ."*

It's not enough to receive Christ by faith into our hearts. We must continue in the faith. It's not how we begin but how we end that matters most. Jesus said: *"He that endureth to the end shall be saved"* (Matthew 10:22).

Don't let what people say turn you away from your faith in God. Because many people are saying something different does not mean that it is the truth. Romans 3:4 always challenges me: *"Let God be true, but every man a liar."* Will I continue to follow God's truth, even if everyone else is doing or saying something different? Will I walk in God's truth even if it may be a different step to everyone else?

Don't let disappointments and hardships move you away from your faith in God. Let's face it. Life isn't easy. Life isn't perfect. Just because you believe in God doesn't exempt you from difficulties. Paul encouraged the new believers *"to **continue in the faith**, and that we must through much tribulation enter into the kingdom of God"* (Acts 14:22). When writing to the Thessalonian believers, he exhorted them not to be moved or shaken by afflictions (1 Thessalonians 3:3).

3. IF YOU CONTINUE IN FAITH, LOVE, HOLINESS, AND SELF-CONTROL

1 Timothy 2:15 (NET) says that women will be *"delivered through child-bearing, if she **continues** in faith and love and holiness with self-control."*

This is a wonderful promise for mothers, isn't it? The word "childbearing" is *teknogonia* and not only means birthing a child, but embraces the whole aspect of mothering— nursing, rearing children, and all our mothering duties in the home. The Bible promises that we will be preserved (physically, emotionally, and spiritually) when we embrace this lifestyle. But there's more. We must also *"continue in faith and love and holiness with self-control."*

The word self-control is *sophrosume* in the Greek and means "soundness of mind or self-control." We as mothers should not be pulled this way or that way by the fashions and dictates of the world and society but should understand and exercise sound judgment on all matters. Most versions of the Bible translate it "self-control."

These wonderful attributes of faith, love, holiness, and self-control should be the testimony of a mother's life. You may not feel they are your testimony at this present time. Perhaps you have felt the way is too hard and you've stopped along the way. You've given up on your vision. Dear mother, come now, get up again. Continue!

A mother's life is a life of continuance. Don't give up. Remain strong in the truth. Don't be sidetracked. Continue on, little by little. Press through your problems, your heartaches, your fears, and your inadequacies. Strive for holiness in your personal and family life.

Keep your eyes on the finishing line!

PRAYER:
"Dear Lord Jesus, please give me grace to continue in the race. Please give me courage to keep on with the vision You have given to me, no matter what obstacles loom before me. Please help me to stand fast in the faith and not be moved. Increase my desire to abide in Your Word, to obey Your Word, and to continue in it. Thank You for Your faithful promises to me as I continue in Your ways. Amen."

AFFIRMATION:
No matter what, I will keep on "keeping on."

84

THE ATMOSPHERE OF YOUR HOME

*"Your wife shall be like a fruitful vine in the very heart of your house,
your children like olive plants all around your table"*
(PSALM 128:3 NKJV).

There are many important aspects to mothering and homebuilding—planning, teaching, nurturing, cooking, cleaning, and the list goes on. They are all important but there is something that overrides them all. I believe it is the atmosphere we create. To permeate your home with a pleasant and peaceful atmosphere is more powerful than anything else you can do. It is the atmosphere that your children will remember when they grow older. It is the atmosphere that creates precious memories. It is the atmosphere of your home that will shape their lives—for good or for bad.

S. D. Gordon in his book, *Quiet Talks on Home Ideals*, writes: "The influence exerted by the mother is great beyond the power of our minds to think or of our words to tell. The making of the child's character is in the mother's hands to a degree that is nothing short of startling."

Again, he writes: "The atmosphere of the home is breathed in by the child, and exerts an influence in his training more, by far, than all other things put together. The child receives more by unconscious absorption than in any other way. He is all ears and eyes and open pores. He is open at every angle and point and direction, and all between. He is an absorbing surface; he takes in constantly; he takes in what is there; and what he takes in makes him. The spirit of the home then is the one thing on which the keen mind and earnest heart of the father and mother will center most, for the child's sake."

To create an atmosphere of harmony and joy in your home is more important than keeping up with all the curriculums you have planned to teach your children. Alfred Edershaim in his book, *The Life and Times of Je-*

sus the Messiah writes: "Education begins in the home . . . it is imparted by influence and example, before it comes by teaching; it is acquired by what it seen and heard, before it is laboriously learned from books; its real object becomes instinctively felt, before its goal is consciously sought."

Your children will learn and thrive in an atmosphere of rest far more than finishing all their work in an atmosphere of tension. True education is not completing workbooks, it is gaining an understanding about life and truth. The greatest gift you can give your children is an insatiable love for learning. They will be turned on to learning in a loving and restful atmosphere. They will be turned off where there is tension and stress.

They will forget most of the facts and figures you try to cram into their brains, but they won't forget your attitude or the atmosphere. That's right, it is your attitude that makes the atmosphere. The **attitude** of your heart will determine the **atmosphere** of your home, which will affect the **actions** of each member of your family.

You, dear mother, set the tone for the home. Keep your eyes upon the Lord and cry out to Him to fill your home with His blessed presence. There is nothing more beautiful than the presence of the Lord. Your house may seem too small, you may feel that you haven't got all the things you need, but you are rich if you have the presence of God in your home.

There is nothing richer that you can give your children. Your children will not be deprived if they don't have all the material things that others have, but they will be deprived if they don't experience the presence of God.

It starts with you. Start the day with God yourself. Saturate, satiate, and soak yourself in God's presence. Start the day speaking forth God's peace. Minister God's peace to each of your children. As you wake up Johnny and ruffle his hair, say, "Johnny, God's peace is upon you. You will live in peace all through the day."

"Peace to you, Sam."

"Monica, we are going to have such a joyful day today, Won't it be fun?"

"Children, I love being your mother. I love teaching you. I love being with you. Aren't we going to have a wonderful day together?"

Your confession sets the atmosphere for the day. You determine a miserable atmosphere or a life-giving atmosphere by the words you speak. You know the words of Proverbs 18:21 but let's be reminded again: *"Death and life are in the power of the tongue."*

The NLT states: *"The tongue can bring death or life; those who love to talk will reap the consequences."* It's interesting that "death" is mentioned before "life" in this Scripture. Maybe because we speak more words of death than life! Do you think you can change that in your life? Make it a habit to eliminate all negative words and speak only life-giving words. What an amazing difference this will make to the atmosphere of your home.

Setting a lovely table and preparing meals for your family also provide a wonderful and welcoming atmosphere. Gathering your family to sit around the table is one of the greatest ways to make memories for your children. It is the foundation of family life and too many families are too busy to sit together for their meals these days. Don't let this happen in your home.

PRAYER:

"Dear Father, help me to create a lovely atmosphere in my home. Most of all, I need You to come and fill our home with Your presence. I want You to come to our table as we eat our meals together. Please saturate our home with Your love and peace and joy. Amen."

AFFIRMATION:

I'm tired of the rat race. I'm slowing down to create a loving and restful atmosphere in our home.

FROM DOUBT TO DECEPTION

"Now the serpent was more subtle than any beast of the field which the LORD God had made. And he said unto the woman, Yea, hath God said, Ye shall not eat of every tree of the garden?"
(GENESIS 3:1).

Satan doesn't blatantly deceive us. He does it subtly. He puts doubts in our mind about what God says. The first temptation to the first man and woman was: *"Hath God said?"* He still tries it on each one of us. God speaks His truth into our lives through His Word and the voice of the tempter whispers in our ear, "Did God really say that? I think it means something else!"

We must constantly watch out for the doubts of the deceiver. Because you love the Lord, he will not tempt you with blatant sin. You wouldn't even be tempted. You would tell him to leave in the name of Jesus. Instead, he tries to get you by doubts and questions. Or he will make the truth sound true when it is not really true. He makes his temptation sound very plausible. When he tempted Eve, he made it sound so good, pleasant, and desirable. He even made his temptation sound wise!

Genesis 3:6 says: *"When the woman saw that the tree was **good** for food, and that it was **pleasant** to the eyes, and a tree to be **desired to make one wise**, she took of the fruit thereof and did eat, and gave also unto her husband with her; and he did eat."*

This is why we must constantly keep up our antennas against deception. Charles Spurgeon writes: "Discernment is not knowing the difference between right and wrong. It is knowing the difference between right and almost right."

Satan always makes his temptations seem very good and wise according to this world's ways. That's why we must become very familiar with God's Word. It is the antidote to deception. Those who study how to discover fraud do not train to become familiar with fraudulent bills (which keep changing all the time). Instead, they learn to become familiar with the feel of the genuine note. It is only when they know it thoroughly that they will detect the fraudulent.

It is the same with us. It is only when we are truly acquainted with what God says that we will detect the deceit. Otherwise, we can easily be fooled.

Let's begin with the first words God spoke into the ears of man. We see an example of this in the matter of trusting God for our children. Genesis 1:28 says: *"Be fruitful, and multiply, and replenish the earth."* God is the author of life. God loves life. Satan, who comes to "steal, kill and destroy" is the destroyer of life and is against this command. Therefore, he puts doubts in the hearts of God's people. "Does God really mean that? I have a son and a daughter. I have done my part."

It seems wise to delay your family or limit your family. You will have more time to fulfill your career or do things you have planned. You will have more money to build a better house, buy a better car, and save for college education for your children. It feels **good** because you will have less work to do and won't have to go through so many sleepless nights. It seems **desirable** because it will be less work and give you more time to do want you want in life. But it is deception, and it is contrary to God's Word.

It is amazing that the Christian church has imbibed this deception and now thinks that it is truth. Pre-marital counseling in most churches includes teaching on birth control! What Scriptures do they have for this? There are none. How incredibly Satan has imbedded his deceptions into the church!

Once Satan has sown the seed of doubt in our hearts, he then begins to deliberately contradict God's Word. We would not receive this contradiction if we didn't first have doubts about what God says. In Genesis 3:4 we read that the serpent said: *"Ye shall not surely die."* This was in total rebellion to God's direct word: *"Ye shall not eat of it, neither shall ye touch it, lest ye die."*

We see how Satan works. He begins with doubts which lead to deception. This distortion of God's truth leads to defecting and disobeying His commands. Then we experience the degenerating. And then the final destructing of His design.

I love to recite the following lines. They are good lines to teach your children too:

If Jesus said it, I'll believe it, I'll believe it till I die!
It is written in the Bible; His Word can never lie!
Though the mountains be removed and cast into the sea,
If Jesus said it, I'll believe it, I'll believe eternally!

PRAYER:

"God of Truth, please save me from deception. Please save my children from the deceptions of this world. Please help me, by the power of Your Holy Spirit dwelling in me to make time each day to read God's Word to our children. I want them to be richly filled with Your Word so they will recognize deception when they face it. Amen."

AFFIRMATION:

If Jesus said it, I'll believe it, I'll believe it till I die!

86

CAN YOU KEEP YOUR HONOR?
Part 1

"A gracious women retaineth honor
(PROVERBS 11:16).

Every woman likes to be respected and honored. She wants her husband and children to praise her. The wonderful thing is that God has already given honor and glory to women.

Proverbs 11:16 tells us that a gracious woman retains her honor and glory. Our job is to hold on to this glory that God gave us by divine creation. God created us female to reveal God's maternal anointing to our families and to the world. The word retain means to "lay hold of, to keep fast, to maintain." We must lay hold of this honor and not let it go.

Revelation 3:11 says: *"Hold that fast which thou hast, that no man take thy crown."*

The glory and crown of womanhood is easy to lose. In fact, it is fading away in our feminist society. As the modern woman lays down her God-given honor and pursues the man's world, she loses her respect. I can remember a time when men immediately gave up their seat for a woman when riding buses and trains, etc. I rarely see this happen today. Men rarely open the door for a woman. They seldom make way for her to go first.

Instinctively, a man wants to be the knight in shining armor who protects and saves his princess. It is his privilege and prerogative to protect and honor women, especially a nursing mother or mother with child. But today many women would rather fight for their own rights. They want to find their identity in the corporate world rather than in the home, but in doing so, they lose the honor and glory God ordained for them. And man loses his gallantry to protect the woman.

We should not take our honor lightly. The Hebrew word for honor is *kabod* and means "weighty, to carry an authority in speech and demeanor, esteem, glory, majesty." It comes from a root word that means "to be heavy." God did not create women to be insignificant. No, we can "carry a lot of weight." I'm not talking about physical weight, but the weight of honor and glory. We have the power to influence the world mightily for God.

How can we reveal this graciousness? Let's look at five areas beginning with M.

1. OUR MATERNALNESS

We walk in graciousness when we embrace our maternalness. Our greatest honor comes from being who God created us to be, and that is maternal. God has innately put a motherly instinct in women. It is the very core of our being. It is the heart of womanhood. When poets and song-writers want to portray tenderness, they speak of motherhood or create paintings of mothers and babies. The Bible uses the same Hebrew word for a woman's womb as it does to describe God's tenderhearted compassion.

We all know about the Titanic disaster. Who did they seek to save first? The women and children. They did not need a conference to decide this matter. It was their first thought. Women are the life-givers of the world and children are the future generation and are therefore to be honored.

God created us to mother, to nurture, and to reach out to the needy in love and compassion. When we lay aside our inherent maternity to pursue the man's role of providing for the family, we lose honor. When we lay aside having children for the sake of career, we deny who we are. Society has tried to reverse this basic law, but it hasn't worked. As women have left the home in droves, we have reaped an epidemic divorce rate and the weakening of the family.

It is true that there are some women who do not marry, and many who are not able to conceive children. Are they denied maternalness? No. This does not alter their innate maternity. They will be fulfilled in their woman-ly glory as they pour out their compassionate hearts to the lonely, needy, and those whom God lays upon their hearts.

I think of some of the women who have influenced the world for God—Susanna Wesley, Sarah Edwards, Catherine Booth, Mary Slessor, Gladys Aylward, Corrie Ten Boom, and Mother Theresa, and the list goes on. Some of these women were great mothers; others never married or had children of their own, but they all poured out their lives to the needy and ministered out of their motherly instinct. And in turn we honor them as mothers.

God commands children: *"Honor thy father and thy mother; which is the first commandment with promise; That it may be well with thee, and thou mayest live long on the earth"* (Ephesians 6:1). God first gave this command in Exodus 20:12.

Mothers have honor, not only because they are good or diligent, but because of the state of motherhood itself. Fatherhood and motherhood are the first careers God gave to men and women. All other careers serve this foremost God-given commission.

2. OUR MEEKNESS

"Meekness?" I hear you question. It's not a very popular word, is it? But it is a godly word. In fact, meekness in women is something that is very precious to God. It is a mark of godly womanhood. 1 Peter 3:4 has been a challenge to me all my life: *"But let it be the hidden man of the heart, in that which is not corruptible, even the ornament of a meek and quiet spirit, which is in the sight of God of great price."* Another translation says that God *"delights in it."*

Meekness is not weakness. Someone has said, "If you think it is weak to be meek, try to be meek for a week!" Meekness is not a personality type. I know quiet people who are very stubborn. I know exuberant people who have a soft and tender spirit. Jesus was *"meek and lowly in heart"* and yet he changed the course of history (Matthew 11:29). Moses was *"very meek, above all the men which were upon the face of the earth"* and yet he was a mighty leader (Numbers 12:3).

This gentle humility does not belong to our flesh. It belongs to the new life of Christ who lives within us. It is only the Holy Spirit who can make this happen in our lives. Wuest's Word Studies comments that this meekness "is that temper of spirit in which we accept God's dealings with us as good and therefore without disputing or resisting. It is the humble heart which is also the meek; and which, as such, does not fight against God and struggle and contend with Him."

The Scriptures reveal God's heart about this subject: *"God resisteth the proud, and giveth grace to the humble. Humble yourselves therefore under the mighty hand of God, that he may exalt you in due time"* (1 Peter 5:5, 6). Also read James 4:6; 10; Isaiah 57:15; and 66:2.

A proud spirit is ugly and takes away our graciousness, but a meek and humble spirit will ultimately bring honor.

"The reward of humility and the fear of the LORD are riches, honor and life" (Proverbs 22:4 NASB).

PRAYER:

"Dear Father, thank You for creating me to be a woman to show forth the glory of Your compassionate and nurturing heart. Help me to stand fast in the truth and in the purpose for which You created me. I want to be faithful to reveal You glory to my family and to the world. Amen."

AFFIRMATION:

I am walking in the glory of who God created me to be.

CAN YOU KEEP YOUR HONOR?
Part 2

"Favor is deceitful, and beauty is vain; but a woman that feareth the LORD, she shall be praised"
(PROVERBS 11:16).

Today we look at three more areas where we reveal our graciousness.

3. OUR MARRIAGE

Marriage certainly exposes our graciousness or ungraciousness! It is no use acting piously at church or at the supermarket if you are "out of sorts" with your husband at home. There are many women who think it is degrading to submit to a man. They would rather jump up and down and demand their own way, do their own thing, and be free from any protective authority. But this kind of behavior is childish. Three-year-old children like to demand their own way. It is a mature woman who learns to submit with meekness. It is something we learn to do as we allow the Holy Spirit to have His way in our lives.

It is interesting that the New Testament exhorts the wife to honor her husband but also commands the husband to honor his wife. Both are a different kind of honor. Let's look at them, shall we?

Ephesians 5:33: *"The wife see that she reverence her husband."* The word reverence means "to be in awe, to revere." We get the full meaning as we read the Amplified Classic version of the Bible: *"However, let each man of you (without exception) love his wife as (being in a sense) his very own self and let the wife see that she respects and reverences her husband (that she notices him, regards him, honors him, prefers him, venerates, and esteems him; and that she defers to him, praises him, and loves and admires him exceedingly)."* Wow!

269

Well, what about the man? 1 Peter 3:7 directs the husband: *"Likewise, ye husbands, dwell with them according to knowledge, giving honor unto the wife, as unto the weaker vessel, and as being heirs together of the grace of life; that your prayers be not hindered."* The word "honor" in this passage means "to buy with a price, the highest degree, valuable, esteem, dignity, preciousness." The husband must see his wife as his most precious and valuable possession and honor her in the highest degree.

The husband in Proverbs 31:29 praises his wife, not only personally, but to all the elders in the gates of the city with these words: *"Many daughters have done virtuously, but thou excellest them all."* What greater honor could a woman receive? It is more blessed to receive honor from an appreciative husband than all the organizations in the world.

4. OUR MANNER OF LIFE

We reveal graciousness through our comportment—the way we walk, dress, sit, smile, and speak. We show our graciousness by the we talk to our husbands and children, the way we welcome people to our home, and the way we react when things don't go our way. I love the way Milton describes Eve in *Paradise Lost* . . .

> "Grace was in all her steps, heaven in her eye,
> In every gesture dignity and love."

A woman of graciousness and glory will not wear scanty or tight clothes. She dresses beautifully, but modestly. She glories in her femininity. She seeks to be gracious in every department of her life.

5. OUR MOUTH

This is where we make it or break it; keep it or lose it! Every time we open our mouths, we lift up or downgrade the dignity of womanhood. There is nothing more unattractive than seeing a mother shouting at her children in a supermarket. There is nothing more hideous than seeing a wife stand up to her husband or degrade him.

It was recorded of Jesus: *"All bare him witness, and wondered at the gracious words which proceeded out of his mouth"* (Luke 4:22). They marveled because they were not used to hearing such words. The Greek word for gracious is *charis*. My husband loves this word and gave it to our daughter,

Serene as her second name. It pictures God's salvation for us. It speaks of a favor given without expectation of return. It portrays God's lovingkindness to sinners. What was His motive? Nothing but His free-hearted, abandoning love to us who do not deserve it.

When Jesus returned to His Father, He sent the Holy Spirit to indwell us so He could manifest His life in us on earth. When we are born again, Jesus Christ comes to live in us by His Spirit and He wants to continue speaking these gracious words through us.

These are words we speak even when the listener doesn't deserve them. Has your husband been nasty to you? Shouted at you? Instead of shouting back, could you try and answer with soft and tender words? When someone speaks hurtfully to you, could you retaliate with kind words? Give them words of blessing, not because they deserve it, but because the grace of God fills your heart and pours out from your lips.

Ephesians 4:29 (NKJV): *"Let no corrupt word proceed out of your mouth, but what is good for necessary edification, that it may impart grace to the hearers."*

Ephesians 4:29 (TPT): *"Never let ugly or hateful words come from your mouth, but instead let your words become beautiful gifts that encourage others; do this by speaking words of grace to help them."*

Colossians 4:6 (TPT): *"Let every word you speak be drenched with grace."*

The testimony of the Above Rubies woman is that: *"She openeth her mouth with wisdom; and in her tongue is the law of kindness"* (Proverbs 31:26).

This is our greatest mark of graciousness. When we open our mouths, we retain or lose our glory.

PRAYER:
"Dear God and Father, please touch my lips with Your holy fire. Please set a guard upon my lips. I often say words I wished I'd never said. I need Your anointing upon my lips. Amen."

AFFIRMATION:
Moment by moment I'm yielding my mouth to God's holy anointing.

88

ON THE SHELF OR IN YOUR HEART?

"I have more understanding than all my teachers:
for thy testimonies are my meditation. I understand
more than the ancients, because I keep thy precepts"
(Psalm 119:99, 100).

How big a place does the Bible have in your home? Although 87 percent of American homes have at least one Bible, Gallup calls the United States "a nation of Biblical illiterates." The Bible is on the shelf but not in the heart.

Horace Greeley, founder of the *New York Tribune*, stated, "It is impossible to mentally or socially enslave a Bible-reading people." Is this why most "Christians" are vulnerable to deception? They own Bibles but don't read them. This great freedom-loving nation of America is already enslaved by the deceptive ideologies of humanism and aggressive socialism.

It is time for the Bible to come off the shelf. It is time to read the Bible personally. It is time to read it to our children. The Bible is our greatest constitution. It is the basis for our mindset. It is the foundation for our nation. It is the blueprint for our success. God encouraged Joshua: *"This Book of the Law shall not depart from your mouth, but you shall meditate in it day and night that you may observe to do according to all that is written in it. For then you will make your way prosperous, and then you will have good success"* (Joshua 1:8 NKJV).

How much of God's Word is in your heart? How much is in your children's hearts? Or perhaps I should ask a more pointed question? How much of God's Word is in your mouth and your children's mouths? God's mandate to parents is for us to not only get His Word into their hearts, but their mouths. Are you and your children familiar with God's Word? Can you speak out with your mouth the basic Scriptures?

Check your children. Try them out. Tonight, at your table begin reciting a common Scripture and ask your children to finish it. Get them to raise their hands rather than calling out. For example . . .

"*Thy word have I hid in mine heart . . .*" Who can finish this Scripture?

"*The wages of sin is death . . .*" First hand up to finish this Scripture.

"*If thou shalt confess with thy mouth the Lord Jesus . . .*" Who knows the rest of this verse?

"*Put on the whole armor of God . . .*" What's next?

"*Behold, I stand at the door and knock . . .*" Who can say the rest of this Scripture?

This will be a fun test with your children. I hope they do well. If not, may you be spurred on to read the Scriptures more faithfully to your children and even do some memory work with them. God's mandate to parents in Isaiah 59:21 is to get His word into the **mouths** of our children, our grandchildren, our great-grandchildren, and the following generations. Did you notice that it does not say their hearts, but their **mouths**? Look up this Scripture to make sure I am telling you the truth.

Don't let the Bible be a "strange" thing in your home. Hosea 8:12 is a sad Scripture: "*I have written to him the great things of my law, but they were counted as a strange thing.*"

Apart from our personal devotions, my husband reads the Bible to our household each morning and evening at our Family Devotions. The concept of "Family Devotions" or the "Family Altar" are forgotten words in most modern "Christian" homes today. And yet this was the normal lifestyle in the early God-fearing homes of our nation.

Isn't it shocking that 50 percent of Christian marriages end in divorce and 47 percent are contaminated by pornography? What an indictment against God's people who are meant to be His holy representatives, shining like lights in this dark and deceived world.

It is time for families to come back—back to sitting at the table together for their meals, especially the evening meal when everyone arrives home from the day's activities. It's time to come back to reading God's Word and praying together before we leave the table. If we do not have time to have Bible reading and prayer with our families, we are too busy! It should be the crowning moment of every day.

If you did not grow up enjoying this blessing and have no idea how to go about it, there's an answer for you. In our home we use *"The Daily Light on the Daily Path,"* which is a compilation of Scriptures on a specific theme for the morning and evening. You don't have to wonder about what to read. You turn to the date and It's all there for you.

To read the Bible daily to your children and to make it a priority in your home is not just a good idea. It is imperative for the saving of our nation. It is crucial for the preservation of future generations—our children, grand-children, and great-grandchildren.

What are you doing about it?

PRAYER:

"Dear Father, please forgive us for not being faithful to read Your Living Word to our family each day. Please help me to be proactive about establishing the time and place each day for this important meeting with You. Please help us to be faithful to impart Your Word into the hearts and mouths of our children. Amen."

AFFIRMATION:

I'm making our family times with God the priority of each day.

SCRIPTURE REFERENCES FOR BIBLE QUESTONS:

In case you don't know where to find the Scripture questions you will ask your children, here they are for you: Psalm 119:11; Romans 6:23; Romans 10:9, Ephesians 6:11; and Revelation 3:20. If your children can tell you the rest of the Scripture, you could then ask them if they know which book of the Bible it is in.

THE DAILY LIGHT ON THE DAILY PATH

This daily devotional is purely God's Word for every morning and evening of the year. If you don't know where to start, this is the book to get. It also has creative ideas for you at the beginning of each month to help make it exciting for your children.

Go to: http://tinyurl.com/CreativeIdeasToReadBible

START BEFORE BIRTH

"Then Manoah entreated the LORD, and said . . .
teach us what we shall do unto the child that shall be born . . .
How shall we order the child, and how shall we do unto him?"
(JUDGES 13:8, 12).

This prayer is from the story of Samson when the angel came to Mano-ah and his wife to tell them they would have a son. Manoah's wife was infertile and unable to conceive so this was a great miracle. God also told them that this son was to be dedicated to God as a Nazarite from his birth and that he would rise up to deliver God's people from the Philistines who had subdued them for the last forty years.

There are three things we notice about Manoah's prayer:

1. HE ENTREATED THE LORD

This was not a formal prayer but an imploring, beseeching, and desper-ate plea to know what to do. How we need God's wisdom and anointing as we parent our children. Cry out to God for your children, dear mother. He will hear your cry. When you ask for wisdom, He will give it to you (James 1:5).

2. HE PRAYED FOR THE CHILD BEFORE HE WAS BORN

Don't wait until your child is born to start praying. Start praying for your child as soon as you conceive. Bathe your unborn child in prayer. Ask your husband to lay your hands on your womb and pray over him/her. Read the Scriptures to your unborn child. Seek God for the destiny of this child. This will help you in the naming of your child too.

You don't even have to wait until you conceive to get a vision for chil-dren and to pray for your future children. God gave Abraham a vision for children when there was no earthly hope of him having children. God told him to look at the stars in the heavens and try to count them and He promised: *"So shall thy seed be."* Abraham believed God's unimaginable promise and God counted it to him for righteousness (Genesis 15:3-5).

God gave Jacob a vision for children when he was a young unmarried man. Before he even had a girlfriend and wasn't even thinking about marriage, God said to him: *"Thy seed shall be as the dust of the earth, and thou shalt spread abroad to the west, and to the east, and to the north, and to the south: and in thee and in thy seed shall all the families of the earth be blessed"* (Genesis 28:14).

3. HE SOUGHT GOD'S GUIDANCE ON HOW TO RAISE HIS CHILD

The margin of the King James Bible and other translations write the question in verse 12 this way: *"What will be the boy's rule of life, and his work?"* The word rule or order is the Hebrew word *mishpat* and usually translated justice. Justice means the use of authority to uphold what is right. It relates to all functions of government.

Justice is a particularly important part of parenting. As parents, we must seek to know and understand justice. We must have a true knowledge of what is right and wrong in the eyes of the Lord so we can train our children to know justice. We must execute justice in the training of our children, or they will not know the true knowledge of God.

God's favor was upon Abraham because he ordered his household in the ways of justice. God said: *"Shall I hide from Abraham that thing which I do . . . For I know him, that he will command his children and his household after him, and they shall keep the way of the LORD, to do justice and judgment"* (Genesis 18:17-19). Because justice is a primary attribute of God, it is important to Him and in the raising of our families.

PRAYER:
"Oh God, please teach me how to train my children in Your ways. Help me to teach them justice. Help me to raise children who are not "wishy-washy" but strong in their convictions. Amen."

AFFIRMATION:
I am seeking to understand justice so I can execute it rightly.

90

WHICH KINGDOM?

"Seek ye first the kingdom of God, and his righteousness;
and all these things shall be added unto you"
(MATTHEW 6:33).

What is the kingdom of God? It is the rule and reign of Christ in our individual hearts, families, the church, and the nation. You will know when you are at odds with the kingdom of Satan because God's kingdom is opposite to Satan's kingdom. Neither of the two do meet. If we fit in nicely with the world, we better check if we are really part of God's kingdom. We can only belong to one kingdom or the other. And sorry, belonging to God's kingdom will not make us popular with the world.

GOD'S KINGDOM IS A KINGDOM OF TRUTH

Satan's kingdom is one of lies and deception; God's kingdom is a kingdom of truth. Satan is the father of lies (John 8:44). When we are part of God's kingdom we passionately seek after truth. We discern what are lies and deception and depart from them.

GOD'S KINGDOM IS A KINGDOM OF LIFE

Satan's kingdom is a kingdom of death; God's kingdom is a kingdom of life. When we belong to God's kingdom, we embrace life. We open our hearts to the children He wants to give us. We are life-givers and not life-stoppers. Life-stoppers are antithesis to God's kingdom.

Matthew 19:14 (GW): *"Jesus said, 'Don't stop children from coming to me! Children like these are part of God's kingdom."* Children are at the center of the kingdom of God. If we don't want children, we are opposite to the kingdom of God. Also read Mark 10:15, 16.

GOD'S KINGDOM IS A KINGDOM OF HOLINESS

God has laws and commandments for His kingdom, and we can only enter His kingdom on His terms (1 Corinthians 6:9-11). The devil's kingdom loves to compromise God's ways and preaches we must tolerate evil and never judge. The devil deceives us by convincing us that we can have eternal life without repenting from our sin.

The devil's kingdom does not stand for judging sin. Read Ephesians 5:5; 1 Peter 1:15-17; Hebrews 12:14; Revelation 21:8; and 22:15. Did you know that there is one Scripture that all the homosexuals, sex-traffickers, and adulterers love? It's *"Judge not, that ye be not judged."* Isn't it amazing how they all know and love that Scripture even though they don't believe the Bible?

GOD'S KINGDOM IS AN UNSHAKEABLE KINGDOM

Satan's kingdom has no surety, but God's kingdom is an unshakeable kingdom (Hebrews 12:28). When things in our lives begin to shake and fall apart around us, we continue rejoicing because we belong to an unshakeable kingdom that will never pass away. We will not be moved by our circumstances.

GOD'S KINGDOM IS A KINGDOM OF RIGHTEOUSNESS, PEACE, AND JOY IN THE HOLY GHOST

Satan's kingdom is riddled with anxiety, worries, fears, depression, and destruction. God's kingdom is filled with *"righteousness, and peace, and joy in the Holy Ghost"* (Romans 14:17).

GOD'S KINGDOM IS A ROYAL KINGDOM

Satan's kingdom is a usurping kingdom. God's kingdom is a glorious, majestic, and royal kingdom (Psalm 145:11, 12). He is King of kings and Lord of lords and to Him every knee will bow (Philippians 2:9-11).

Because we belong to a royal kingdom, we are no longer normal citizens. Because Christ dwells in us we bear the image of the heavenly. We walk in majesty and dignity. We die to our flesh and live the life of Christ which abides in us. God has *"delivered us from the power of darkness, and hath translated us into the kingdom of his dear Son"* (Colossians 1:13).

Therefore, we live like royalty. We live in a way that is conducive to those who belong to a royal kingdom. We are now *"kings and priests unto God"* (Revelation 1:6).

GOD'S KINGDOM IS A KINGDOM OF FAITH

People seek after riches in Satan's kingdom, but God's kingdom is a kingdom of faith (Mark 10:23, 24).

GOD'S KINGDOM IS AN EVERLASTING KINGDOM

The kingdoms of this world will all pass away but we belong to an everlasting kingdom! Hallelujah! Doesn't this make you shout for joy?

Psalm 145:13: *"Thy kingdom is an everlasting kingdom, and thy dominion endureth throughout all generations."*

Psalm 146:10: *"The LORD shall reign forever, even thy God, O Zion, unto all generations. Praise ye the LORD."*

Daniel 7:14b: *"His dominion is an everlasting dominion, which shall not pass away, and his kingdom that which shall not be destroyed."*

Let's allow God to rule and reign in our lives and in every room of our homes.

PRAYER:

"Dear Father, thank You that You have redeemed me by Your precious blood and accepted me into Your eternal kingdom. I thank You that I live in Your kingdom now. Please anoint me to live by Your kingdom principles and live the victorious kingdom lifestyle that You have planned for me. Amen."

AFFIRMATION:

No matter what happens in my home, no matter what happens all around me, no matter what happens in the nation, I belong to an unshakeable kingdom. I cannot be moved.

91

JOYFUL
MOTHERING

*"For whosoever will save his life shall lose it; but whosoever
shall lose his life for My sake and the gospels, the same shall find it"*
(MARK 8:35).

As mothers talk with me about their concerns and problems, the more I realize we must come back to a basic, fundamental, biblical, and eternal principle. Without it we can't succeed. What is it?

It's found in Mark 8:35: *"For whosoever will save his life shall lose it; but whosoever shall lose his life for my sake and the gospels, the same shall save it."*

Dear mother, the secret to blessing lies in laying down our lives. Oh no! We don't like that secret, do we? However, we may as well face it. Motherhood is not self-serving. Motherhood is pouring out our lives in self-sacrificial love and service. If we think we should be able to continue the lifestyle we lived before having children, we'll be miserable. While we try to hang on to our own rights and desires, we will never experience the true fulfillment God intends for us.

But dear mother, don't get too down in the dumps. Forgetting about yourself and your needs is not the end of the world. In fact, it's when you forget about yourself and lose your own life that you truly find peace, joy, and LIFE! This is when you truly begin to live as God purposes.

There is joy, glory, and an anointing of motherhood that God desires us to walk in, but most women have never entered it. They have been too busy trying to have it their way. When you try to hang on to your own life and all that you think you deserve, you lose! When you lay down your life and have the same attitude that Jesus revealed in Philippians 2:5-8 you win!

The following revelation set me free into the fullness of enjoying motherhood and it has set many mothers free. Are you waiting for it? Here it is . . .

Every mother loves her children but not every mother loves the career of motherhood. There is a big difference. All mothers love their children, but many think the career of motherhood is insignificant. They think they could be doing something more important. They think their children are a hindrance to their serving the Lord. They can't wait until they grow up so they can do something great for God!

Dear mother, motherhood is your highest calling. It is a God-given mandate. It is God's perfect will for you. He created you to mother. He chose you to mother. He commissioned you to mother. And He consecrated you to mother.

As you lay down your life and embrace the career of motherhood with all your heart, you will find true fulfillment. Instead of groaning about staying home with your children, change your confession to "I love motherhood!" Say it aloud. Say it when you get up in the morning. You may not feel like it, but don't worry about your feelings—they change like the wind. The power of your confession will affect your attitude, your behavior, and your whole life.

When you come to prepare breakfast for your children each morning, greet them with positive statements. Tell them, "Children, I love being your mother!" Or "I'm so blessed to be your mother!" Or "Children you are all my favorites. You are the most amazing children in the world!" Remind them again when you are driving them in the car. Confess these words aloud when you start to feel frustrated during the day.

You'll be amazed at the joy that comes into your life as you not only love your children, but as you embrace the divine career of motherhood that God has given to you.

You'll be amazed at the difference in the behavior of your children too!

PRAYER:

"*Dear Father God, I am sorry that I have not embraced this powerful and divine calling that You have given to me. I thought my career and my ministry were more important than mothering my children in my home. Please forgive me. Father God, with all my heart I embrace motherhood. I thank You that before the foundation of the world You determined that I would be a mother and bear children for Your glory. You chose me to train these precious children for Your highest purposes. This is my highest calling in life. Thank You for giving me the gift of motherhood. I embrace it to my heart. By Your grace I will love it. I will make it my highest priority. I will constantly tell my children that I love being their mother. I will tell the world that I love being a mother. Thank You, Father, for Your grace and enabling. Amen.*"

AFFIRMATION:

"*I intend to make myself fit to be a mother and being that in every sense, I will be ready for any destiny that God may put upon me.*"
~ *Catherine Booth*

92

I AM MY HUSBAND'S CROWN!

"A virtuous woman is a crown to her husband:
but she that maketh ashamed is as rottenness in his bones"
(PROVERBS 12:4).

You have most probably read Matthew Henry's famous quote on the creation of the woman, "The woman was made of a rib out of the side of Adam, not made out of his head to rule over him, nor out of his feet to be trampled upon by him, but out of his side to be equal with him, under his arm to be protected, and near his heart to be beloved."

The Word of God also tells us in 1 Corinthians 11:7 that the *"woman is the glory of the man."* As the glory of the man, she is also a crown to honor her husband.

I love the Amplified version of Proverbs 12:4: *"A virtuous and worthy wife – earnest and strong in character – is a crowning joy to her husband."* Isn't it interesting that God says a virtuous woman is a crown? God does not want her to be trodden underfoot. He does not want her to be looked down upon. She is not inferior. She is a crown.

A crown is worn upon the head. A crown is something that is dazzlingly beautiful. Crowns are usually made of gold and ornamented with precious gems. It is a token of honor.

Noah Webster's 1828 dictionary says to crown means "to invest with royalty, to bestow something upon as a mark of honor or dignity, to adorn, dignify, to award first rank." Point five of Webster's says: "Anything which imparts beauty, splendor, honor, or finish; also, the highest state or quality of anything." And on this point, he quotes Proverbs 12:4.

A virtuous woman adds distinction and dignity to her husband. He is proud to wear her. He wants to show her off. He praises her before others.

When she honors him as king of her home, he rises to kingly heights in his manhood.

When she awards him "first rank" he becomes free to reach his full potential and will do things he never thought possible. And in return he will treat his wife like a queen with dignity and respect.

Have you crowned your husband? The more richly you crown him the more he will crown you.

What does the crown look like with which you adorn your husband? Is it tarnished? Are many jewels are missing? Or is it filled with precious gems? What are some of the gems that can make your husband proud to wear you as his crown?

Is your crown decorated with diamonds of devotion, dedication, dignity, and diligence as a wife and mother?

Have you set in sapphires that shine and sparkle with a serving, sacrificial, and submissive spirit? Are you sweet to him? Are you a strength and support to his vision and goals in life? Are you sensitive to his needs? Are you steadfast in your loyalty and commitment to your marriage?

Have you positioned pearls in your crown—pearls of patience, peace, perseverance, and prayers for your husband and family?

Don't forget the rubies, the rarest of all gems. Is your crown radiating with rubies of reverence and respect for your husband?

Is your crown ornamented with opals of openness, obedience, overflowing love, and the oil of joy?

Don't forget the emeralds that emanate esteem, earnest commitment, encouragement, and endurance.

Is your crown adorned with amethysts of admiration, affection, affirmation, approval, appreciation, and attentiveness?

Just a minute! You can't forget the crowning jewel of all—contentment! This jewel adds luster to your crown. This jewel releases your husband from bondage and pressure. Sadly, it is often a missing jewel. It's easy to be content when you have everything you want. But can you learn to be content when you don't have everything you want? Can you be content with what your husband provides for you? I love Psalm 128:3 (TLB) where it talks about the "*contented*" wife in the home.

"If I do all this, he'll walk all over me," you say. "He'll become proud, and he's already got a big enough head!" It doesn't work that way, dear one. When you forget about yourself and seek to bless your husband, you not only crown him with dignity and honor, but you become his crown. You won't be subservient. You'll be worn on his head as his most treasured possession.

PRAYER:

"Father God, I confess my sin to You of not crowning my husband. I am so busy thinking of myself that I forget to crown him with blessings. Help me to be a crown upon his head that will cause him to shine for the glory of God and to "sit in the gate of the city." Save me from doing things that will make him ashamed. Amen."

AFFIRMATION:

I am becoming a glorious crown for my husband to wear.

HOW DOES THE VIRTUOUS WOMAN CROWN HER HUSBAND?

She . . .

C Cherishes her husband (Titus 2:4).

R Reverences her husband (Ephesians 5:33).

O Obeys her husband (Titus 2:5).

W Watches over her husband to do him good. (Proverbs 31:11-12).

N Never nags her husband. (Proverbs 19:13; 21:9,19; and 27:15).

93

FRIENDSHIP WITH GOD

"Oh that I were . . . in the days when God preserved me; When his candle shined upon my head, and when by his light I walked through darkness . . . when the secret of God was upon my tabernacle, when the Almighty was yet with me, when my children were about me"
(JOB 29:2-5).

Job is going through his time of intense suffering, and he thinks back to the days when God's blessing was upon him. What a beautiful description he gives. There can be no greater blessing than to have our children about us and God's presence filling our homes. That sounds like heaven on earth, doesn't it?

What is *"the secret of God"*? The Hebrew word for secret is *sod*. It has different shades of meaning, "a group of intimate people who share confidential matters, a friendly conversation among friends, a cushion, a pillow, a couch, a familiar acquaintance, the counsel of the Lord."

It is the same word used in Psalm 55:14: *"We took sweet counsel (sod) together, and walked into the house of God in company."* From this we see that the "secret of God" in Job's home was nothing less that the intimate presence of God. It was like God was sitting on a cushion or low couch (as they did in those days) fellowshipping with Job, giving him counsel and telling him His secrets. It speaks of their intimate relationship.

Don't you long for this? Job lost this for a time when God gave Satan permission to attack him, but it was not for long and God restored a double portion of all His blessings to him.

Let's look at some other translations:

MSG: *"Oh how I miss those golden years when God's friendship graced my home."* What blessing to have our precious children sitting around our table. What joy to have dear friends stay in our home and grace our table as we richly fellowship together. But oh, how much more to have God's presence grace our home.

NLT: *"The friendship of God was felt in my home."*

MLB: *"The friendship of God lingered in my tent."* Oh, how I love these words. We don't want God to grace our home only on the odd occasion. Do you want His presence to linger in your home? Do you want His presence to be felt in every room, by every person in the family, and everyone who comes into the home? I long for this.

How does God come to our homes? By His Holy Spirit. But remember how easy it is to grieve the Holy Spirit? He is likened to the dove that is easily "frightened" and turned away by sin. God wants our homes to be an intimate, secret place. To keep the preciousness of His lingering presence, we must protect our homes from the harshness of the world outside. We must guard our homes from the ugliness of sin, deception, and vice, the biting winds of hardness and strife that can beat against us, and the glitzy lightning of worldliness.

A home ceases to be a home when we allow the storms inside. It is a roof and some walls but cannot be called a home. A home is a haven, a hiding place from the storm, a sanctuary! And a place for the intimate friendship of God.

Perhaps you have allowed storms into your home. It's never too late to repair the damage, build strong walls of protection, and keep out the intruding elements. God loves to heal. God loves to restore. He wants to help you make your home a haven instead of being vulnerable to every outside influence.

Make your home a secret place from the world.

PRAYER:

"Oh, Lord God, I long for Your lingering presence in my life and in my home. Please come into my home and fill every room with Your presence. I want You to be a familiar guest in my home. I welcome You to sit on a cushion and fellowship with me. I ask You to grace our table when we eat together. Amen."

AFFIRMATION:

I am keeping my home as a place of safety for my family. I will keep out everything that grieves the Spirit of God.

A FUTILE LIFE

*"Do not turn away from following the LORD, but serve the LORD
with all your heart. You must not turn away, for then you would go after
futile things which cannot profit or rescue, because they are futile."*
(1 SAMUEL 12:20, 21 AMP).

This Scripture tells us that when we turn from the Lord, we tend to follow futile things. When we keep close to the Lord, through prayer and guidance of His Word, He keeps our hearts in the right place and guards us from confusion. When we turn aside to our own ways, we have nothing to deter us from walking after vain things and running into deception.

Romans 1:21-28 tells us that when people turned aside from God and focused all their attention on themselves, worshipping *"the creature more than the Creator,"* they became *"futile in their thinking"* and God gives them over to a *"reprobate mind"* which is a mind that is void of all judgment and understanding.

The word futile in the above Scripture is *tohu* in the Hebrew and means "desolate, worthless, confusion, emptiness, vanity, waste, useless, nothingness, and false. It always has negative connotations. This word has no parallel in other languages and therefore we can only determine its meaning in the light of the Scripture passages where it is used. Let's look at some of them:

A WILDERNESS

Psalm 107:40: *"He poureth contempt upon princes, and causeth them to wander in the wilderness (tohu), where there is no way."* Also read Deuteronomy 32:10 and Job 12:24.

To go a different way than God has planned for us is to waste our lives. I have always thought that the saddest thing anyone can do is to go through life doing their own thing and not fulfil the destiny God planned for them before the foundation of the world. It's a wasted and wilderness life going nowhere.

CONFUSION

Isaiah 41:29: *"Their works are nothing: their molten images are wind and confusion (tohu)."*

We live in a society that is deceived and deluded. Because we are engulfed by humanist thinking—in the media, the education system, and the mindset of the majority around is, it can seem normal to us. Unless we keep close to the Lord and live in His Word, we can also be deceived and confused without knowing it.

VANITY

Isaiah 44:9: *"They that make a graven image are all of them vanity (tohu)."*

Isaiah 59:4: *"None calleth for justice, nor any pleadeth for truth: they trust in vanity (tohu), and speak lies; they conceive mischief, and bring forth iniquity."* If we are not trusting in the Lord, we are trusting in vanity! And what a futile way to live!

When the children of Israel wanted to turn back to the Lord, Samuel said to them: *"Fear not: ye have done all this wickedness: yet turn not aside from following the LORD, but serve the LORD with all your heart; And turn ye not aside: for then should ye go after vain (tohu) things, which cannot profit nor deliver; for they are vain (tohu)"* (1 Samuel 12:20, 21).

It is a vain thing to pursue our own way. It has no eternal reward.

NOTHINGNESS

Job 6:18: *"The paths of their way are turned aside: they go to nothing (tohu) and perish."* There is only nothingness at the end of a life spent only on itself. Luke 12:8-21 reveals the nothingness at the end for the one *"who lays up treasure for himself, and is not rich towards God."*

However, although *tohu* is usually a negative word, we read of a positive in Genesis 1:2 where it tells us that God created the earth from nothing!

Job 26:7: *"He stretcheth out the north over the empty (tohu) place, and hangeth the earth upon nothing."* God not only created the earth out of nothing, but also the heavens. Many Scriptures reveal that Heaven is somewhere in the recesses of the north. Scientists believe there is an empty space in the north of our universe that is so large that it could contain 2,000 milky ways and perhaps it is somewhere there that Heaven is located.

Now if God can create the earth and the heavens out of nothing, He can also restore our lives from nothingness and worthlessness and create His beautiful life in us. He delights to take us from uselessness, conform us into His image, and make our lives worthwhile.

EMPTINESS

Some versions of the Bible translate *tohu* as "empty." Many people try to fill their lives with pleasures and material possessions. They fill their homes with stuff—TVs, beautiful décor, and every new thing they see advertised. And yet their homes are empty of people—empty of babies and children, the true riches that we can take into eternity with us.

I think of God's words about Israel when they walked in their own ways: *"Israel is an empty vine, he bringeth forth fruit unto himself"* (Hosea 10:1). When we focus on ourselves and our own aspirations, we are empty. We have nothing to give to anyone else. We have nothing to take into eternity.

The word empty in Hosea 10:1 is *baqaq* and means "to empty, to depopulate." Isn't that interesting? This is what has been happening in the church over the last few decades. As people have turned away from God's truths to fill their lives with the pleasures of this world, they have depopulated the church. Thousands and thousands of godly children who God intended to come forth to bring God's light and salvation into the world are not here. Not only have we depopulated the church, but we have depopulated the land.

In turning from God's ways, we have become empty.

PRAYER:
"Oh God, please keep me on Your narrow way. I don't want to waste my life. Amen."

AFFIRMATION:
Not my way, but God's way.

95

GOD WANTS TO TURN OUR HEARTS

"Behold, I will send you Elijah the prophet before the coming of the great and dreadful day of the LORD: And he shall turn the heart of the fathers to the children, and the heart of the children to their fathers, lest I come and smite the earth with a curse"
(MALACHI 4:5, 6).

As we read the above Scriptures, we feel God's heart for families. God longs for the turning of the hearts to children. This should also be our prayer and longing.

We know that that this Scripture was fulfilled in the life of John the Baptist of whom it was said: *"And many of the children of Israel **shall he turn** to the Lord their God. And he shall go before him in the spirit and power of Elijah, **to turn the hearts of the fathers to the children**, and the disobedient to the wisdom of the just; to make ready a people prepared for the Lord"* (Luke 1:16, 17).

God chose John the Baptist to prepare the people for the first coming of Jesus by turning the hearts of the fathers to the children. But Jesus is coming a second time and the way must be prepared again. God is going to do it the same way, by turning the hearts of the fathers (and this also includes the mothers) back to the children. This issue is so important to the heart of God that He says that if it doesn't happen, He will smite the earth with a curse. This is not something we can take lightly.

God started this human race with the mandate *"Be fruitful and multiply"* and He is going to finish it the same way. God hasn't changed His attitude toward children. He loves children. He calls them a blessing. When Jesus was on earth, He embraced the children to Him and severely reprimanded those who turned them away.

Mark 10:13, 14: *"And they brought young children to him, that he should* *touch them: and his disciples rebuked those that brought them. But when Jesus saw it, he was **much displeased** and said unto them, Suffer the little children to come unto me, and forbid them not: for f such is the kingdom of God."*

How can we be followers of God and yet have a different attitude about children than He does? Are we on God's agenda or the devil's agenda? Truly it is time for God's people to turn back to His ways. Will we turn or will we have the curse?

Malachi 3:18: *"Then shall ye return, and discern between the righteous and the wicked, between him that serveth God and him that serveth him not."* Do you notice that it is in returning that we receive understanding and discernment? While we continue to live according to our own agenda, we are often oblivious to what God really wants. It is when we turn from our own way and turn back to Him and obedience to His Word that we begin to understand truth we have not seen before.

Discernment comes after turning and heading back to God.

It is time for us to turn from pride, stubbornness, prayerlessness, disobedience, mediocrity, passiveness, and following the spirit of this world.

Jesus came to turn us away from ungodliness: *"God, having raised up his Son Jesus, sent him to bless you, in **turning away every one of you from his iniquities**"* (Acts 3:26).

*"To open their eyes, and to **turn them from darkness to light**, and from the power of Satan unto God, that they may receive forgiveness of sins"* (Acts 26:18).

*"There shall come out of Zion the Deliverer, and shall **turn away ungodliness** from Jacob"* (Romans 11:26).

*"I thought on my ways, and **turned my feet unto thy testimonies**"* (Psalm 119:59).

*"Let us search and try our ways, and **turn again to the LORD**"* (Lamentations 3:40).

*"Turn thou us unto thee, O LORD, and **we shall be turned; renew our days as of old**"* (Lamentations 5:21).

Which way are we going to turn? This generation and future generations hinge upon our decision.

PRAYER:

"Oh God please save me from being deceived. Help me to turn completely to You so that I will discern what is truth and what is Your way. Amen."

AFFIRMATION:

I'm daily turning my heart toward the Lord, to His ways, and His Word.

FURTHER STUDY: Go to page 314.

96

A TALE OF TWO CULTURES
Part 1

"Do everything without grumbling and arguing, so that you may blameless and pure, children of God who are faultless in a crooked and perverted generation, among whom you shine like stars in the world"
(PHILIPPIANS 2:14, 15 HCSB).

We live in a world of two cultures—the "normal humanistic culture," which seems very normal to most people, and the "normal biblical culture," the way of life which is not so popular. Many of us often go between the two.

The folk who live in the "normal humanistic culture" are mostly delightful people—intelligent, kind, caring, involved in the community, and good citizens. Many of them are born again believers. Their hearts are cleansed by the blood of Jesus, and they love God. There's only one problem. Their minds have not yet caught up with their renewed hearts. They are influenced by this society with its socialist and progressive agenda and think like a humanist. It is so normal to their thinking pattern that they think any other way is strange, even if it's biblical.

TWISTED TRUTH

The Knox translation of Philippians 2:15 states: *"You live in an age that is twisted out of its true pattern, and among such people you shine out, beacons to the world, upholding the message of life."*

God spoke to His people, Israel, saying: *"Though I wrote for him ten thousand precepts of my law, they are regarded as a strange thing"* (Hosea 8:12 NASB).

Again, He said to them: *"You turn things upside down"* (Isaiah 29:16 AMP). God's ways seem strange because they are not familiar. Therefore, they would rather trust in their own reasoning than God's counsel (Psalm

81:11-14).

In the "normal humanistic culture" couples usually wait a few years until they consider having children. They plan to someday, but they want time to further their studies, their careers, solicit material possessions, and of course, to "get to know one another more." When they eventually decide to have children (if they have not waited too long to conceive) they limit the number to two. Sometimes they may go for a third. After that, it's "the snip!" Isn't that what the majority are doing? And we must keep up with the Joneses!

Sometimes the mother may stay home with her newborn for a while, but soon she sends her child to daycare while she continues her career. Once children reach school age it is "normal" to send them to public education (and they wouldn't want to be considered different.) Everything looks great on the surface, but many parents are not aware of the hidden agenda of the socialists to take over our country by infiltrating the minds of our children.

DIMMING LIGHT

From 1962 God has been continually excommunicated from our state schools, due to court rulings from our U.S. Supreme Court.

On June 25, 1962, students were forbidden to do what they had been doing since the founding of our nation, publicly pray at the beginning of each school day, "Almighty God, we acknowledge our dependence on Thee and beg Thy blessing over us, our parents, our teachers, and our nation." Can the demise of our nation be traced to the cessation of daily prayer in schools?

In 1963 the U.S. Supreme court banned the school-directed recital of the Lord's Prayer and reading of Bible passages as part of "devotional exercises" in public schools.

In 1980 the Ten Commandments were prohibited from being posted on public school classroom walls.

In 1985 observance of "daily moments of silence" were banned from public schools when students were encouraged to pray during the silent periods.

In 1992 they banned prayers led by members of the clergy at public school graduation ceremonies.

And on June 19, 2000, the U.S. Supreme Court outlawed student-led pre-kickoff prayers at high school football games.

Christianity was the foundation of this nation but now our children are taught the religion of secular humanism. They are taught evolution as a fact, sex-education, and the "goodness" of other anti-Bible religions, including Islam. Homosexual activists have lobbied successfully for their lifestyle to be taught as part of the school curriculum. Already the California Teachers Association supports abolishing gender stereotypes in schools and doing away with all distinctions between male and female. The light of God's truth wanes as each generation is hooked more and more into the "normal humanistic culture," masterminded by the devil.

Philippians 2:14, 15 (Fenton): *"Do all without grudging and disputes; so that you may become blameless and pure, beautiful children of God, in the midst of a deformed, degenerate race—among whom you will shine like bright lights to the whole world."*

PRAYER:

"Dear God of truth, please save me from being pulled into the twisted thinking of this age. Help me to keep in Your Word daily, becoming more and more familiar with the truth. Amen."

AFFIRMATION:

I belong to God's kingdom of marvelous light and will not be lured back into the darkness of deception.

97

TALE OF TWO CULTURES
Part 2

"And be not conformed to this world: but be ye transformed
by the renewing of your mind, that ye may prove what is that good,
and acceptable, and perfect, will of God"
(ROMANS 12:2).

The humanistic lifestyle is quite predictable and very "safe" because humanists and socialists demand control of their own lives—their bodies, their finances, and their future. Many in this culture depend upon government programs and finances. They believe it is their "right" to receive "handouts."

ORDINARY TO EXTRAORDINARY

On the other hand, it is quite scary to live in the "normal biblical culture." First, you will be a misfit. You are a stranger and pilgrim. You believe what God says rather than what man says. You move out of the ordinary into the extraordinary. You move from the predictable into a life of faith! You move out of being in control of your own life and future to trust in God's sovereignty. You move into a sphere where the "normal culture" thinks you are strange because you live a completely different lifestyle.

Because you no longer trust in your own wisdom and resources, you are cast upon God to sovereignly direct your life. This means you believe the Bible rather than the popular voice of society. This means you believe God when He says that children are a blessing. This takes faith and you move into miraculous living.

When you conceive, God visits you (Genesis 21:1, 2 and I Samuel 2:21). Doesn't a *"visitation of God"* call for rejoicing?

And when you birth your baby, you experience another miracle. Talking about birth, God said in Genesis 18:14: *"Is anything too hard for the LORD."*

The phrase *"too hard"* is the Hebrew word *pala* and means "extraordinary, wonderful, miraculous, astonishing, marvelous, and beyond the bounds of human powers or expectations." It is also the name that is given to Jesus in Isaiah 9: 6: *"For unto us a child is born, unto us a son is given: and the government shall be upon his shoulder: and his name shall be called **Wonderful** . . ."*

This is just the beginning of your life of faith and watching God do miracles. Your baby is God's gift to you. Are you going to give your precious gift away to someone else to look after while you do something secondary? No, you and your husband trust God to provide, even beyond your husband's hard-working income. You trust His Word that when He blesses the womb, He promises to bless you with all you need to provide for His child (Deuteronomy 28:1-14). You begin the adventurous life of faith.

CONTINUAL CELEBRATIONS

We should more correctly call this lifestyle the "extraordinary biblical culture." It's certainly not a kill-joy lifestyle. We enjoy continual celebrations of weddings, babies, and all the exciting adventures of life which each new baby leads us into. We live in a culture of life, not death. We live in a culture of covenant-keeping and marriage commitment.

The Bible tells us that out of the dwelling places of Zion *"shall proceed thanksgiving and the voice of them that make merry: and I will multiply them, and they shall not be few; I will also glorify them, and they shall not be small"* (Jeremiah 30:19).

God's culture is one of wedding celebrations where we hear *"the voice of joy, and the voice of gladness, the voice of the bridegroom, and the voice of the bride"* (Jeremiah 33:11). This is not a languishing life. It's full of challenges and hard work, but the fruit is joy, fulfillment, and knowing you are walking in the perfect will of God. Your career is eternity impacting!

Because you are concerned that your children and grandchildren may be pulled in to the "normal humanistic culture" that permeates the whole of society, you think very carefully about how you will educate them. You do not want them to sit in the company of the scornful each day (Psalm 1:1). Instead, you teach your children the ways of truth, integrity, righteousness, wisdom, and justice. You daily fill them with God's Word, so His ways, thoughts, and plans will be "normal" to them and not "a strange thing."

GOD MANDATED CAREER

You know God's plan for you. This is your affirmation which you confess every morning:

I am not languishing. I am not deceived. I have a vision. I know who I am and who God created me to be. I know my purpose. I am walking in the perfect will of God. I know it's not easy, but I've counted the cost. My goal is set.

How could my career be easy when I am influencing a nation for God, generations to come, and eternity?

How could it be easy when I am destroying the plans of the devil? Such is the power of my God-mandated career, the highest calling ever given to women—motherhood.

I have embraced my calling. I am not intimidated by my antagonists. I will not be moved. My heart is fixed. I may be hidden in my home but look out world! I am sharpening my arrows. I am getting them ready to shoot forth and destroy the adversary.

In the power and anointing of God, I am advancing God's Kingdom.

PRAYER:

"Thank You dear Father, for calling me out of darkness into Your marvelous light. I praise You continually that I belong to Your kingdom. Because You have made me a child of Your kingdom, I want live according to the statutes of Your kingdom. Please pour out Your Holy Spirit upon me to fully walk in Your ways. Amen."

AFFIRMATION:

I'm walking the narrow way that's filled with life and leads to the ultimate eternal life.

98

FRIENDS SHAPE FRIENDS

"He that walketh with wise men will be wise:
but the companion of fools shall be destroyed"
(PROVERBS 13:20).

Isn't it amazing how our children grow up so quickly? It seems like one blink of my eyes that our eldest son (who is in his late fifties) was born. I don't know where the years have flown.

I remember when my children were babies, and as I experienced the beautiful moments with them, I thought I would remember them forever. But now they are fading from my memory. My little babies grew up. They married and raised children and now their children are raising a new generation.

When my children were teens, I raised them on the above Scripture. I like the Knox translation which says: *"Wise company brings wisdom; fool he ends that fool befriends."* How true this is. Peer pressure is a big pull upon children in their teen years. You can be the godliest parents in the world, but if your children get into the wrong company, your parental influence is weakened.

The thing we must guard more than anything else in the teen years is the company our children keep. We must encourage godly Christian friends for our children. We must watch they do not become involved in situations where there is bad company. Homeschooling is a great blessing in this regard. And of course, if your teens are part of a big family, they have friends right in their own home. Teens love company. They love socializing and what a great blessing it is when they have their best friends continually on tap!

If your children establish solid friendships with those who are a good influence before they are teens, they will be off to a good start. How can you do this? One of the greatest blessings Colin and I found as we raised our children was to have loads of hospitality, especially with those of "kindred spirits." The more functions and gatherings you can have in your home that include "good influencing" young people, the more blessed your teens will be. They love fun and loads of people around.

This was one of the complaints of a girl I talked to recently. She was homeschooled but got into a bad crowd in her teens. She said her parents didn't like to have people to their home and therefore she missed the company of good young people through the ministry of hospitality. Because of her own experience she said that when she raises her family, she wants to freely show hospitality to provide friendships for her children.

Our sons are still best friends with their best friends of their youth. They went to church together, played together, camped together, made go-karts together, and later did moto-cross together. And most of all, served the Lord together. And now, after all these years, they are still doing projects together for the kingdom of God.

Another important thing is to get involved in a good church or prospering home fellowship that has other families the ages of your children. How true are the words of Proverbs 27:17 (Knox): *"Iron whets iron, friend shapes friend."* Our children will become like their friends.

This applies to us too. We become like the people we associate with. What a blessing to rub shoulders with and discuss the things of God with the wise and godly. It's one of my favorite things of life.

I remember when one of my children had his first opportunity to prepare a message for a youth group. The Scripture he chose was Proverbs 13:20! He knew it by heart as I had drummed it into him. Use this Scripture to encourage your children and here are a few more for your children and teens to memorize:

Proverbs 12:11: *"He that followeth vain persons is void of understanding."*

Proverbs 14:7: *"Go from the presence of a foolish man, when thou perceivest not in him the lips of knowledge."*

Proverbs 22:24, 25: *"Make no friendship with an angry man; and with a furious man thou shalt not go: Lest thou learn his ways, and get a snare to thy soul."*

1 Corinthians 5:6: *"Know ye not that a little leaven leaveneth the whole lump?"*

1 Corinthians 15:33 (ESV): *"Bad company ruins good morals."*

May God pour out His wisdom upon you as you raise godly children for His kingdom.

PRAYER:

"*My Lord God, I ask that You please help me to find godly friends for my children and help my children to be a positive influence on their friends. Amen.*"

AFFIRMATION:

I'm seeking and praying for wholesome friends for my children.

99

WHAT IS YOUR GLORY?
Part 1

"And the very God of peace sanctify you wholly;
and I pray God your whole spirit and soul and body be preserved
blameless unto the coming of our Lord Jesus Christ"
(1 THESSALONIANS 5:23).

Are you preparing for the coming Day? The day when our Lord Jesus Christ returns from Heaven? What will we present to Him on that day? Paul writes about what He is preparing for the Lord Jesus. He doesn't mention any material things or aspirations of building a great organization. Instead, he talks about his babes in Christ.

When writing to the new Thessalonian believers, he says: *"For what is our hope or joy or crown of boasting before our Lord Jesus at his coming? Is it not you? For you are our glory and joy"* (1 Thessalonians 2:19, 20 ESV). What will be your glory when Jesus comes?

What a challenge to us as mothers. We have such a powerful ministry in our homes. It's right at our doorsteps. We don't have to go any further. God has given us precious lives to lead to salvation and to nurture, train, and teach to be ardent disciples of the Lord. We have the responsibility to pray and pour into their lives so we can present our children to the Lord at His coming—sanctified and blameless in body, soul, and spirit (1 Thessalonians 5:23).

We have no greater ministry. The Lord Jesus will not be interested in our presenting our career to Him. Or our material possessions. Or the great name we made for ourselves. He looks for cleansed, purified, and holy sons and daughters. They will be our *"crown of boasting."* They will be our *"glory"* and *"joy"* on that day.

This doesn't happen without our intercession, dedication, sacrifice, and pouring out our lives. As we read the entire epistle of Thessalonians, we find Paul's example of what it takes for this to happen.

NURTURING

Paul was like a *"nursing mother"* to these new babes in Christ. He says in 1 Thessalonians 2:7, 8 (ESV): *"We were gentle among you, like a nursing mother taking care of her own children. So, being affectionately desirous of you, we were ready to share with you not only the gospel of God but also our own selves, because you had become very dear to us."*

If Paul could be like a nursing mother, giving up his own self, surely, we can embrace our mothering role with all our hearts. We know that a nursing mother is available to her little baby day and night. She pours out her life for her little one. She doesn't try to save her own life; she loses her life to find it (Mark 8:35).

Be encouraged, dear mother, you begin discipling your children from the moment they are born. You not only nurture your babe with sustenance from your breast, but with powerful thoughts, visions, and prayers from your heart. Every moment of nursing is powerful and ministers into the life of your child who is an eternal soul. Not one moment is lost.

Preparing your child to present to Jesus at His coming begins as a nursing mother.

LIFE EXAMPLE

As our children grow, they learn more from watching our lifestyle than what we teach them. They emulate our way of life. Because of Paul's lifestyle, he could say: *"Be ye followers of me, even as I also am of Christ"* (1 Corinthians 11:1). Can we confidently say this to our children? Read how many other times he said this or similar words: 1 Corinthians 4:15, 16; Philippians 3:17; 4:9; 1 Thessalonians 1:6; and 2 Thessalonians 3:9.

Paul could also say to these young Christians: *"You are witnesses, and God also, how **holy** and **righteous** and **blameless** was our conduct toward you"* (1 Thessalonians 2:10 ESV). Not only for our own sake, and for God's sake, but for our children's sake we must seek to live holy lives.

TEACH AND COMMAND

Nothing happens in life without making it happen. Our children do not become our *"glory"* by hoping it will happen. What was Paul's example? He says: *"For you know how like a father with his children, we exhorted each one of you and encouraged you and **charged** you to walk in a manner worthy of God, who calls you into his own kingdom and glory"* (1 Thessalonians 2:11,

12 ESV). It takes constant encouraging, urging, teaching, and even commanding. Read further Scriptures were Paul commands the new believers: 2 Thessalonians 3: 4, 6, 10, and 12.

Abraham was a great example of parenting. God said that all the nations of the earth would be blessed because of Abraham and one of the reasons was because of his parenting. God said in Genesis 18:19: *"For I know him, that he will **command** his children and his household after him, and they shall keep the way of the LORD, to do justice and judgment."* He didn't let his household work things out for themselves. He commanded them in the ways of the Lord.

It's our daily duty. Read Deuteronomy 4:9; 6:6-9; Psalm 78:1-8; and Isaiah 28:10, 12.

PRAYER:

"Dear Father, I want to be ready for Your coming. I want my children to be ready for Your coming. Please strengthen me to be a responsible mother as I prepare my children to present them to You. I want them to be my joy and crown at Your appearing. Amen."

AFFIRMATION:

I have a royal command to prepare my children for the coming of the Lord.

WHAT IS YOUR GLORY?
Part 2

"Holding forth the word of life; that I may rejoice in the day of Christ,
that I have not run in vain neither labored in vain"
(PHILIPPIANS 2:16).

We continue our study about preparing our children for the coming of the Lord Jesus.

4. GOD'S WORD OF TRUTH

We must have a healthy fear of God's Word. That means we revere it as the living, breathing, active Word of God. We read it as though God is personally speaking to us. We listen to Him through His Word. We obey Him. We tremble at His word. If we have this attitude to God's Word, our children will imbibe the same attitude.

If we carelessly treat God's Word, our children will be careless about it. Our children notice if we rarely pick up the Bible. They see what importance we place on His Word by how much we read it and talk about it. Do we read it with them every morning and evening? They soon become aware that we either take it with a grain of salt or *"tremble"* at His Word (Isaiah 66:2). What is your testimony before them?

In preparing the new Christians to be his *"crown of boasting"* when Jesus comes, Paul lifted God's Word to its high level. 1 Thessalonians 2:13 says: *"When ye received the word of God which ye heard of us, ye received it not as the word of men, but as it is in truth, the word of God, which effectually worketh also in you that believe."*

When writing to these believers, Paul shared how he longed to see their faces again so he *"might perfect that which is lacking in your faith"* (1 Thessalonians 3:10). How did he do this? By continuing to teach them more of

God's Word of truth. It is the Word that builds up faith and fills up the areas we lack in our lives and our children's lives.

God's Word is the most powerful tool to fill up the weaknesses in your children lives!

When you see an area of lack in any of your children, fill it up with God's Word. Find the Scriptures that apply to that area of need. Read those Scriptures with your children. Write them out and pin them up in big colorful letters in appropriate places in the home. Encourage your children to memorize these Scriptures. You will find that there is nothing else that is as effective of God's Word to fill up their weaknesses.

5. PRAYER

Prayer is the last point but the most important of all. And the one we use the least. Do you and your husband pray together each day for your children? It takes much prayer and intercession to get them through life in victory and holiness—and for them to become your *"glory"* and *"joy."* Never give up praying. Find a time that is suitable for your husband to pray with you each day. Paul prayed *"night and day exceedingly"* (1 Thessalonians 3:10). If Paul could to this for these young believers who were not his flesh and blood, surely, we can at least find one time in the day to pray together for our children who are our own flesh and blood!

He prayed that God would establish their hearts *"unblameable in holiness before God"* 1 Thessalonians (3:13). We live in an evil and deceived world, and it takes prayer to keep our children and grandchildren walking in holiness. He also prayed: *"And the very God of peace sanctify you wholly, and I pray God your whole spirit and soul and body be preserved blameless unto the coming of our Lord Jesus Christ"* (1 Thessalonians 5:23).

He not only prayed but travailed in prayer for the believers in Galatia (Galatians 4:19).

He prayed many blessings for the Ephesian believers and that they would be *"filled with all the fullness of God"* (Ephesians 3:14-19).

He did *"not cease to pray"* for the Colossians believers (Colossian 1:9-12).

He prayed for the Philippian believers who he also called *"my joy and crown"* (Philippians 1:4, 9-11 and 4:1).

We must continually lift our children up before the Lord for He is the only One who is able to keep them from falling and present them faultless *"before the presence of his glory with exceeding joy"* (Jude 1:24).

Are your children your boast in the Lord? Paul confessed in 1 Thessalonians 3:8: *"For now we live, if ye stand fast in the Lord."* Is this how you feel too? You feel that you can only really live if your children are standing fast, walking in holiness, and overcoming the temptations of this evil world.

May our children be our *"glory"* and *"joy"* at His coming. May we not live in vain.

PRAYER:

"Dear Father, Thank You for showing me the tools I need to prepare my children for Your coming. Help me to use them faithfully. Help me to give them a LOVE for Your precious Word. Help my husband and me to be faithful in praying for them each day. Amen."

AFFIRMATION:

I am filling up the weaknesses of my children with God's powerful Word.

Further Study

DAY 65

Please look up and meditate on the following Scriptures. Each one is powerful. Teach them to your children. Use them as a study in your Family Devotions. We must know that God is truth in the very essence of our beings.

GOD IS TRUTH

Exodus 34:6; Numbers 23:19; Deuteronomy 32:4; 1 Samuel 15:29; Psalm 25:5; 31:5; 57:3, 10; 86:15; 89:14; 96:13; 100:5; 108:4; 146:6; Jeremiah 4:2; 10:10; John 3:33; 7:28; 17:3; Romans 1:25; Titus 1:2; Hebrews 6:17, 18; and 1 John 5:20.

JESUS CHRIST IS TRUTH

Matthew 22:16; John 1:14, 17; and 14:6.

THE HOLY SPIRIT IS TRUTH

John 14:16-18; 15:26; 16:13; 1 John 2: 27; and 5:6.

GOD'S WORD IS TRUTH

Psalm 19:9-11; 33:4, 5; 43:3; 111:7, 8; 117:2; 119:142, 151, 160; 138:2; John 17:17; Proverbs 30:5; Daniel 10:21; John 5:39; 8:31, 32; Romans 15:4; Ephesians 1:13; 2 Timothy 2:15; 3:15-17; James 1:18; 1 Peter 1:23; and 2 Peter 1:20, 21.

THE DEVIL IS THE DECEIVER AND FATHER OF LIES

Isaiah 14:12-14; Matthew 13:19; John 8:44; 2 Corinthians 2: 11; 11:3, 14; Ephesians 2:2; 6:11, 12; 2 Thessalonians 2:9-12; 2 Timothy 2:26; 1 Peter 5:8, 9; 1 John 3:8; and Revelation 12:9.

NO. 4: TRUTH BELIEVERS

John 3:15, 16, 18, 36; 5:24; 6:35, 40, 47; 7:38, 39; 11:26, 27; 14:12; and 20:31.

DAY 69

NO. 23. TRUTH KEEPERS

2 Timothy 1:14 (NLT): "Through the power of the Holy Spirit who lives within us, carefully guard the precious truth that has been entrusted to you."

You will notice how many Scriptures there are about keeping God's truth. As you read these Scriptures, look out for **ALL the blessings** *God gives when we observe and keep His truths and statutes. Write down the blessings and share them with your children. You will be amazed.*

Genesis 18:19; Exodus 20:5, 6; Leviticus 18:26-30; 19:37; 20:8, 22; 22:31; 25:18; 26:3-13; 1 Kings 2:3; 3:14; 6:12; 8:61; 9:4-7; 11:38; 2 Kings 17:37; and 21:8.

Deuteronomy 4:2, 6, 40; 5:1, 10, 8:1; 6:2, 17; 7:9, 11, 12; 8:2, 6, 11; 10:12, 13; 11:1, 8, 22; 13:4, 18; 26:16-19; 27:1; 28:9, 45; 29:9; 30:10, 16; Joshua 22:5 and Nehemiah 1:9.

Psalm 19:7-11; 105:43-45; 119:2, 4, 5, 8, 17, 22, 33, 34, 44, 55-57, 60, 63, 67, 69, 88, 100, 101, 106, 115, 129, 134, 136, 145, 146, 167, and 168.

Proverbs 3:1; 4:13, 20-23; 6:20-23; 7:1-3; 8:32, 33; 10:17; 19:16; 28:7; 29:18; Ecclesiastes 8:5; 12:13; Ezekiel 11:20; 20:19; 36:27; and 44:24.

Luke 11:28; John 8:51; 14:15, 21, 23, 24; 15:10; 1 Timothy 6:14; 1 John 2:3-5; 3:24; 5:2, 3; and Revelation 22:7.

NO. 26. TRUTH OBEYERS

Psalm 119:166; Matthew 7:21-23, 24-27; Luke 6:46-49; Galatians 3:1; 5:7; James 1:22-25; 1 Peter 1:22; and 1 John 3:7, 18.

DAY 70

NO. 31. TRUTH PREACHERS

Jesus preached: *Isaiah 61:1-3 (Luke 4:16-20); Matthew 4:17, 23; 9:35;11:1-5 (Luke 7:22); Mark 1:4, 15, 38, 39; 2:2; Luke 4: 43, 44; 8:1;20:1; and 1 Peter 3:19.*

Jesus commanded His disciples to preach: *Matthew 10:5- 8, 27; 24:14; Mark 3:14; 6:7, 12; Mark 16:15-20; Luke 3:3-18; 9:1, 2, 6; Acts 1:8; 5:42; 8:4, 5, 25, 35-40; and 10:42. Remember, the disciples were not older men; they were teenagers! They were preaching in their teens!*

Paul preached boldly: *Acts 9:18-20; 9:27; 13:5; 14:5-7; 15:35; 20:7, 24-27; 28:30, 31; Romans 1:15, 16; 10:13-15; 15:18-21; 16:25; 1 Corinthians 1:17, 18, 21-24; 2:4, 5; 9:16; 15:1-4, 11; 2 Corinthians 1:19, 20; 10:16; 11:7; Galatians 1:8, 9, 15, 16, 23, 24; 4:13; Ephesians 3:8; Colossians 1: 27, 28; 1 Thessalonians 2:9; 1 Timothy 2:7; 2 Timothy 1:11; and 2 Timothy 4:17; and Titus 1:3.*

We are all commanded to preach the gospel wherever we go: *Psalm 40:9, 10; Isaiah 40:9; Matthew 24:14; Mark 16:15-18; Luke 16:16; 24:45-47; Acts 11:19-21; Romans 1:15, 16; 10:14, 15; 1 Corinthians 1:18-24; 9:16; 15:1-4; 2 Corinthians 4:5; and 2 Timothy 4:2.*

Do you want beautiful feet? Preach the good tidings: *Isaiah 52:7; Nahum 1:15; and Romans 10:15.*

DAY 72

NO. 39. TRUTH SPEAKERS

1 Kings 17:24; Psalm 15:2; 29:9; 35:28; 37:30; 119:172; 145:4-7; Proverbs 12:17; 14:5; Isaiah 50:4; Jeremiah 1:7, 8, 17; Ezekiel 2:7; Zechariah 8:16, 17; Acts 4: 29-31; 1 Timothy 2:7; 1 John 3:18; and 1 John 4:5, 6.

We don't only speak to those who want to hear, but those who don't want to hear:

Jeremiah 7:27, 28: "Therefore thou shalt speak all these words unto them; but they will not hearken to thee: thou shalt also call unto them; but they will not answer thee. But thou shalt say unto them, This is a nation that obeyeth not the voice of the LORD their God, nor receiveth correction: truth is perished, and is cut off from their mouth."

Ezekiel 2:6, 7: "Be not afraid of them, neither be afraid of their words, though briers and thorns be with thee, and thou dost dwell among scorpions: be not afraid of their words, not be dismayed at their looks, though they be a rebellious house. And thou shalt speak y words unto them, whether they will hear, or whether they will forbear; for they are most rebellious."

Galatians 4:16: "Am I therefore become your enemy, because I tell you the truth?"

TWO POEMS FOR YOUR CHILDREN TO LEARN

ALWAYS SPEAK THE TRUTH

Here's a secret for the girl and boy
Who wants to live a life of joy—
ALWAYS SPEAK THE TRUTH

When you tell a lie, you please the devil,
He's the father of lies and wants you a rebel—
ALWAYS SPEAK THE TRUTH

Do not try to cover the mess you're in
By telling a lie God says is sin—
ALWAYS SPEAK THE TRUTH

Every lie you tell makes matters worse,
It leads to another and becomes a curse—
ALWAYS SPEAK THE TRUTH

Confess the truth although hard to do,
It's the way to go and God will bless you—
ALWAYS SPEAK THE TRUTH.

There are no liars in heaven, did you know?
Stop telling them now, it's the way to go!
ALWAYS SPEAK THE TRUTH.

Break the habit of lies while in your youth,
To follow God, you must speak the truth—
ALWAYS SPEAK THE TRUTH

WHO IS BRAVE?

Who is brave and very wise?
And deserves to get a prize?
THE ONE WHO TELLS THE TRUTH!

Who can lift their head up high?
And does not need to hide and cry?
THE ONE WHO TELLS THE TRUTH!

Who can smile with open face?
And never bring himself disgrace?
THE ONE WHO TELLS THE TRUTH!

Who will grow up straight and true?
And be successful in all they do?
THE ONE WHO TELLS THE TRUTH!

DAY 95

Exhortations to turn back to God:

2 Chronicles 7:14; Job 36:10; Proverbs 1:23; Isaiah 44:22; Jeremiah 3:14a; 4:1; 19, 22; 18:11; 25:5-6; 36:3, 7; Ezekiel 14:6; 18:30-31; 33:11; Hosea 6:1; 12:6; 14:1-2; Joel 2:12-13; Zechariah 1:3-4; and Malachi 3:7.

We have a responsibility to exhort people to turn back to God:

Jeremiah 23:22; 26:2, 3; Ezekiel 33:7-9; Daniel 12:3; Malachi 2:6, 7; Acts 14:15; and 26:16-18.

Prayers of turning back to God:

1 Kings 8:35, 36; 2 Chronicles 6:24-27; Psalm 80:3, 7, 19; 119:37; Jeremiah 31:18, 19; Lamentations 5:21; and Hosea 14:1, 2.

Examples of turning back to God:

1 Kings 18:37, 38; Malachi 3:18; 1 Thessalonians 1:9; and 1 Peter 2:25.

Examples of not turning away from God:

1 Kings 15:4, 5; 2 Kings 22:1-2; 23:25; Psalm 44:18; and Isaiah 50:5.

Examples of turning away from God:

Leviticus 20:6; Numbers 14:43; Deuteronomy 31:18; Judges 8:33; 1 Kings 11:1-11; 2 Chronicles 25:27; 29:6-8; Psalm 78:9, 41, 56, 57; Proverbs 28:9; Isaiah 53:6; 44:20; 59:14, 15; Jeremiah 2:21, 27; 3:10;

5:3; 11:9-11; 15:6, 7; 23:14, 15; 32:33; 50:6; Lamentations 1:8, 9; Hosea 7:9-16; Amos 4:6, 9-11; Zephaniah 1:4-6; Haggai 2:17; Acts 7:39; and 2 Timothy 4:4.

Examples of turning quickly away from God:

Exodus 32:8; Deuteronomy 9:12, 16; and Judges 2:17.

Exhortations to turn from evil:

Deuteronomy 5:32, 33; 11:16, 17; 26-28; 28:14; 29:18-20; 30:17, 18; Joshua 1:7; 23: 6; 1 Samuel 12:20,21; 1 Kings 9:6, 7; 2 Kings 17:13; 2 Chronicles 7:14; 19, 20; Psalm 85:8; 125:5; Proverbs 4:27; Ezekiel 18:24-28; 33:12-20; 2 Timothy 3:5; and Hebrews 12:25

God promises and blessings to us if we turn back to Him:

Deuteronomy 4:30, 31; 30:9, 0; 1 Kings 18:37, 38; 2 Chronicles 6:24-27, 37-39; 7:14; 7:19, 20; 15:4; 30:6, 9; Nehemiah 1:9; Job 22:23; Isaiah 55:7; 59:20, 21; Jeremiah 15:19, 20; 18:7-10; 4:6-7; 26:2, 3; Ezekiel 18:21-23; 33:14-16, 19; Joel 2:12-14; Zechariah 1:3; and Malachi 4:5-6.